Canadian Perinatal Health Report

2003

Canadian **Perinatal** Surveillance System

Our mission is to help the people of Canada
maintain and improve their health.

Health Canada

Copies of this report are available from:

Maternal and Infant Health Section
Health Surveillance and Epidemiology Division
Centre for Healthy Human Development
Population and Public Health Branch
Health Canada
Jeanne Mance Building #19, 10th Floor, A.L. 1910C
Tunney's Pasture
Ottawa, Ontario
K1A 0K9

Telephone: (613) 941-2395
Fax: (613) 941-9927

This publication can also be accessed electronically via the Internet at:
http://www.hc-sc.gc.ca/pphb-dgspsp/rhs-ssg/index.html

Également disponible en français sous le titre :
Rapport sur la santé périnatale au Canada, 2003

Suggested citation: Health Canada. Canadian Perinatal Health Report, 2003.
Ottawa: Minister of Public Works and Government Services Canada, 2003.

Published by authority of the Minister of Health

Table of Contents

Section A: Determinants of Maternal, Fetal and Infant Health

1. Behaviours and Practices

2. Health Services

Section B: Maternal, Fetal and Infant Health Outcomes

3. Maternal Health Outcomes

4. Fetal and Infant Health Outcomes

Bibliography

Section C: Appendices

List of Figures and Tables

Figures

List of Figures and Tables

Tables

Acknowledgements

This report could not have been completed without the dedication and cooperation of many individuals. The Division of Health Surveillance and Epidemiology would like to thank the following people:

Ora Kendall and Wai Ming Chan of the Data Development and Exchange Program, Public Health Training and Applications Division, Health Canada, for their management of the acquisition and maintenance of most of the vital statistics and hospital datasets used in this report;

The Vital Statistics Registrars of the provinces and territories for providing us, through Statistics Canada, with the provincial and territorial births, stillbirths and deaths data;

Michel Pageau, Marc Ferland and Louis Rochette of the Direction de santé publique de la Régie régionale de la santé et des services sociaux de Québec for providing us with hospital discharge data for Quebec. We would also like to thank Mr. Pageau and Mr. Ferland for their collaboration in reviewing the French *Rapport sur la santé périnatale au Canada, 2003*;

Deborah Malazdrewicz and Penny Brown of Manitoba Health's Health Information Management group for providing us with hospital discharge data for Manitoba;

Megan Rogers of Dalhousie University's Population Health Research Unit for providing us with hospital discharge data for Nova Scotia;

Eleanor Paulson and her colleagues, Scientific Publication and Multimedia Services, Health Canada, for the initial editing and proofreading;

Allium Consulting Group Inc., and Paraphrase rédaction et communication inc., for their essential role in editing and proofreading.

Finally, we would like to thank the authors, editors and members of the Canadian Perinatal Surveillance System (CPSS) Steering Committee and Study Groups for their continued dedication to the work of the CPSS.

Contributors

Authors

Sharon Bartholomew, MHSc
Jennifer Crain
Susie Dzakpasu, MHSc
Ruth Kohut, RN, MSc
Shiliang Liu, MB, PhD
I.D. Rusen, MD, MSc, FRCPC
Shi Wu Wen, MB, PhD

Editors

Susie Dzakpasu, MHSc
K.S. Joseph, MD, PhD
Catherine McCourt, MD, MHA, FRCPC
Hajnal Molnar-Szakács, MD, MSc
Reg Sauve, MD, MPH, FRCPC

Research Assistants

Jean-François Cayer
Jennifer Crain
Ling Huang, MD, MSc
Louie Macleod
Kathleen Moss, MA
Jocelyn Rouleau
Martine Tardif
Barbara Xiao, MSc

Administrative Support

Ernesto Delgado

Graphic Design and Layout

Gina Marin

Canadian Perinatal Surveillance System Steering Committee and Study Group Members (2003)

CPSS Chair

Reg Sauve, MD, MPH, FRCPC
Professor of Paediatrics and Community
    Health Sciences
University of Calgary
Calgary, Alberta
Visiting Scientist to Health Canada
Ottawa, Ontario
SC, FIHSG, MESG, MHSG

Representatives

Alexander Allen, MD, FRCPC
Canadian Perinatal Programs
    Coalition
Halifax, Nova Scotia
SC, FIHSG (Co-chair)

Madeline Boscoe, RN
Canadian Women's Health Network
Winnipeg, Manitoba
SC, MESG

Jane Evans, PhD, FCCMG
Canadian College of Medical
    Geneticists
Winnipeg, Manitoba
SC, FIHSG

Nonie Fraser-Lee, MHSA
Canadian Public Health Association
Edmonton, Alberta
SC, FIHSG, MESG

Karen Fung Kee Fung, MD
Society of Obstetricians and
    Gynaecologists of Canada
Ottawa, Ontario
SC, FIHSG

Vania Jimenez, MDCM, CCFP, FCFP
College of Family Physicians of Canada
Montréal, Quebec
SC, MESG

Nizar Ladak, MEd
Canadian Institute for Health
    Information
Toronto, Ontario
SC

Shoo K Lee, PhD, MBBS, FRCPC
Canadian Paediatric Society
Vancouver, British Columbia
SC, FIHSG

Miriam Levitt, PhD
Canadian Institute of Child Health
Ottawa, Ontario
SC, MESG

Robert Liston, MB, ChB, FRCSC,
    FRCOG
Society of Obstetricians and
    Gynaecologists of Canada
Vancouver, British Columbia
SC, FIHSG, MHSG (Co-chair)

Jennifer Medves, RN, PhD
Canadian Nurses Association
Association of Women's Health,
  Obstetric and Neonatal Nurses,
  Canada
Kingston, Ontario
SC, FIHSG

Beverley O'Brien, RM, DNSc
Canadian Association of Midwives
Edmonton, Alberta
SC, FIHSG, MESG

Catherine Royle, RN, MN
Canadian Perinatal Programs
  Coalition
St. John's, Newfoundland
SC, FIHSG, MESG

Individual Experts

Thomas F. Baskett, MB, FRCS
Department of Obstetrics and
  Gynaecology
Dalhousie University
Halifax, Nova Scotia
MHSG

Beverley Chalmers, DSc(Med), PhD
The Centre for Research in Women's
  Health
University of Toronto
Toronto, Ontario
SC, MESG (Co-chair)

Kinga David, MHSc
Hospital Morbidity & Therapeutic
  Abortions Databases
Canadian Institute for Health
  Information
Toronto, Ontario
FIHSG, MHSG

William Fraser, MD
Département d'Obstétrique-
  Gynécologie
Université de Montréal
Hôpital Ste-Justine
Montréal, Quebec
MHSG

Maureen Heaman, RN, MN, PhD
Faculty of Nursing
University of Manitoba
Winnipeg, Manitoba
MESG, MHSG

K.S. Joseph, MD, PhD
Perinatal Epidemiology Research Unit
Departments of Obstetrics and
  Gynecology and of Pediatrics
Dalhousie University and the IWK
  Health Centre
Halifax, Nova Scotia
SC, FIHSG, MHSG

Janusz Kaczorowski, PhD
Departments of Family Medicine
  and of Clinical Epidemiology
  and Biostatistics
McMaster University
Centre for Evaluation of Medicines
St. Joseph's Healthcare
Hamilton, Ontario
MESG

Robert Kinch, MD
Department of Obstetrics and
  Gynaecology
McGill University Health Centre
Montréal, Quebec
MHSG

Michael Kramer, MD
Departments of Pediatrics and of
  Epidemiology and Biostatistics
McGill University
Faculty of Medicine
Montréal, Quebec
SC, FIHSG, MHSG

Cheryl Levitt, MBBCh, CCFP, FCFP
Department of Family Medicine
McMaster University
Hamilton, Ontario
MESG

Judith Lumley, MB, PhD
Centre for the Study of Mothers'
  and Children's Health
La Trobe University
Carlton, Victoria, Australia
SC, FIHSG, MESG

Brian McCarthy, MD
Centers for Disease Control
  and Prevention
Atlanta, Georgia
SC, FIHSG

Arne Ohlsson, MD, MSc, FRCPC
Departments of Paediatrics, Obstetrics
  and Gynaecology, and Health
  Policy, Management and Evaluation
University of Toronto
Toronto, Ontario
Canadian Cochrane Network and Centre
McMaster University
Hamilton, Ontario
SC, FIHSG

Robert Platt, PhD
Departments of Pediatrics and of
  Epidemiology and Biostatistics
McGill University
Faculty of Medicine
Montréal, Quebec
FIHSG

Janet Smylie, MD, CCFP, MPH
Department of Family Medicine
University of Ottawa
Ottawa, Ontario
SC, FIHSG, MESG

Federal Government Representatives

Gary Catlin
Health Statistics Division
Statistics Canada
Ottawa, Ontario
SC

Margaret Cyr
Occupational and Environmental
  Health Research Section
Statistics Canada
Ottawa, Ontario
FIHSG, MHSG

Martha Fair, MSc
Occupational and Environmental
  Health Research Section
Statistics Canada
Ottawa, Ontario
SC, FIHSG, MHSG

Sharon McMahon, MA
Community Acquired Infections
  Division
Population and Public Health Branch
Health Canada
Ottawa, Ontario
MESG

Nicki Sims-Jones, RN, MScN
Children's Environmental Health
  Division
Healthy Environments and Consumer
  Safety Branch
Health Canada
Ottawa, Ontario
MESG

Christina Stanford, PhD (c)
Division of Childhood and
  Adolescence
Population and Public Health Branch
Health Canada
Ottawa, Ontario
SC, MESG

Susan Taylor-Clapp, RN, MSc
Health Information and Analysis
    Division
First Nations & Inuit Health Branch
Health Canada
Ottawa, Ontario
SC, FIHSG, MESG, MHSG

Russell Wilkins, BA, BEd, MUrb
Health Analysis and Measurement
    Group
Statistics Canada
Department of Epidemiology and
    Community Medicine
University of Ottawa
Ottawa, Ontario
FIHSG

FIHSG — Fetal and Infant Health Study Group
MESG — Maternity Experiences Study Group
MHSG — Maternal Health Study Group
SC — CPSS Steering Committee

Introduction

The *Canadian Perinatal Health Report, 2003* is the third national perinatal surveillance report from the Canadian Perinatal Surveillance System (CPSS), continuing an important initiative of the Maternal and Infant Health Section, Health Canada. In 1995, the Section and the CPSS Steering Committee developed the conceptual framework for the CPSS, identified appropriate perinatal health indicators and their data sources, and undertook analysis and interpretation of the data. In 2000, the first *Canadian Perinatal Health Report*[1] was published. The second report, *Congenital Anomalies in Canada — A Perinatal Health Report*,[2] was published in 2002. This third report provides updates on the indicators from the 2000 report, describing temporal trends and differences observed at the national and provincial/ territorial levels.

In 2000, the CPSS also published *Perinatal Health Indicators for Canada: A Resource Manual*.[3] This document provides detailed information on the indicators being monitored by the CPSS and is intended as a reference guide for readers of the national surveillance report and for those undertaking perinatal health data collection, analysis, interpretation, and response at provincial, territorial or regional levels.

CPSS Conceptual Framework

The CPSS considers a health surveillance system to be a network of people and activities that maintain the surveillance process.[4] The surveillance itself is a continuous and systematic process of collection, analysis and interpretation of descriptive information for monitoring health problems[4] with the aim of reducing health disparities and promoting health. Figure A on the next page depicts the cycle of surveillance, adapted from a conceptual framework described by Dr. Brian McCarthy, Centers for Disease Control and Prevention (CDC), Atlanta, Georgia.[5]

Overlying this concept of health surveillance is the concept of the determinants of health: that health status is influenced by a range of factors including, but not limited to, health care.[6] Therefore, it is important to monitor not only health outcomes but also factors — such as behaviours, physical and social environments, and health services — that may affect those outcomes. The aim of health surveillance is to contribute to improved health outcomes. Information on trends in and patterns of various risk and protective factors helps to explain patterns of morbidity and mortality, and may point the way to effective interventions and appropriate allocation of health resources. Monitoring of health determinants and monitoring of health outcomes are strongly interrelated in health surveillance systems.

It is important to monitor not only health outcomes but also factors — such as behaviours, physical and social environments, and health services — that may affect those outcomes.

FIGURE A **National Health Surveillance**

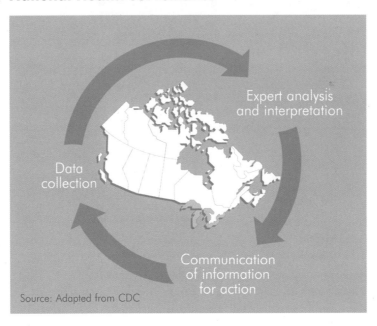

Source: Adapted from CDC

CPSS Structure

The mandate of the CPSS is to contribute to improved health for pregnant women, mothers, and infants in Canada through ongoing monitoring and reporting on perinatal health determinants and outcomes. The CPSS collaborates with Statistics Canada, the Canadian Institute for Health Information (CIHI), provincial and territorial governments, health professional organizations, advocacy groups and university-based researchers. Representatives of these groups and several international experts serve on the CPSS Steering Committee and its study groups: the Fetal and Infant Health Study Group (FIHSG), the Maternal Health Study Group (MHSG) and the Maternity Experiences Study Group (MESG) (see Figure B). The principles and objectives of the CPSS are described in more detail elsewhere.[7,8]

FIGURE B **Structure of the Canadian Perinatal Surveillance System**

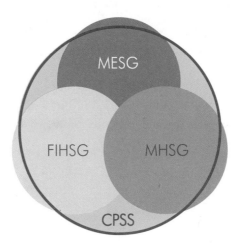

Fetal and Infant Health Study Group (FIHSG)

The mandate of the FIHSG is to conduct surveillance on fetal and infant mortality and morbidity. The FIHSG primarily uses existing data sources for its surveillance efforts. The FIHSG is also working toward developing a national perinatal database. Other projects include studies on preterm birth, fetal growth, perinatal mortality and infant mortality.

Maternal Health Study Group (MHSG)

The mandate of the MHSG is to conduct surveillance on key behaviours, health services and outcomes related to maternal health. The MHSG primarily uses existing data sources for its surveillance efforts. Current maternal health surveillance projects include the surveillance of induced abortion, cesarean delivery, and severe maternal morbidity. The MHSG is also conducting a review of maternal deaths in Canada. The results of the maternal death review will be presented as the fourth national perinatal surveillance report.

Maternity Experiences Study Group (MESG)

The mandate of the MESG is to guide the development, implementation, expert analysis and reporting of a national Maternity Experiences Survey (MES). The primary objective of the MES is to document Canadian women's knowledge, experiences and practices during pregnancy, birth, and the early postpartum months and their perceptions of perinatal care, as an integral component of perinatal health surveillance. The first survey of its kind in Canada, the MES will also provide information for an in-depth examination of selected population subgroups, such as recent immigrants and teenage mothers, deemed to be at a higher risk of adverse perinatal health outcomes. A pilot study was conducted in the fall of 2002, and planning for national implementation is currently under way.

CPSS Indicators

A health indicator is a measurement that, when compared with either a standard or desired level of achievement, provides information regarding a health outcome or important health determinant.[7] The Maternal and Infant Health Section and the CPSS Steering Committee undertook a process to identify the perinatal health indicators that should be monitored by a national perinatal surveillance system.[3] The group considered the importance of the health outcome or determinant, the scientific properties of the indicator, such as its validity in measuring that outcome or determinant, and the feasibility of collecting the data required to construct it. *Appendix B* provides the set of indicators that resulted from this process. The first 43 indicators listed are ranked according to the Steering Committee's assessment of health importance. Nine additional indicators were added to the list after subsequent consultations.

Outline of the Report

This report contains information on 27 perinatal health indicators for which we currently have national data. These are grouped as indicators of health determinants (behaviours and practices, and health services) and indicators of outcomes (maternal, fetal, and infant health). As in the previous report, for each indicator, surveillance results are presented, data limitations discussed, and key references listed. Statistics for each indicator consist mainly of temporal trends at the national level and interprovincial/territorial comparisons for the most recent year for which data were available. However, there are important differences between the two reports, which have contributed to an improved reporting on the determinants and outcomes related to perinatal health in Canada. The most important differences are described in the *Overview* section.

Perinatal health surveillance provides both a measurement tool and a stimulus to action.

The principal data sources used for this perinatal health report are vital statistics, hospitalization data and the National Longitudinal Survey of Children and Youth (NLSCY). Population estimates and induced abortion statistics from Statistics Canada are also used. A detailed description of these data sources, including data quality, is presented in the *Data Sources and Methods* section of the report. This section also presents the methods for calculating each indicator based on the data source.

Summary

Perinatal health surveillance has an important and fundamental role in providing the necessary information to be used to improve the health status of pregnant women, mothers and infants in Canada. It comprises a dynamic, integrated system of ongoing data collection, linkage, validation, analysis and interpretation on vital perinatal health issues. The result is information that permits identification of "red flags," tracking of temporal and geographic trends and disparities, as well as assessment of the effect of changes in clinical practice and public health policy. Perinatal health surveillance provides both a measurement tool (where we have been in the past, where we are at present) and a stimulus to action (where we need to be in the future).

Reg Sauve, MD, MPH, FRCPC
Professor of Paediatrics and
  Community Health Sciences
University of Calgary
Visiting Scientist to Health Canada
Chair, CPSS Steering Committee

Hajnal Molnar-Szakács, MD, MSc
Chief, Maternal and Infant Health Section
Centre for Healthy Human Development
Population and Public Health Branch
Health Canada

References

1. Health Canada. *Canadian Perinatal Health Report, 2000*. Ottawa: Minister of Public Works and Government Services Canada, 2000 (Catalogue No. H49-142/2000E). URL: <http://www.hc-sc.gc.ca/pphb-dgspsp/rhs-ssg/index.html>.

2. Health Canada. *Congenital Anomalies in Canada — A Perinatal Health Report, 2002*. Ottawa: Minister of Public Works and Government Services Canada, 2002 (Catalogue No. H39-641/2002E). URL: <http://www.hc-sc.gc.ca/pphb-dgspsp/rhs-ssg/index.html>.

3. Health Canada. *Perinatal Health Indicators for Canada: A Resource Manual*. Ottawa: Minister of Public Works and Government Services Canada, 2000 (Catalogue No. H49-135/2000E). URL: <http://www.hc-sc.gc.ca/pphb-dgspsp/rhs-ssg/index.html>.

4. Buehler J. Surveillance. In: Rothman KJ, Greenland S (Eds.), *Modern Epidemiology*, 2nd Edition. Philadelphia: Lippincott-Raven, 1998.

5. McCarthy B. The risk approach revisited: a critical review of developing country experience and its use in health planning. In: Liljestrand J, Povey WG (Eds.), *Maternal Health Care in an International Perspective. Proceedings of the XXII Berzelius Symposium, 1991 May 27-29, Stockholm, Sweden*. Sweden: Uppsala University, 1992:107-24.

6. Federal, Provincial and Territorial Advisory Committee on Population Health. *Strategies for Population Health: Investing in the Health of Canadians*. Ottawa: Minister of Supply and Services Canada, 1994.

7. Health Canada. *Canadian Perinatal Surveillance System Progress Report*. Ottawa: Minister of Supply and Services Canada, 1995.

8. Health Canada. *Canadian Perinatal Surveillance System Progress Report 1997-1998*. Ottawa: Minister of Public Works and Government Services Canada, 1999.

Perinatal Health in Canada: An Overview

The *Canadian Perinatal Health Report, 2003* continues an important initiative of the Canadian Perinatal Surveillance System (CPSS) and provides an updated description of determinants and outcomes related to fetal, infant and maternal health in Canada. As in the previous report,[1] the focus is on documenting the magnitude of specific indicators of perinatal health and describing temporal trends and interprovincial/territorial differences in indicator values. There are several important differences between the two reports, however.

Temporal trends examined in this report, with the exception of the ones in this *Overview* and the indicator on maternal mortality, use 1991 as the base year in order to avoid excluding Newfoundland from tabulations. (Data on the characteristics of mothers and infants are not available in Statistics Canada's files for births that took place in Newfoundland before that year.) Second, indicators based on hospital discharge data now include information from Nova Scotia, Quebec and Manitoba. Hospital discharge data from these provinces are not available to Health Canada for all years, and this had resulted in the exclusion of these provinces from some tabulations previously. The omission has now been rectified by obtaining data directly from the provinces involved. Another notable change is that the algorithm used for identifying obstetric records in the Discharge Abstract Database (DAD) of the Canadian Institute for Health Information (CIHI) has been modified. Finally, vital statistics data from Ontario, previously excluded from all tabulations because of concerns regarding data quality, are presented in *Appendix G* of this report. These changes have resulted in a more comprehensive and higher quality *Canadian Perinatal Health Report*. The CPSS recognizes that careful examination and tabulation of perinatal data at the national and provincial/territorial levels will ensure improvements in data quality, besides facilitating informed decision making at the clinical, public health and health policy levels.

This *Overview* discusses specific areas of perinatal health that are of contemporary concern and highlights a few topics requiring attention from a public health, health care or surveillance standpoint.

Global Ranking of Infant Mortality

Organizations such as the United Nations Children's Fund (UNICEF) and the Organisation for Economic Cooperation and Development periodically rank countries on the basis of infant mortality rates or mortality rates among children under five years of age. These rankings receive widespread attention in the news media and are not infrequently the basis of political rhetoric. In recent years, Canada has not scored particularly well in such rankings: in the 2003 UNICEF report[2] Canada ranked behind several other countries both in terms of infant mortality in 2001 (cited as 5 per 1,000 live births) and under-five mortality in 2001 (cited as 7 per 1,000 live births). Sweden led the rankings with an infant mortality rate of 3 per 1,000 live births in 2001 and an identical under-five mortality rate (3 per 1,000 live births).

Other countries with infant and under-five mortality rates between 3 and 4 per 1,000 live births in 2001 included Denmark, Iceland, Norway and Singapore. Several countries with under-five mortality rates between 5 and 7 per 1,000 live births also ranked ahead of Canada.

Does this ranking indicate better perinatal health and high quality health care elsewhere, or is it a reflection of poor health and a deficient health care system in Canada? This question cannot be answered on the basis of the available information. Although infant and under-five mortality rates are useful indices for assessing the health status of populations, various factors limit their usefulness for international rankings, such as those provided by UNICEF. First, UNICEF estimates of Canadian infant mortality and under-five mortality for 2001 are projected estimates. In fact, Statistics Canada had not released infant mortality rates for 2000 and 2001 when UNICEF published its international rankings. Second, and more importantly, international comparisons of infant mortality and under-five mortality are seriously flawed as a result of enormous regional differences in the registration of live births.

International comparisons of infant mortality and under-five mortality are seriously flawed as a result of enormous regional differences in the registration of live births.

The World Health Organization (WHO) defines a live birth as "a product of conception, irrespective of the duration of the pregnancy, which . . . breathes or shows any other evidence of life . . .".[3] Despite being generally accepted, this definition is not the basis for birth registration in many countries where considerations regarding viability affect decisions related to birth registration. Thus, countries that tend to register live births according to the WHO definition of live birth tend to have an excess of births (and consequently infant deaths) at the borderline of viability when compared with countries that have more pragmatic birth registration policies.[4-7] For instance, studies have shown that the registration of live births with a birth weight of < 500 g varies 50-fold between country and population groups, ranging from < 1 per 10,000 live births in Sweden and Israel to 3 per 10,000 in Norway and over 10 per 10,000 in the United States.[7] Birth registrations of infants < 500 g is more frequent in Canada than in many other countries and has been increasing over the last 15 years, despite no concurrent change in other low birth weight categories.[8-10] There were 8.6 per 10,000 live births of < 500 g in Canada (excluding Ontario) in 1997-1999, and the infant mortality rate in this birth weight category was 943 per 1,000 live births.

Differences in birth registration policies are also evident in the frequency of registration of live births weighing between 500 g and 749 g.[7] As a consequence of these differences in birth registration, infant deaths among live births < 1,000 g vary from less than 10% of all infant deaths in some countries to over 35% in others.[6] Approximately 44 per 10,000 live births in Canada in 1997-1999 were < 1,000 g, and 40% of all infant deaths occurred among live births in this birth weight category.

The WHO has long recognized that the validity of international comparisons of infant mortality can be compromised by the differential exclusion of extremely low birth weight live births and recommends the restriction of comparative statistics to those involving live births with a birth weight of ≥ 1,000 g.[3] When birth weight information is missing, the WHO recommends using the corresponding gestational age (28 completed weeks) or body length (35 cm crown to heel). It has been suggested that similar restricted analyses be employed for temporal and regional comparisons within Canada, given temporal changes and interprovincial differences in birth registration policies.[8,9]

Perhaps the greatest impediment to the implementation of such birth weight-specific comparisons of infant mortality (i.e., infant mortality among live births ≥ 1,000 g) arises because such information is not routinely available for many countries. A shift from "period-based" infant mortality rates (ratio of infant deaths in a given year to live births in the same year) to "birth cohort-based" infant mortality rates (infant deaths among all live births that occur in a given year, expressed as a proportion) is a prerequisite for such birth weight-specific infant mortality calculations. This report includes detailed tables providing birth cohort-based infant mortality rates in Canada among all live births and among live births ≥ 500 g and ≥ 1,000 g in order to facilitate valid international comparisons of infant mortality (Figure 1 and *Appendix E*, Tables E1 and E2). Similar tabulations are provided for provinces and territories to enable within-Canada comparisons (Figure 2 and *Appendix E*, Tables E3 and E4). Stillbirth rates, which are affected by similar registration biases,[11] are also presented with and without birth weight restrictions (page 87).

FIGURE 1 **Birth cohort-based crude infant mortality rates (IMR) and IMR among live births ≥ 1,000 g,**
Canada (excluding Ontario), 1991-1999*

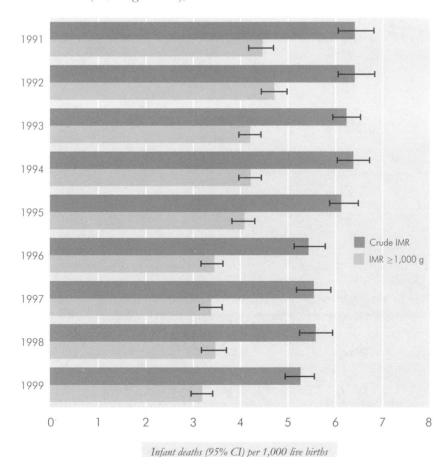

Infant deaths (95% CI) per 1,000 live births

Source: Statistics Canada. Canadian Vital Statistics System, 1991-1999 (birth-infant death linked files).
*Data for Ontario were excluded because of data quality concerns.
CI — confidence interval.

FIGURE 2 **Birth cohort-based crude infant mortality rates (IMR) and IMR among live births ≥ 1000 g, by province/territory,**
Canada (excluding Ontario), 1997-1999*

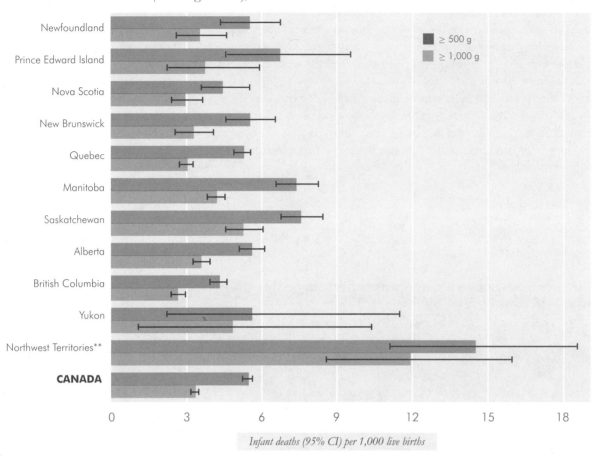

Infant deaths (95% CI) per 1,000 live births

Source: Statistics Canada. Canadian Vital Statistics System, 1997-1999 (birth-infant death linked files).
*Data for Ontario were excluded because of data quality concerns.
**Nunavut is included in the Northwest Territories in the data for 1999.
CI — confidence interval.

Fetal and infant mortality rates in Canada have declined steadily over the last 15 years.

Facilitation of valid international and other comparisons of infant mortality rates notwithstanding, it is necessary to introduce a cautionary note regarding the meaning and purpose of rankings based on infant mortality rates. Analyses restricted to live births ≥ 1,000 g eliminate a substantial burden of mortality from Canadian infant death statistics. The complexities inherent in interpreting birth weight-specific comparisons of mortality constitute another reason for de-emphasizing such international comparisons of infant mortality.[12-14] Finally, ranking of countries or provinces/territories may not be as helpful as careful and detailed examinations of the causes and circumstances of infant mortality, carried out specifically with the purpose of identifying preventable causes of death.

Temporal Trends in Fetal and Infant Mortality in Canada

Fetal and infant mortality rates in Canada have declined steadily over the last 15 years. Figures 3A, 3B and 3C show birth cohort-based stillbirth, neonatal, perinatal, infant and fetal-infant mortality rates among singleton, twin and triplet births in Canada (excluding Newfoundland and Ontario) between 1985 and 1999. Only births ≥ 500 g were included in the calculation of these rates, and three-year moving averages (two-year averages for the extreme years) were employed for trends among twin and triplet births in order to obtain stable estimates. Among singleton births, fetal-infant mortality rates decreased by 31% (95% confidence interval [CI] 26% to 35%), from 12.0 per 1,000 total births in 1985 to 8.3 per 1,000 total births in 1999 (*Appendix E*, Table E5). Meanwhile, fetal-infant mortality rates among twins declined by 41% (95% CI 32% to 49%), from 53.3 per 1,000 total births in 1985-1986 to 31.5 per 1,000 total births in 1998-1999 (*Appendix E*, Table E6). Fetal-infant mortality rates among triplet births, while substantially higher than among singleton and twin births, decreased by 58% (95% CI 22% to 77%) between 1985-1986 and 1998-1999, from 109.9 to 46.2 per 1,000 total births. Note: variance estimates (and 95% CI) for changes in twin and triplet death rates provided here and elsewhere have not been corrected for the potential non-independence in outcomes among members of a multiple birth set.

FIGURE 3A **Birth cohort-based fetal and infant mortality rates among singleton births ≥ 500 g,** *Canada (excluding Newfoundland and Ontario),* * *1985-1999*

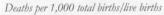

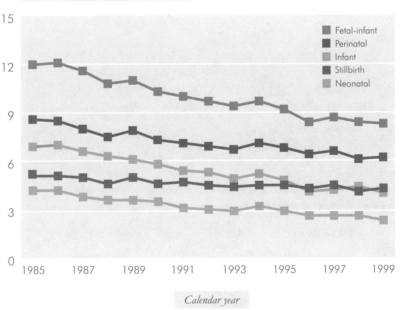

Source: Statistics Canada. Canadian Vital Statistics System, 1985-1999 (birth-infant death linked files).
*Data for Newfoundland were excluded because data were not available nationally prior to 1991.
Data for Ontario were excluded because of data quality concerns.

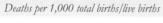 **Birth cohort-based fetal and infant mortality rates* among twin births ≥ 500 g,** *Canada (excluding Newfoundland and Ontario),** 1985-1999*

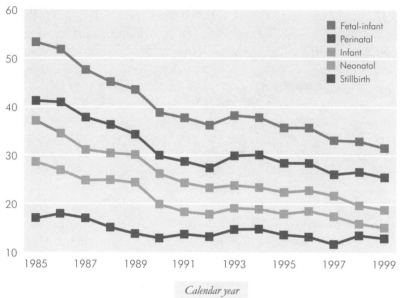

Source: Statistics Canada. Canadian Vital Statistics System, 1985-1999 (birth-infant death linked files).
*Rates represent moving averages.
**Data for Newfoundland were excluded because data were not available nationally prior to 1991.
  Data for Ontario were excluded because of data quality concerns.

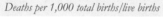 **Birth cohort-based fetal and infant mortality rates* among triplet births ≥ 500 g,** *Canada (excluding Newfoundland and Ontario),** 1985-1999*

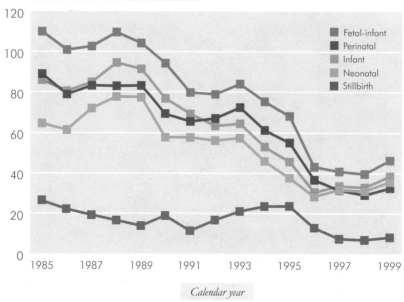

Source: Statistics Canada. Canadian Vital Statistics System, 1985-1999 (birth-infant death linked files).
*Rates represent moving averages.
**Data for Newfoundland were excluded because data were not available nationally prior to 1991.
  Data for Ontario were excluded because of data quality concerns.

Cause-Specific Reductions in Fetal and Infant Mortality

Fetal Deaths (Stillbirths)

Among births of singletons ≥ 500 g, significant temporal reductions were observed in stillbirths due to complications of the placenta, cord and membranes (ICD-9 762), and intrauterine hypoxia and birth asphyxia (ICD-9 768). The rate of stillbirth due to complications of the placenta, cord and membranes declined from 1.93 per 1,000 total births in 1985-1988 to 1.38 per 1,000 total births in 1996-1999 (29% reduction, 95% CI 23% to 34%), while rates of stillbirth due to intrauterine hypoxia and birth asphyxia decreased from 0.36 in 1985-1988 to 0.26 per 1,000 total births in 1996-1999 (28% reduction, 95% CI 15% to 40%). Figure 4A and *Appendix E*, Table E7, show temporal changes in cause-specific stillbirth rates.

FIGURE 4A **Cause-specific rates of stillbirth among singleton births ≥ 500 g,** *Canada (excluding Newfoundland and Ontario),* 1985-1988, 1989-1992, 1993-1995 and 1996-1999*

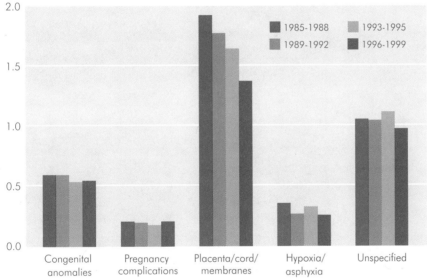

Stillbirths per 1,000 total births

1985-1988 1993-1995
1989-1992 1996-1999

Cause of stillbirth

Source: Statistics Canada. Canadian Vital Statistics System, 1985-1999 (birth-infant death linked files).
*Data for Newfoundland were excluded because data were not available nationally prior to 1991.
Data for Ontario were excluded because of data quality concerns.

FIGURE 4B **Cause-specific rates of stillbirth among twin births ≥ 500 g,**
Canada (excluding Newfoundland and Ontario), 1985-1988, 1989-1992, 1993-1995*
and 1996-1999

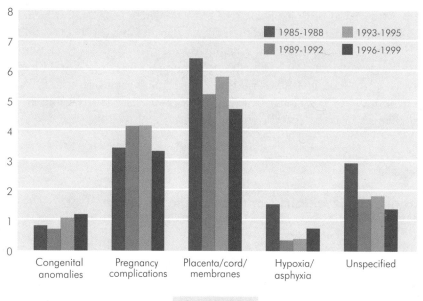

Source: Statistics Canada. Canadian Vital Statistics System, 1985-1999 (birth-infant death linked files).
*Data for Newfoundland were excluded because data were not available nationally prior to 1991.
Data for Ontario were excluded because of data quality concerns.

Stillbirths due to complications of the placenta, cord and membranes also declined among births of twins ≥ 500 g, from 6.42 per 1,000 total births in 1985-1988 to 4.74 per 1,000 total births in 1996-1999 (26% reduction, 95% CI 3% to 44%). Stillbirths due to unspecified causes (ICD-9 779.9) also decreased significantly, from 2.94 to 1.41 per 1,000 total births (52% reduction, 95% CI 24% to 70%), and there was a 51% reduction (CI 9% to 74%) in stillbirths due to intrauterine hypoxia and birth asphyxia (Figure 4B and *Appendix E,* Table E8).

Infant Deaths

Congenital anomalies (ICD-9 740 to 759) as a cause of infant death fell by 43% (95% CI 38% to 47%), from 2.31 per 1,000 live births in 1985-1988 to 1.32 per 1,000 live births in 1996-1999 among live births of singletons ≥ 500 g (Figure 5A and *Appendix E,* Table E9). The considerable decline in the birth prevalence of congenital anomalies observed in Canada and elsewhere,[9,15-21] and the consequent reduction in their contribution to late fetal and infant death are unprecedented. Other causes of infant death among singletons also decreased in frequency between 1985-1988 and 1996-1999, including respiratory distress syndrome (RDS) (ICD-9 769), sudden infant death syndrome (SIDS) (ICD-9 798.0), and disorders relating to short gestation and unspecified low birth weight (ICD-9 765), which decreased by 69% (95% CI 63% to 74%), 53% (95% CI 47% to 59%) and 25% (95% CI 8% to 39%), respectively. Among live births of twins ≥ 500 g, infant deaths due to maternal complications of pregnancy decreased by 44% (95% CI 19% to 61%), and those due to short gestation and unspecified low birth weight, and RDS decreased by 55% (95% CI 24% to 73%) and 65% (95% CI 52% to 75%), respectively (Figure 5B and *Appendix E*, Table E10). Also, infant deaths due to SIDS decreased by 56% (95% CI 19% to 76%), and those due to intrauterine hypoxia and birth asphyxia decreased by 63% (95% CI 10% to 85%).

FIGURE 5A **Cause-specific infant mortality rates (IMR) among singleton live births ≥ 500 g,** *Canada (excluding Newfoundland and Ontario),* 1985-1988, 1989-1992, 1993-1995 and 1996-1999*

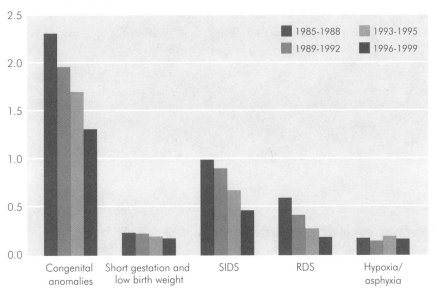

Infant deaths per 1,000 live births

Legend:
- 1985-1988
- 1989-1992
- 1993-1995
- 1996-1999

Cause of infant death

Source: Statistics Canada. Canadian Vital Statistics System, 1985-1999 (birth-infant death linked files).
*Data for Newfoundland were excluded because data were not available nationally prior to 1991.
Data for Ontario were excluded because of data quality concerns.

Congenital anomalies as a cause of infant death fell by 43%, from 2.31 per 1,000 live births in 1985-1988 to 1.32 per 1,000 live births in 1996-1999.

FIGURE 5B **Cause-specific infant mortality rates (IMR) among twin live births ≥ 500 g,** *Canada (excluding Newfoundland and Ontario),* 1985-1988, 1989-1992, 1993-1995 and 1996-1999*

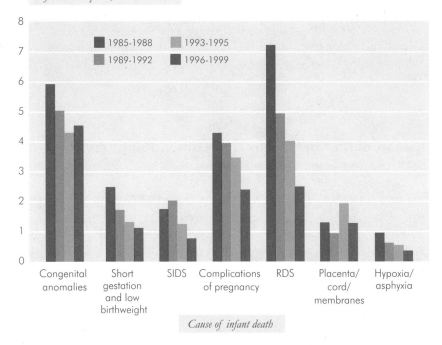

Infant deaths per 1,000 live births

Legend:
- 1985-1988
- 1989-1992
- 1993-1995
- 1996-1999

Cause of infant death

Source: Statistics Canada. Canadian Vital Statistics System, 1985-1999 (birth-infant death linked files).
*Data for Newfoundland were excluded because data were not available nationally prior to 1991.
Data for Ontario were excluded because of data quality concerns.

The Role of Obstetric Intervention in the Decline in Fetal and Infant Mortality

The causes of the declines in fetal and infant mortality in Canada are multi-factorial. The success of SIDS prevention, through interventions that have reduced the prevalence of the prone sleeping position, is a striking example of simple knowledge translation.[22] On the other hand, technologically sophisticated advances in neonatal care have reduced infant mortality at gestational ages as early as 24 to 25 weeks.[23] Obstetric intervention is another factor that has played a substantial role in the temporal reduction in late fetal and infant mortality rates over the last 15 years. Two broad and distinct modalities of obstetric intervention have been primarily responsible, namely, prenatal diagnosis of congenital anomalies (coupled with selective termination of affected pregnancies), and labour induction and/or cesarean delivery.

Prenatal Diagnosis of Congenital Anomalies and Selective Termination

The rate of late fetal and infant deaths due to major congenital malformations has declined dramatically in Canada and elsewhere in recent years.[9,15-21] This has been a consequence of increases and improvements in prenatal screening and diagnosis (maternal serum screening, ultrasonography), and selective termination of pregnancies with serious congenital anomalies. Although the introduction of such technology has meant an increase in pregnancy termination for serious congenital malformations at very early gestational ages, it has been responsible for substantial declines in late fetal deaths due to neural tube defects (60% to 70% decrease), cardiovascular malformations (20% to 25% decrease), urinary tract anomalies (45% to 50% decrease), and multiple congenital anomalies (40% to 45% decrease) between 1981-1985 and 1994-1998.[20] Similarly, there has been a substantial drop in infant deaths due to congenital anomalies of the central nervous system (60% to 65% decrease), the cardiovascular system (40% to 50% decline) and the urinary tract (55% to 60% decline).[20] However, unlike declines in late fetal deaths due to congenital anomalies, which can be mostly attributed to prenatal diagnosis, the reduction in infant deaths due to congenital anomalies also reflects improvements in the surgical treatment of serious congenital anomalies.[24]

Population uptake of prenatal diagnosis is probably uneven across Canada because of differences in provincial/territorial programs and regional differences in rates of acceptance of prenatal diagnosis.[9] The provincial/territorial rate of infant death due to congenital anomalies is inversely related to the rate of fetal death due to congenital anomalies/pregnancy termination at 20 to 23 weeks' gestation.[9] As prenatal diagnostic testing improves and second trimester testing is replaced by first trimester tests, it is expected that the uptake of prenatal diagnosis will increase in both urban and rural areas of Canada. This is likely to lead to further declines in lethal congenital anomalies as a cause of late fetal and infant death.

Labour Induction and/or Cesarean Delivery

The other form of obstetric intervention that has increased dramatically in recent years is labour induction and/or cesarean delivery.[25-27] This increase has sparked concerns over costs and benefits, especially since labour induction rates in many industrialized countries have increased because of both medical and non-medical indications.[26,27] In Canada, the rate of medical induction of labour increased from 12.9% in 1991-1992 to 19.7% of hospital deliveries in 2000-2001, and the rate of surgical induction of labour increased from 6.3% in 1991-1992 to 7.7% of hospital deliveries in 2000-2001 (page 30). In fact, increases in labour induction have been largely responsible for the recent increase in preterm births observed in Canada and other industrialized countries.[28-31] However, the largest absolute increase in labour induction has occurred at term and postterm gestation in response to the results of studies contrasting the benefits and risks of labour induction and expectant management at term gestation.[32,33]

It is important to note that the increase in labour induction and/or cesarean delivery at preterm gestation has occurred principally between 34 and 36 weeks' gestation. Further, increases in labour induction have varied by risk status. For instance, preterm labour induction and/or cesarean delivery rates among low-risk pregnancies in Nova Scotia[31] increased slightly, from 0.34 to 0.41 per 100 live births, between 1988-1993 and 1994-1999 (absolute increase < 0.1%). Meanwhile, these rates increased from 3.0 to 3.9 per 100 live births among pregnancies at moderate-risk (absolute increase 0.9%) and from 16.6 to 20.1 per 100 live births among high-risk pregnancies (absolute increase 3.5%).[31] Another example of the differential increase in labour induction rates by risk status of pregnancy is observed when singleton, twin and triplet pregnancies are compared. Figures 6A, 6B and 6C show the incidence of birth at each gestational age (births at any gestation divided by fetuses at risk of

Prenatal diagnosis of congenital anomalies and selective termination has been responsible for dramatic declines in late fetal and infant death rates.

birth at that gestation, expressed per 1,000 fetuses at risk[14,34]). Birth rates between 33 and 36 weeks' gestation have increased to a much larger extent among triplet births relative to twin births (because of increases in labour induction and/or cesarean delivery), and this reflects the much higher risk of perinatal death among triplet births. Similarly, increases in birth rates among twins at 34 to 36 weeks' gestation have been far greater than those observed among singletons, and again this is because of a differential increase in labour induction and/or cesarean delivery among pregnancies at higher risk of perinatal death.

FIGURE 6A **Gestational age-specific birth rates among singleton births,**
Canada (excluding Newfoundland and Ontario), 1985-1988 and 1996-1999*

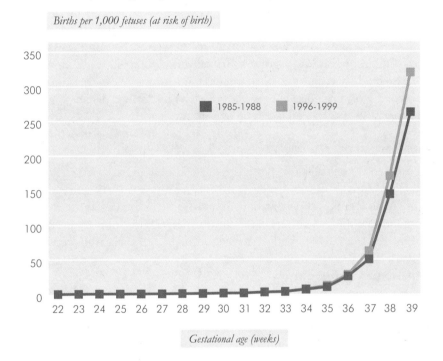

Source: Statistics Canada. Canadian Vital Statistics System, 1985-1999 (birth-infant death linked files).
*Data for Newfoundland were excluded because data were not available nationally prior to 1991.
Data for Ontario were excluded because of data quality concerns..

FIGURE 6B **Gestational age-specific birth rates among twin births,**
Canada (excluding Newfoundland and Ontario),* 1985-1988 and 1996-1999

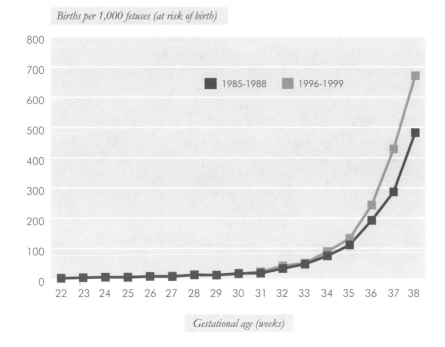

Births per 1,000 fetuses (at risk of birth)

■ 1985-1988 ■ 1996-1999

Gestational age (weeks)

Source: Statistics Canada. Canadian Vital Statistics System, 1985-1999 (birth-infant death linked files).
*Data for Newfoundland were excluded because data were not available nationally prior to 1991.
Data for Ontario were excluded because of data quality concerns.

FIGURE 6C **Gestational age-specific birth rates among triplet births,**
Canada (excluding Newfoundland and Ontario),* 1985-1992 and 1993-1999

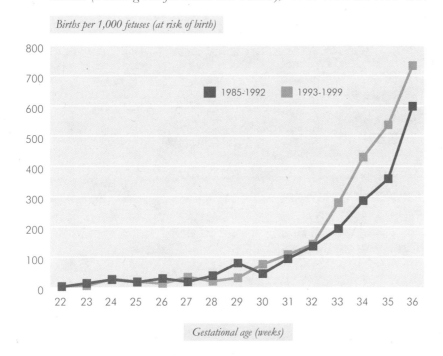

Births per 1,000 fetuses (at risk of birth)

■ 1985-1992 ■ 1993-1999

Gestational age (weeks)

Source: Statistics Canada. Canadian Vital Statistics System, 1985-1999 (birth-infant death linked files).
*Data for Newfoundland were excluded because data were not available nationally prior to 1991.
Data for Ontario were excluded because of data quality concerns.

Overview

Temporal increases in labour induction and/or cesarean delivery appear to be associated with reductions in perinatal mortality.[35] Figures 7A and 7B (also *Appendix E*, Tables E11 and E12) show that the magnitude of the temporal decrease in perinatal mortality was larger at later gestational ages, when the largest increases in labour induction and/or cesarean delivery occurred. For instance, among singletons (Figure 7A), the temporal decline in perinatal mortality between 1985-1988 and 1996-1999 among pregnancies reaching 40 weeks' gestation (32%, 95% CI 26% to 38%) was slightly larger than that among pregnancies reaching 34 weeks (28%, 95% CI 24% to 32%), which in turn was larger than that among pregnancies reaching 22 weeks' gestation (24%, 95% CI 22% to 27%). However, it is important to note that the reductions in mortality attributed to labour induction and/or cesarean delivery may be confounded by temporal increases in prenatal diagnosis and selective pregnancy termination. Also, temporal trends in perinatal mortality provide an incomplete picture and need to be complemented with studies of trends in serious neonatal morbidity.

FIGURE 7A **Percentage decline in stillbirth, neonatal and perinatal mortality among singleton births, by gestational age,** *Canada (excluding Newfoundland and Ontario),* 1985-1988 vs. 1996-1999*

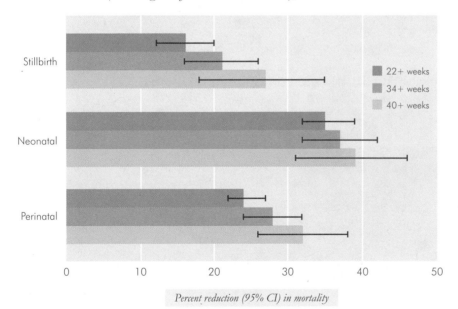

Percent reduction (95% CI) in mortality

Source: Statistics Canada. Canadian Vital Statistics System, 1985-1999 (birth-infant death linked files).
*Data for Newfoundland were excluded because data were not available nationally prior to 1991.
 Data for Ontario were excluded because of data quality concerns.
CI — confidence interval.

FIGURE 7B **Percentage decline in stillbirth, neonatal and perinatal mortality among twin births, by gestational age,** *Canada (excluding Newfoundland and Ontario),* 1985-1988 vs. 1996-1999*

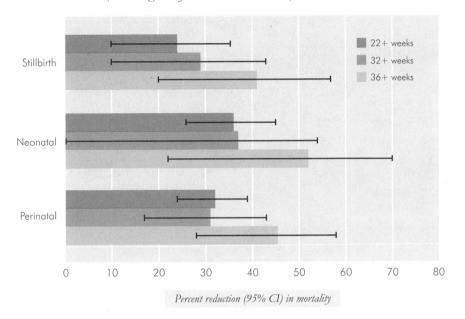

Percent reduction (95% CI) in mortality

Source: Statistics Canada. Canadian Vital Statistics System, 1985-1999 (birth-infant death linked files).
*Data for Newfoundland were excluded because data were not available nationally prior to 1991.
Data for Ontario were excluded because of data quality concerns.
CI — confidence interval.

Early delivery of the compromised fetus remains a cornerstone of modern obstetrics.

The increases in labour induction and cesarean delivery have occurred against a backdrop of technological advances in neonatal care, including the introduction of surfactant therapy and improvements in assisted ventilation. These advances in neonatal care have permitted prompt delivery in carefully selected cases in order to prevent serious perinatal morbidity and mortality. Early delivery of the compromised fetus remains a cornerstone of modern obstetrics. In fact, early delivery in a high-risk pregnancy showing unambiguous signs of serious fetal compromise is the raison d'être for antenatal care, high-risk labeling and careful monitoring of high-risk pregnancies.

This population perspective on the role of labour induction and cesarean delivery has little bearing on the appropriateness of labour induction or cesarean delivery in any single individual case. Labour induction and cesarean delivery are medical/ surgical procedures that carry risks to both the fetus and the mother. Early delivery without a justifiable indication can lead to an increased risk of serious neonatal morbidity or mortality, especially when carried out at preterm gestation. For these reasons, it is imperative that indications for labour induction and cesarean delivery be monitored by the clinical community in order to guard against compromising maternal or fetal safety.[36,37]

Behaviours and Practices in Pregnancy

There has been an enormous change in maternal characteristics in Canada over the last two decades. Some of these changes are well recognized, such as increases in older maternal age. In Canada (excluding Ontario), live births to mothers 35 to 39 years of age increased from 7.6% of live births in 1991 to 12.4% of live births in 2000 (page 25). The proportion of live births to women 30 to 34 years of age also increased, and the proportion of live births to women ≥ 40 years of age more than doubled. On the other hand, live births to women < 20 years of age have declined, from 6.7% of live births in 1991 to 6.1% of live births in 2000 (page 20).

The rate of maternal cigarette smoking has decreased substantially in recent years. Data from the National Longitudinal Survey of Children and Youth (NLSCY) show that in 1994-1995, 23.5% of children aged 0 to 2 years had mothers who smoked during pregnancy (page 4). This proportion fell to 19.4% in 1998-1999. Another positive development is the steady increase in breastfeeding initiation and duration (page 10). The NLSCY showed that the proportion of infants who were breastfed increased from 75.1% in 1994-1995 to 81.9% in 1998-1999. Among mothers who breastfed, the proportion who did so for three or more months also increased, from 58.7% to 63.0% over the same period. However, there are large regional differences in prenatal smoking and breastfeeding rates across Canada (pages 4 and 11).

There have been other dramatic changes in maternal characteristics in recent years that have been less publicized. Educational attainment has increased considerably, and the proportion of mothers with less than high school education decreased from 17.2% in 1994-1995 to 13.4% in 1998-1999 (page 14). This probably reflects higher educational status among more recent birth cohorts. The implications of this change are evident, given the strong associations between level of education and behaviours such as prenatal smoking and breastfeeding (pages 14, 15), and also perinatal mortality.[38]

Other changes in maternal characteristics that have an important bearing on perinatal health include changes in pre-pregnancy weight and weight gain in pregnancy. These are important determinants of perinatal health, and changes in them have been documented in several industrialized countries.[39-45] Although increases in pre-pregnancy weight in Canada have not been adequately studied, this trend probably corresponds to the general increase in weight among Canadian women of reproductive age.[46] Trends in pre-pregnancy weight and weight gain in pregnancy have not been adequately described in Canada, mainly because our national sources of perinatal health data do not capture such information. Several of these deficiencies will be addressed by the Maternity Experiences Survey (being developed by the Maternity Experiences Study Group of the CPSS), which will be interviewing a large number of women about their experiences in pregnancy, labour and delivery, and new parenthood.

Health Service Issues

Cesarean delivery rates in Canada decreased from 18.2% of hospital deliveries in 1991-1992 to 17.5% in 1994-1995 before increasing to 21.2% in 2000-2001. This overall increase is largely a consequence of increases in primary cesarean deliveries, from 12.4% in 1991-1992 to 15.6% in 2000-2001. The proportion of women with a previous cesarean delivery increased from 9.5% in 1991-1992 to 10.2% in 2000-2001, while the rate of repeat cesarean delivery decreased from 73.2% in 1991-1992

Cesarean delivery rates in Canada increased from 18.2% of hospital deliveries in 1991-1992 to 21.2% in 2000-2001.

to 64.7% in 1995-1996 before rising to 70.1% in 2000-2001 (page 33). These increases have occurred as a result of various influences, including changes in maternal characteristics (e.g., maternal age, parity, pre-pregnancy weight[47]), changes in obstetric practice due to concerns regarding fetal and maternal safety (e.g., regarding mid-pelvic forceps use,[48] vaginal birth after cesarean delivery[49]) and changes due to other factors (including potential increases in cesarean delivery for non-medical reasons). There is a lack of consensus on the relative contributions of these different influences, and detailed studies are required in order to address this controversial topic dispassionately. Nevertheless, it is safe to predict higher rates of cesarean delivery in the future, given the evidence supporting new indications for cesarean delivery,[50] links between pelvic floor dysfunction and mode of delivery,[51,52] and possible increases in elective primary cesarean delivery.[53]

The rate of operative vaginal deliveries has remained approximately constant (17.4% in 1991-1992 versus 16.3% of vaginal deliveries in 2000-2001), although this belies a large decline in the rate of forceps use (11.2% to 6.2%) and the concurrent increase in vacuum extractions (6.8% to 10.6%, page 37). Episiotomy rates continued to decrease, from 49.1% of vaginal deliveries in 1991-1992 to 23.8% in 2000-2001 (page 41). Regional differences in episiotomy rates are partly (but not entirely) explained by regional differences in rates of operative vaginal delivery (page 38). The average maternal length of stay in hospital appears to have stabilized in the last three years after both vaginal (average 2.4 days) and cesarean delivery (average 4.5 days, page 44). Similarly, neonatal length of hospital stay was approximately 8 days among newborns weighing 1,000-2,499 g and approximately 2.3 days among newborns of normal birth weight in each of the last few years (page 48).

Maternal Health

Maternal mortality ratios have declined from 6.1 maternal deaths per 100,000 live births in 1979-1981 to 2.5 per 100,000 in 1997-1999 (page 54). Maternal mortality tends to be under-reported in Canada, as in other countries;[54,55] nevertheless, the rates in Canada are among the lowest in the world. Rates of other life-threatening conditions in pregnancy are more appropriate indicators in the surveillance of maternal health and maternal health care. Temporal trends in one such condition, namely, postpartum hemorrhage requiring hysterectomy, show an increase in recent years: from 23.3 per 100,000 deliveries in 1991-1992 to 46.9 per 100,000 deliveries in 1999-2000 and 44.2 per 100,000 deliveries in 2000-2001 (page 58). This was not associated with an increase in case fatality rates. Direct maternal deaths due to postpartum hemorrhage in Canada (excluding Ontario) have declined from 4.1 per 100,000 live births in 1979-1984 to 3.4, 1.4 and 1.6 per 100,000 live births in 1985-1990, 1991-1996 and 1997-1999, respectively (page 55). In Ontario, maternal deaths due to postpartum hemorrhage decreased from 8.0 per 100,000 live births in 1979-1984 to 7.2, 1.1 and 0.0 per 100,000 live births in 1985-1990, 1991-1996 and 1997-1999, respectively (pages 216). The increase in postpartum hemorrhage requiring hysterectomy probably reflects obstetric practice changes, increases in older maternal age or increases in adherent placenta due to higher rates of previous cesarean delivery.[56] Further study into the increase in this index of severe maternal morbidity is currently being undertaken by the Maternal Health Study Group of the CPSS.

Maternal mortality ratios have declined from 6.1 maternal deaths per 100,000 live births in 1979-1981 to 2.5 per 100,000 in 1997-1999.

Fetal and Infant Health Outcomes

Indicators of fetal growth show a substantial temporal decline in small-for-gestational age live births and an increase in large-for-gestational age live births (pages 81 and 84). These trends appear to be due primarily to improved fetal growth among term live births and are a consequence of increases in maternal pre-pregnancy body mass index, reductions in cigarette smoking and changes in other socio-demographic factors, such as maternal age, parity and weight gain in pregnancy.[57-59] The multiple birth rate increased steadily from 2.1% of births in 1991 to 2.7% in 2000 (page 98). This increase can be attributed to a higher proportion of pregnancies in older women, and to increases in infertility treatments, including use of ovarian stimulation and assisted reproduction.[60,61] The contribution of the latter two technologies is of particular public health concern as twin and especially higher-order multiple births are at very high risk of preterm birth and perinatal morbidity and mortality. Unfortunately, precise information on the frequency of use of infertility treatments is not routinely available in Canada, in part because of the absence of public funding for this enterprise.

The declines in fetal and infant mortality discussed in earlier sections are complemented by modest declines in the rate of RDS (page 95). Rates of neonatal sepsis have increased, however, and may reflect increased survival and prolonged hospitalization of very low gestational age infants in neonatal intensive care units.[62] However, regional differences in sepsis rates are striking (especially as compared with the approximately similar rates of RDS, page 96) and may be due to variations in factors other than infant morbidity (e.g., diagnosis and coding).

Regional variations in prenatal smoking and breastfeeding initiation can provide an impetus for increased public education.

Conclusion

The *Canadian Perinatal Health Report, 2003* documents various phenomena of perinatal interest. These range from regional variations in pregnancy-related behaviours and health services to temporal trends in perinatal outcomes. Regional variations in prenatal smoking and breastfeeding initiation can provide an impetus for increased public education, while regional variations in health services such as operative vaginal or cesarean delivery can lead to a re-examination of routines and standards in medical practice. Temporal trends in obstetric intervention, fetal growth, preterm birth, fetal and infant mortality, and maternal morbidity and mortality provide a comprehensive picture of perinatal health trends in Canada. Besides providing new information and illuminating several areas of perinatal concern, this report also identifies weaknesses in our knowledge of perinatal health in Canada. It will therefore inform decision making at the clinical, public health and policy levels and also serve to focus surveillance efforts in perinatal health.

K.S. Joseph, MD, PhD
Perinatal Epidemiology Research Unit
Departments of Obstetrics and Gynecology and of Pediatrics
Dalhousie University and the IWK Health Centre
Member, Steering Committee, Canadian Perinatal Surveillance System

References

1. Health Canada. *Canadian Perinatal Health Report, 2000*. Ottawa: Minister of Public Works and Government Services Canada, 2000 (Catalogue No. H49-142/2000E). URL: <http://www.hc-sc.gc.ca/pphb-dgspsp/rhs-ssg/index.html>.

2. United Nations Children's Fund. *The State of the World's Children 2003*. New York: UNICEF, 2002.

3. World Health Organization. *International Statistical Classification of Diseases and Related Health Problems*, 10th Revision, Vol. 2. Instruction manual. Geneva: WHO, 1993:129-34.

4. Howell EM, Blondel B. International infant mortality rates: Bias from reporting differences. *Am J Pub Health* 1994;84:850-2.

5. Sepkowitz S. International rankings of infant mortality and the United States' vital statistics natality data collection system — failure and success. *Int J Epidemiol* 1995;24:583-8.

6. Sachs BP, Fretts RC, Gardner R, Hellerstein S, Wampler NS, Wise PH. The impact of extreme prematurity and congenital anomalies on the interpretation of international comparisons of infant mortality. *Obstet Gynecol* 1995;85:941-6.

7. Kramer MS, Platt RW, Yang H, Haglund B, Cnattingius S, Bergsjo P. Registration artifacts in international comparisons of infant mortality. *Paediatr Perinat Epidemiol* 2002;16:16-22.

8. Joseph KS, Kramer MS. Recent trends in Canadian infant mortality rates: Effect of changes in registration of newborns weighing less than 500 g. *Can Med Assoc J* 1996;155:1047-52.

9. Liu S, Joseph KS, Kramer MS, Allen A, Sauve R, Rusen ID, et al. for the Fetal and Infant Health Study Group of the Canadian Perinatal Surveillance System. Relationship of prenatal diagnosis and pregnancy termination to overall infant mortality in Canada. *JAMA* 2002;287:1561-7.

10. Nault F. Infant mortality and low birth weight, 1975 to 1995. *Health Rep* 1997;9:39-46.

11. Joseph KS, Allen AC, Kramer MS, Cyr M, Fair ME, for the Fetal and Infant Mortality Study Group of the Canadian Perinatal Surveillance System. Changes in the registration of stillbirths less than 500 g in Canada, 1985-95. *Paediatr Perinat Epidemiol* 1999;13:278-87.

12. Golding J. Birthweight-specific mortality rates — are they meaningful? *Paediatr Perinatal Epidemiol* 1994;8:256-7.

13. Wilcox AJ, Skjœrven R, Buekens P, Kiely J. Birth weight and perinatal mortality: a comparison of the United States and Norway. *JAMA* 1995;272:709-11.

14. Joseph KS, Liu S, Demissie K, Wen SW, Platt RW, Ananth CV, et al. for the Fetal and Infant Health Study Group of the Canadian Perinatal Surveillance System. A parsimonious explanation for intersecting perinatal mortality curves: understanding the effect of plurality and of parity. *BMC Pregnancy and Childbirth* 2003;3:3. URL: <www.biomedcentral.com/1471-393/3/3>.

15. EUROCAT Working Group. Prevalence of neural tube defects in 20 regions of Europe and the impact of prenatal diagnosis, 1980-1986. *J Epidemiol Community Health* 1991;45:52-8.

16. Cragan JD, Roberts HE, Edmonds LD, Koury MJ, Kirby RS, Shaw G, et al. Surveillance for anencephaly and spina bifida and the impact of prenatal diagnosis — United States, 1985-1994. *MMWR* 1995;44:1-13.

17. Forrester MB, Merz RD, Yoon PW. Impact of prenatal diagnosis and elective termination on the prevalence of selected birth defects in Hawaii. *Am J Epidemiol* 1998;148:1201-11.

18. Wen SW, Liu S, Joseph KS, Trouton K, Allen A. Regional patterns of infant mortality caused by congenital anomalies. *Can J Public Health* 1999;90:316-9.

19. Wen SW, Liu S, Joseph KS, Rouleau J, Allen A. Patterns of infant mortality caused by congenital anomalies. *Teratology* 2000;61:342-6.

20. Liu S, Joseph KS, Wen SW, Kramer MS, Marcoux S, Ohlsson A, et al. for the Fetal and Infant Mortality Study Group of the Canadian Perinatal Surveillance System. Secular trends in congenital anomaly-related fetal and infant mortality in Canada, 1985-1996. *Am J Med Genetics* 2001;104:7-13.

21. Lee KS, Khoshnood B, Chen L, Wall SN, Cromie WJ, Mittendorf RL. Infant mortality from congenital malformations in the United States, 1970-1997. *Obstet Gynecol* 2001;98:620-7.

22. Dwyer T, Cochrane J. Population trends in Sudden Infant Death Syndrome. *Semin Perinatol* 2002;26:296-305.

23. Joseph KS, Kramer MS, Allen AC, Cyr M, Fair M, Ohlsson A, et al. for the Fetal and Infant Mortality Study Group of the Canadian Perinatal Surveillance System. Gestational age- and birth weight-specific declines in infant mortality in Canada, 1985-94. *Paediatr Perinat Epidemiol* 2000;14:332-9.

24. Morris CD, Menashe VD. 25-year mortality after surgical repair of congenital heart defect in childhood. A population-based cohort study. *JAMA* 1991; 266:3447-52.

25. Yawn BP, Wollan P, McKeon K, Field CS. Temporal changes in rates and reasons for medical induction of term labor, 1980-1996. *Am J Obstet Gynecol* 2001;184:611-9.

26. Rayburn WF, Zhang J. Rising rates of labor induction: present concerns and future strategies. *Obstet Gynecol* 2002;100:164-7.

27. Zhang J, Yancey MK, Henderson CE. U.S. national trends in labor induction, 1989-1998. *J Reprod Med* 2002;47:120-4.

28. Joseph KS, Kramer MS, Marcoux S, Ohlsson A, Wen SW, Allen A, et al. Determinants of preterm birth rates in Canada from 1981 through 1983 and from 1992 through 1994. *N Engl J Med* 1998;339:1434-9.

29. Kramer MS, Platt R, Yang H, Joseph KS, Wen SW, Morin L, et al. Secular trends in preterm birth: a hospital-based cohort study. *JAMA* 1998;280:1849-54.

30. Joseph KS, Allen AC, Dodds L, Vincer MJ, Armson BA. Causes and consequences of recent increases in preterm birth among twins. *Obstet Gynecol* 2001;98:57-64.

31. Joseph KS, Demissie K, Kramer MS. Trends in obstetric intervention, stillbirth and preterm birth. *Semin Perinatol* 2002;26:250-9.

32. Hannah ME, Hannah WJ, Hellmann J, Hewson S, Milner R, Willan A, and the the Canadian Multicenter Post-Term Pregnancy Trial Group. Induction of labor as compared with serial antenatal monitoring in post-term pregnancy. A randomized controlled trial. *N Engl J Med* 1992;326:1587-92.

33. Crowley P. Interventions for preventing or improving the outcome of delivery at or beyond term (Cochrane Review). In: *The Cochrane Library*, Issue 1, 2003. Oxford: Update Software.

34. Joseph KS. Core concepts in perinatal epidemiology: incidence of birth, growth-restriction and death. *J Clin Epidemiol* (in press).

35. Matthews TG, Crowley P, Chong A, McKenna P, McGarvey C, O'Regan M. Rising caesarean section rates: a cause for concern? *Brit J Obstet Gynaecol* 2003;110:346-9.

36. Bettiol H, Rona RJ, Chinn S, Goldani M, Barbieri MA. Factors associated with preterm births in Southeast Brazil: a comparison of two birth cohorts born 15 years apart. *Paediatr Perinat Epidemiol* 2000;14:30-8.

37. Silva AA, Lamy-Filho F, Alves MT, Coimbra LC, Bettiol H, Barbieri MA. Risk factors for low birthweight in north-east Brazil: the role of caesarean section. *Paediatr Perinat Epidemiol* 2001;15:257-64.

38. Chen J, Fair M, Wilkins R, Cyr M, and the Fetal and Infant Mortality Study Group of the Canadian Perinatal Surveillance System. Maternal education and fetal and infant mortality in Quebec. *Health Rep* 1998;10:53-64.

39. Johnson JWC, Longmate JA, Frentzen B. Excessive maternal weight and pregnancy outcome. *Am J Obstet Gynecol* 1992;167:353-72.

40. Brost BC, Goldenberg RL, Mercer BM, Iams JD, Meis PJ, Moawad AH, et al. The Preterm Prediction Study: association of cesarean delivery with increases in maternal weight and body mass index. *Am J Obstet Gynecol* 1997;177:333-41.

41. Guilhard P, Blondel B. Trends in risk factors for cesarean sections in France between 1981 and 1995: lessons for reducing the rates in the future. *Br J Obstet Gynaecol* 2001;108:48-55.

42. Lu GC, Rouse DJ, DuBard M, Cliver S, Kimberlin D, Hauth JC. The effect of the increasing prevalence of maternal obesity on perinatal mortality. *Am J Obstet Gynecol* 2001;185:845-9.

43. Kaiser PS, Kirby RS. Obesity as a risk factor for cesarean in a low-risk population. *Obstet Gynecol* 2001;97:39-43.

44. Baeten JM, Bukusi EA, Lambe M. Pregnancy complications and outcomes among overweight and obese nulliparous women. *Am J Public Health* 2001;91;436-40.

45. Cnattingius S, Lambe M. Trends in smoking and overweight during pregnancy: prevalence, risks of pregnancy complications and adverse pregnancy outcomes. *Semin Perinatol* 2002;26:286-95.

46. Katzmarzyk PT. The Canadian obesity epidemic: an historical perspective. *Obes Res* 2002; 10:666-74.

47. Joseph KS, Young DC, Dodds L, O'Connell CM, Allen VM, Chandra S, et al. Changes in maternal characteristics and obstetric practice and recent increases in primary cesarean delivery. *Obstet Gynecol* 2003;102:791-800.

48. American College of Obstetricians and Gynecologists. *Operative vaginal delivery*. Technical Bulletin No. 196, August 1994.

49. McMahon MJ, Luther ER, Bowes WA Jr, Olshan AF. Comparison of a trial of labour with an elective second cesarean section. *N Engl J Med* 1996;335:689-95.

50. Hannah ME, Hannah WJ, Hewson SA, Hodnett ED, Saigal S, Willan AR. Planned caesarean section versus planned vaginal birth for breech presentation at term: a randomized multicentre trial. Term Breech Trial Collaborative Group. *Lancet* 2000;356:1375-83.

51. Hannah ME, Hannah WJ, Hodnett ED, Chalmer B, Kung R, Willan A, et al. Outcomes at 3 months after planned cesarean vs planned vaginal delivery for breech presentation at term: the international randomized Term Breech Trial. *JAMA* 2002;287:1822-31.

52. Rortveit G, Daltveit AK, Hannestad YS, Hunskaar S. Urinary incontinence after vaginal delivery or cesarean section. *N Engl J Med* 2003;348:900-7.

53. Minkoff H, Chervenak FA. Elective primary cesarean delivery. *N Engl J Med* 2003;348:946-50.

54. Turner LA, Cyr M, Kinch RA, Liston R, Kramer MS, Fair M, et al. for the Maternal Mortality and Morbidity Study Group of the Canadian Perinatal Surveillance System. Under-reporting of maternal mortality in Canada: a question of definition. *Chronic Dis Can* 2002;23:22-30.

55. Turner LA, Kramer MS, Liu S, for the Maternal Mortality and Morbidity Study Group of the Canadian Perinatal Surveillance System. Cause-specific mortality during and after pregnancy and the definition of maternal death. *Chronic Dis Can* 2002;23:31-6.

56. Cunningham FG, MacDonald PC, Grant NF, Leveno KJ, Gilstrap LC, Hankins GDV, et al. (Eds.). *Williams Obstetrics*, 21st Edition. Toronto: McGraw-Hill, 2001.

57. Kramer MS, Morin I, Yang H, Platt RW, Usher R, McNamara H, et al. Why are babies getting bigger? Temporal trends in fetal growth and its determinants. *J Pediatr* 2002;141:538-42.

58. Ananth CV, Wen SW. Trends in fetal growth among singleton gestations in the United States and Canada, 1985 through 1998. *Semin Perinatol* 2002;26:260-7.

59. Wen SW, Kramer MS, Platt R, Demissie K, Joseph KS, Liu S, et al. for the Fetal and Infant Health Study Group of the Canadian Perinatal Surveillance System. Secular trends of fetal growth in Canada, 1981 to 1997. *Paediatr Perinat Epidemiol* 2003;17:347-54.

60. Bergh T, Ericson A, Hillensjö T, Nygren KG, Wennerholm UB. Deliveries and children born after in-vitro fertilisation in Sweden 1982-95: a retrospective cohort study. *Lancet* 1999;354:1579-85.

61. Blondel B, Kaminski M. Trends in the occurrence, determinants, and consequences of multiple births. *Semin Perinatol* 2002;26:239-49.

62. Polin RA, Saiman L. Nosocomial infections in the neonatal intensive care unit. *NeoReviews* 2003;4:e81-9.

Determinants of Maternal, Fetal and Infant Health

Behaviours and Practices

Rate of Maternal Smoking During Pregnancy

Author:
Susie Dzakpasu,
MHSc

The rate of maternal smoking during pregnancy is defined as the number of pregnant women who smoked cigarettes during pregnancy expressed as a proportion of all pregnant women (in a given place and time).

Maternal cigarette smoking can have adverse health effects on the fetus and child. It increases the risk of intrauterine growth restriction (IUGR), preterm birth, spontaneous abortion, placental complications, stillbirth and sudden infant death syndrome.[1] It is associated with an overall increased risk of infant mortality and morbidity, due in part to increases in IUGR and preterm birth.

The relation between maternal smoking and adverse pregnancy outcomes is linked to the amount and duration of smoking. Women who stop smoking before becoming pregnant or during their pregnancy are at significantly reduced risk of IUGR and preterm birth compared with women who smoke throughout pregnancy.[1,2] Although pregnant women are more likely to quit smoking and smoke fewer cigarettes than women who are not pregnant, maternal smoking during pregnancy remains a notable public health problem. It is important to continue to promote non-smoking among women in general, and to help pregnant women who smoke to stop or reduce smoking as early as possible.[2,3]

Rates of maternal smoking during pregnancy were estimated using data from the National Longitudinal Survey of Children and Youth (NLSCY).

Results

- Between 1994-1995 and 1998-1999, maternal smoking rates decreased. In 1994-1995, 23.5% of children under the age of two had a mother who reported smoking during her pregnancy compared with 19.4% in 1998-1999. The percentage of children exposed during the third trimester, when the negative effect on fetal growth is greatest, declined from 21.5% to 17.2%. The percentage of children exposed to more than 10 cigarettes per day before birth declined from 8.1% to 5.3%.

- Younger mothers were more likely to report smoking. In 1998-1999, 53.2% of children under two years of age whose mothers were under 20 years of age at the time of the survey were exposed to tobacco prenatally, compared with 11.8% of children whose mothers were 35 years or older at the time of the survey (Figure 1.1). This inverse relation between maternal smoking and maternal age was also present in previous years. Even though mothers under 20 years of age reported the highest rate of smoking, they only accounted for 6.4% of children exposed to tobacco prenatally.

- Reported rates of maternal smoking varied by region. In 1998-1999, rates ranged from lows of 13.0% and 15.8% in British Columbia and Ontario, respectively, to highs of 24.2% in Quebec and 24.8% in the Atlantic provinces (Figure 1.2). *Tabular information is presented in Appendix F.*

FIGURE 1.1 **Rate of maternal smoking, by maternal age,**
Canada (excluding the territories), 1994-1995, 1996-1997 and 1998-1999*

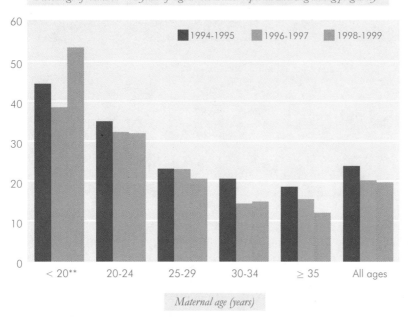

Percentage of children < 2 years of age whose mother reported smoking during pregnancy

■ 1994-1995 ■ 1996-1997 ■ 1998-1999

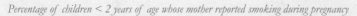

Maternal age (years)

Source: Statistics Canada. NLSCY, 1994-1995, 1996-1997, 1998-1999 (custom tabulations).
*Data from the territories were not available from the NLSCY.
**These estimates have low precision since they are based on a small number of subjects.

FIGURE 1.2 **Rate of maternal smoking, by region/province,**
Canada (excluding the territories), 1994-1995, 1996-1997 and 1998-1999*

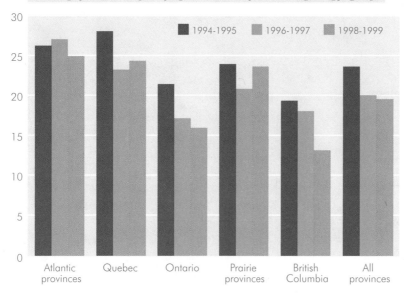

Percentage of children < 2 years of age whose mother reported smoking during pregnancy

■ 1994-1995 ■ 1996-1997 ■ 1998-1999

Region/province

Source: Statistics Canada. NLSCY, 1994-1995, 1996-1997, 1998-1999 (custom tabulations).
*Data from the territories were not available from the NLSCY.

Data Limitations

The knowledge that smoking during pregnancy can adversely affect the outcome of the pregnancy may have led mothers to under-report their smoking behaviour during pregnancy.[4] Therefore, rates of maternal smoking in Canada are probably higher than those reported in the NLSCY. Data from the territories were not available from the NLSCY.

References

1. Office of the Surgeon General. Health consequences of tobacco use among women, reproductive outcomes. In: *Women and Smoking*. Rockville, MD: U.S. Department of Health and Human Services, 2001:272-307.

2. Lumley J, Oliver S, Waters E. Interventions for promoting smoking cessation during pregnancy (Cochrane Review). In: *The Cochrane Library*, Issue 3, 2002. Oxford: Update Software.

3. Heaman M. Smoking cessation in pregnancy: are we doing enough? [guest editorial]. *J Obstet Gynaecol Can* 2002;24:611-3.

4. Patrick DL, Cheadle A, Thompson DC, Diehr P, Koepsell T, Kinne S. The validity of self-reported smoking: a review and meta analysis. *Am J Public Health* 1994;84:1086-93.

Rate of Maternal Alcohol Consumption During Pregnancy

Author:
Susie Dzakpasu,
MHSc

The rate of maternal alcohol consumption during pregnancy is defined as the number of pregnant women who consumed alcoholic beverages during pregnancy expressed as a proportion of all pregnant women (in a given place and time).

Maternal alcohol consumption can result in fetal alcohol spectrum disorder (FASD), a term used to describe a series of birth defects and neurodevelopmental disorders caused by alcohol consumption during pregnancy. FASD includes neurodevelopmental, behavioural and cognitive abnormalities, which persist into adulthood and significantly impair an individual's quality of life. The diagnosis of fetal alcohol syndrome (FAS) is based on a history of prenatal alcohol exposure combined with prenatal and postnatal growth restriction, characteristic facial dysmorphology and central nervous system damage.[1,2] The effects of alcohol on the fetus are thought to depend on numerous factors, including the amount of alcohol consumed, the pattern and timing of drinking, maternal age, the mother's ability to metabolize alcohol and the genetic susceptibility of the fetus.[1,2] Since a safe level of alcohol consumption during pregnancy has not been determined, Health Canada recommends that women who are or may become pregnant abstain from alcohol consumption.[3]

Rates of maternal alcohol consumption during pregnancy were estimated using data from the National Longitudinal Survey of Children and Youth (NLSCY).

Results

- Between 1994-1995 and 1998-1999, there was a decline in the percentage of mothers who reported drinking alcohol during pregnancy. In 1994-1995, 17.4% of children under the age of two had a mother who reported drinking alcohol during pregnancy compared with 14.6% in 1998-1999. This percentage includes all mothers who reported drinking, regardless of amount.

- Older mothers were more likely to report alcohol consumption. In 1998-1999, 14.1% of children less than two years of age whose mothers were under 25 years of age at the time of the survey were exposed to some alcohol prenatally compared with 21.6% of children whose mothers were 35 years and older at the time of the survey (Figure 1.3). Some studies have suggested that binge drinking (consumption of five or more drinks per occasion) may be more prevalent among younger women.[4] The proportion of children exposed to binge drinking could not be determined reliably using NLSCY data.

- Reported rates of maternal alcohol consumption varied by region. In 1998-1999, rates ranged from a low of 7.7% in the Atlantic provinces to a high of 25.1% in Quebec (Figure 1.4). *Tabular information is presented in Appendix F.*

FIGURE 1.3 **Rate of maternal alcohol consumption, by maternal age,**
Canada (excluding the territories), 1994-1995, 1996-1997 and 1998-1999*

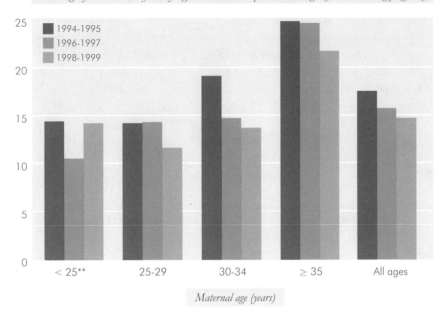

Percentage of children < 2 years of age whose mother reported drinking any alcohol during pregnancy

- 1994-1995
- 1996-1997
- 1998-1999

Maternal age (years)

Source: Statistics Canada. NLSCY, 1994-1995, 1996-1997, 1998-1999 (custom tabulations).
*Data from the territories were not available from the NLSCY.
**Further categorization of age was not possible because of small samples.

FIGURE 1.4 **Rate of maternal alcohol consumption, by region/province,**
Canada (excluding the territories), 1994-1995, 1996-1997 and 1998-1999*

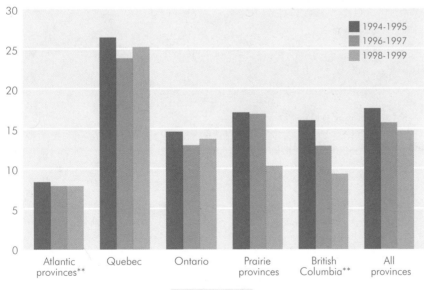

Percentage of children < 2 years of age whose mother reported drinking any alcohol during pregnancy

- 1994-1995
- 1996-1997
- 1998-1999

Region/province

Source: Statistics Canada. NLSCY, 1994-1995, 1996-1997, 1998-1999 (custom tabulations).
*Data from the territories were not available from the NLSCY.
**These estimates have low precision since they are based on a small number of subjects.

Data Limitations

There may be systematic under-reporting of maternal alcohol consumption in surveys, because alcohol consumption during pregnancy is considered socially undesirable and known to incur risk to the fetus.[5] Biological markers offer an alternative to asking women about their prenatal alcohol intake. However, the biomarkers identified to date are not routinely assessed in pregnant women and newborns in Canada.[6] Therefore, rates of maternal alcohol consumption in Canada are probably higher than those reported in the NLSCY. The proportion of children with chronic, heavy prenatal alcohol exposure could not be determined reliably using NLSCY data. Data from the territories were not available from the NLSCY.

References

1. Canadian Pediatric Society. Fetal alcohol syndrome. *Paediatr Child Health* 2002;7:161-74.

2. Roberts G, Nanson J. *Best Practices: Fetal Alcohol Syndrome/Fetal Alcohol Effects and the Effects of Other Substance Use During Pregnancy*. Ottawa: Canada's Drug Strategy Division, Health Canada, 2000.

3. Health Canada. *Joint Statement: Prevention of Fetal Alcohol Syndrome (FAS), Fetal Alcohol Effects (FAE) in Canada*. Ottawa: Health Canada, October 1996 (Catalogue No. H39-348/1996E).

4. Gladstone J, Levy M, Nulman I, Koren G. Characteristics of pregnant women who engage in binge alcohol consumption. *Can Med Assoc J* 1997;156:789-94.

5. Stoler JM, Huntington KS, Peterson CM, Peterson KP, Daniel P, Aboagye KK, et al. The prenatal detection of significant alcohol exposure with maternal blood markers. *J Pediatr* 1998;133:346-52.

6. Hicks M, Sauve RS, Lyon AW, Clarke M, Tough S. Alcohol use and abuse in pregnancy: an evaluation of the merits of screening. *Can Child Adolesc Psychiatry Rev* 2003;12:77-80.

Rate of Breastfeeding

Author:
Susie Dzakpasu,
MHSc

The rate of breastfeeding is defined as the number of women who delivered and ever breastfed a live born child expressed as a proportion of all women who delivered a live born child (in a given place and time).

Breastfeeding is the optimal method of feeding infants. Beneficial effects for the infant include protection from gastrointestinal and respiratory infections and otitis media, and possible enhancement of cognitive development.[1-4] Beneficial effects for mothers include reduced postpartum bleeding, earlier return to pre-pregnancy weight and delayed resumption of ovulation, which helps to increase the spacing between pregnancies. There is also evidence that lactating women have improved postpartum bone remineralization and a reduced risk of ovarian and breast cancers.[2,3] The Canadian Paediatric Society (CPS), Dietitians of Canada (DC) and Health Canada recommend exclusive breastfeeding for at least the first four months of life, and continuing breastfeeding and complementary foods for up to two years of age and beyond.[1] The World Health Organization recommends exclusive breastfeeding for six months, with introduction of complementary foods and continued breast-feeding thereafter.[5]

Breastfeeding rates were estimated using data from the National Longitudinal Survey of Children and Youth (NLSCY).

Results

- Between 1994-1995 and 1998-1999, breastfeeding rates increased. In 1994-1995, 75.1% of children under the age of two had been breastfed for some period of time compared with 81.9% in 1998-1999 (Figure 1.5). In 1998-1999, among children who had been breastfed, 63.0% were breastfed for three months or more.

- Breastfeeding initiation rates varied by maternal age. In all three periods of the NLSCY, rates among older mothers were higher than rates among younger mothers (Figure 1.5). Breastfeeding duration also increased with increasing maternal age. In 1998-1999, 49.1% of breastfed children whose mothers were less than 25 years of age at the time of the survey were breastfed for three months or more, compared with 74.9% of breastfed children whose mothers were 35 years or older at the time of the survey (Figure 1.6).

- Breastfeeding initiation varied by region. In 1998-1999, rates ranged from a low of 64.5% in the Atlantic provinces to a high of 95.2% in British Columbia (Figure 1.7). Mothers in regions with higher breastfeeding initiation rates also tended to breastfeed for a longer duration (Figure 1.8). *Tabular information is presented in Appendix F.*

Data Limitations

The NLSCY could not be used to determine the degree of adherence to the recommendations made by Health Canada and other Canadian organizations to breastfeed exclusively for four months or longer, as the NLSCY did not ask mothers if breastfeeding was exclusive. Furthermore, the breastfeeding duration categories used in the NLSCY do not coincide with the Canadian recommendation. Data from the territories were not available from the NLSCY.

FIGURE 1.5 **Rate of breastfeeding, by maternal age,**
Canada (excluding the territories), 1994-1995, 1996-1997 and 1998-1999*

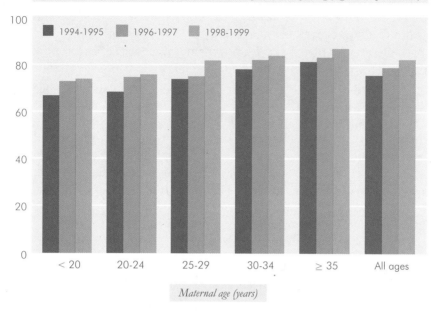

Source: Statistics Canada. NLSCY, 1994-1995, 1996-1997, 1998-1999 (custom tabulations).
*Data from the territories were not available from the NLSCY.

FIGURE 1.6 **Duration of breastfeeding, by maternal age,**
Canada (excluding the territories), 1994-1995, 1996-1997 and 1998-1999*

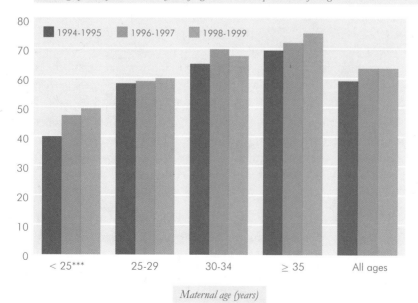

Source: Statistics Canada. NLSCY, 1994-1995, 1996-1997, 1998-1999 (custom tabulations).
*Data from the territories were not available from the NLSCY.
**Estimates based on children who were breastfed, but were no longer being breastfed at the time of the survey.
***Further categorization of age was not possible because of the small sample.

FIGURE 1.7 **Rate of breastfeeding, by region/province,**
Canada (excluding the territories),* 1994-1995, 1996-1997 and 1998-1999

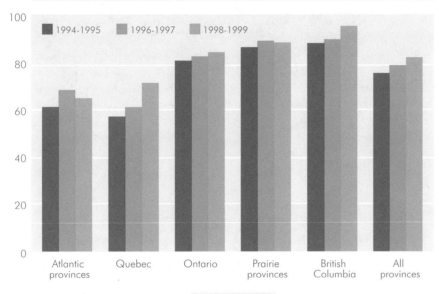

Percentage of children < 2 years of age whose mother reported breastfeeding (regardless of duration)

Source: Statistics Canada. NLSCY, 1994-1995, 1996-1997, 1998-1999 (custom tabulations).
*Data from the territories were not available from the NLSCY.

FIGURE 1.8 **Duration of breastfeeding, by region/province,**
Canada (excluding the territories),* 1994-1995, 1996-1997 and 1998-1999

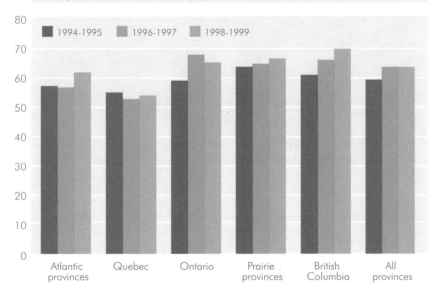

Percentage of breastfed children < 2 years of age whose mother reported breastfeeding three months or more**

Source: Statistics Canada. NLSCY, 1994-1995, 1996-1997, 1998-1999 (custom tabulations).
*Data from the territories were not available from the NLSCY.
**Estimates based on children who were breastfed, but were no longer being breastfed at the time of the survey.

References

1. Canadian Paediatric Society, Dietitians of Canada and Health Canada. *Nutrition for Healthy Term Infants*. Ottawa: Minister of Public Works and Government Services Canada, 1998.

2. American Academy of Pediatrics, Work Group on Breastfeeding. Breastfeeding and the use of human milk. *Pediatrics* 1997;100:1035-9.

3. Lawrence RA, Lawrence RM. *Breastfeeding, a Guide for the Medical Profession*, 5th Edition. St. Louis: Mosby, 1999.

4. Kramer MS, Chalmers B, Hodnett ED, Sevkovskaya Z, Dzikovich I, Shapiro S, et al. Promotion of Breastfeeding Intervention Trial (PROBIT): a randomized trial in the Republic of Belarus. *JAMA* 2001;285:413-20.

5. World Health Organization. *The Optimal Duration of Exclusive Breastfeeding. Report of an Expert Consultation*. Geneva: WHO, 2001.

Rate of Low Maternal Education

Author:
Susie Dzakpasu,
MHSc

The proportion of pregnant women with a low educational level is defined as the number of women with less than 12 years of education who delivered a live born child as a proportion of all women who delivered a live born child (in a given place and time).

A low maternal educational level has been found to be consistently related to poor perinatal health outcomes. For example, preterm birth, small-for-gestational-age, stillbirth and infant mortality rates are higher among women with a low level of education.[1-4] The mechanisms by which maternal education ultimately influences perinatal health outcomes are complex, often involving intermediate variables such as maternal age, health care utilization and the prevalence of risk behaviours such as maternal smoking.[5,6]

Rates of low maternal educational level were estimated using data from the National Longitudinal Survey of Children and Youth (NLSCY). The association between maternal education and three determinants of perinatal health — namely, maternal smoking during pregnancy, maternal alcohol consumption during pregnancy and breastfeeding — is also presented.

Results

- Between 1994-1995 and 1998-1999, there was a decrease in the proportion of new mothers with a low maternal education (Figure 1.9). In 1994-1995, 17.2% of children under the age of two had a mother who had not completed high school compared with 13.4% in 1998-1999. In 1994-1995, 42.9% of children had a mother who was a university or college graduate compared with 46.5% in 1998-1999.

- There was a strong association between maternal education, maternal smoking and maternal alcohol consumption during pregnancy in all three periods of the NLSCY. In 1998-1999, 35.9% of children with mothers with less than a high school education were exposed to tobacco prenatally compared with 9.0% of those whose mothers were university or college graduates (Figure 1.10). The opposite trend was observed with prenatal exposure to alcohol. In 1998-1999, 9.9% of children with mothers with less than a high school education were exposed to alcohol prenatally compared with 17.7% of children whose mothers were university or college graduates (Figure 1.11).

- Breastfeeding initiation and duration rates were also associated with maternal educational levels. In 1998-1999, 70.5% of children with mothers with less than a high school education were breastfed for some time, compared with 89.0% of children of university and college graduates (Figure 1.12). Women with lower educational levels also tended to breastfeed for a shorter period of time (Figure 1.13). *Tabular information is presented in Appendix F.*

Data Limitations

Data from the territories were not available from the NLSCY.

FIGURE 1.9 **Rate of low maternal education and other categories of maternal education,** *Canada (excluding the territories),* *1994-1995, 1996-1997 and 1998-1999*

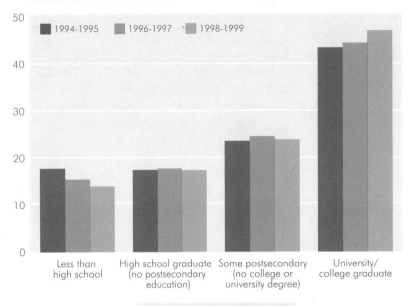

Percentage of children < 2 years of age whose mother had a particular educational level

Source: Statistics Canada. NLSCY, 1994-1995, 1996-1997, 1998-1999 (custom tabulations).
*Data from the territories were not available from the NLSCY.

FIGURE 1.10 **Rate of maternal smoking, by maternal education,** *Canada (excluding the territories),* *1994-1995, 1996-1997 and 1998-1999*

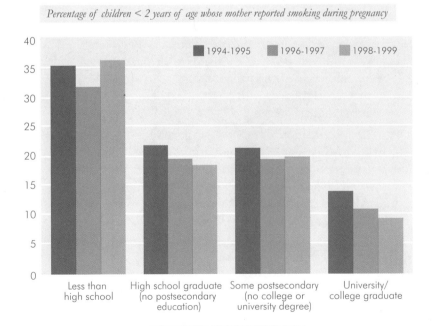

Percentage of children < 2 years of age whose mother reported smoking during pregnancy

Source: Statistics Canada. NLSCY, 1994-1995, 1996-1997, 1998-1999 (custom tabulations).
*Data from the territories were not available from the NLSCY.

FIGURE 1.11 **Rate of maternal alcohol consumption, by maternal education,**
Canada (excluding the territories), 1994-1995, 1996-1997 and 1998-1999*

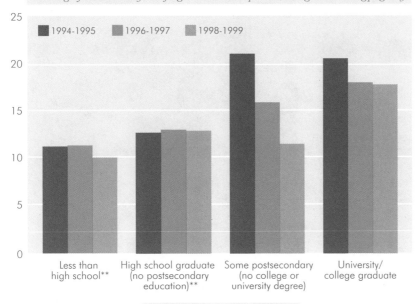

Percentage of children < 2 years of age whose mother reported drinking alcohol during pregnancy

Source: Statistics Canada. NLSCY, 1994-1995, 1996-1997, 1998-1999 (custom tabulations).
*Data from the territories were not available from the NLSCY.
**These estimates have low precision since they are based on a small number of subjects.

FIGURE 1.12 **Rate of breastfeeding, by maternal education,**
Canada (excluding the territories), 1994-1995, 1996-1997 and 1998-1999*

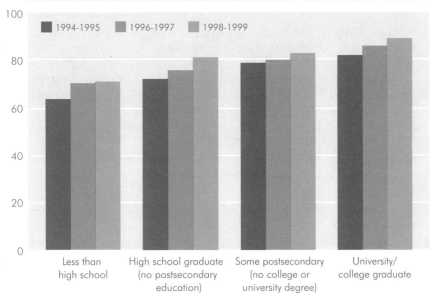

Percentage of children < 2 years of age whose mother reported breastfeeding (regardless of duration)

Source: Statistics Canada. NLSCY, 1994-1995, 1996-1997, 1998-1999 (custom tabulations).
*Data from the territories were not available from the NLSCY.

FIGURE 1.13 **Duration of breastfeeding, by maternal education,**
Canada (excluding the territories),* 1994-1995, 1996-1997 and 1998-1999

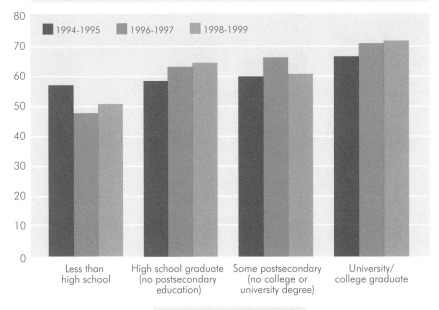

Percentage of breastfed children < 2 years of age whose mother reported breastfeeding three months or more**

Legend: 1994-1995, 1996-1997, 1998-1999

Highest level of maternal education

Source: Statistics Canada. NLSCY, 1994-1995, 1996-1997, 1998-1999 (custom tabulations).
*Data from the territories were not available from the NLSCY.
**Estimates based on children who were breastfed, but were no longer being breastfed at the time of the surveys.

References

1. Claussen B, Cnattingius S, Axelsson O. Preterm and term births of small for gestational age infants: a population-based study of risk factors among nulliparous women. *Br J Obstet Gynaecol* 1998;105:1011-7.

2. Chen J, Fair M, Wilkins R, Cyr M, and the Fetal and Infant Mortality Study Group of the Canadian Perinatal Surveillance System. Maternal education and fetal and infant mortality in Quebec. *Health Rep* 1998;10:53-64.

3. Parker JD, Schoendorf KC, Kiely JL. Associations between measures of socioeconomic status and low birth weight, small for gestational age, and premature delivery in the United States. *Ann Epidemiol* 1994;4:271-8.

4. Kramer MS, McLean FH, Eason EL, Usher RH. Maternal nutrition and spontaneous preterm birth. *Am J Epidemiol* 1992;136:574-83.

5. Sharma RK. Causal pathways to infant mortality: linking social variables to infant mortality through intermediate variables. *J Health Soc Policy* 1998;9:15-28.

6. D'Ascoli PT, Alexander GR, Petersen DJ, Kogan MD. Parental factors influencing patterns of prenatal care utilization. *J Perinatol* 1997;17:283-7.

Rate of Live Births to Teenage Mothers

Author:
Jennifer Crain

The age-specific live birth rate among teenage mothers is defined as the number of live births to mothers aged ≤ 14, 15-17 or 18-19 years per 1,000 females aged 14, 15-17 and 18-19 years, respectively (in a given place and time). A related indicator is the proportion of live births to teenage mothers, which refers to the number of live births to mothers aged ≤ 14, 15-17 or 18-19 years expressed as a percentage of all live births (in a given place and time).

Various adverse maternal and infant outcomes have been associated with teenage pregnancy. Typically, teen pregnancies are characterized by delayed entry into prenatal care and lower rates of prenatal care. Tobacco, alcohol and other substance abuse is reported to be higher among pregnant adolescents.[1] A relatively higher proportion of teenagers report physical and sexual abuse during pregnancy.[2] Compared with mothers 20 to 24 years of age, mothers aged 17 years or younger have an increased risk of delivering babies who are preterm or growth restricted.[3] While socio-demographic factors can influence the outcomes of teenage pregnancies, biologic immaturity of teenage mothers may also play a key role in adverse outcomes, including preterm birth.[3] Other adverse outcomes associated with teen pregnancies include pre-eclampsia, anemia, urinary tract infection and postpartum hemorrhage.[4]

Rates of live births to teenage mothers were calculated using vital statistics data.

Results

- The birth rate among older teenagers is decreasing, but is considerably higher than that among younger adolescents.[5] Among 18 to 19 year olds, the rate declined from 46.8 per 1,000 females in 1991 to 32.4 per 1,000 females in 2000 (Figure 1.14). With the exception of a slight increase in 1992, the age-specific live birth rate among females aged 15 to 17 declined from 15.4 per 1,000 females in 1991 to 9.7 per 1,000 in 2000. The age-specific live birth rate among females aged 14 years or younger declined steadily from 1.9 per 1,000 females in 1991 to 0.9 per 1,000 females in 2000. The higher rate among older teenagers can be partially attributed to the increased likelihood that they will be married, cohabiting or sexually active if unmarried, compared with their younger peers.[6] Younger teens are also more likely to have an induced abortion than to give birth, whereas the majority of pregnancies among older teens end in a live birth.[6] The overall decline in live births to teenage mothers reflects the decline in teenage pregnancy rates, perhaps due to the availability of contraception and the increased awareness of the risks of unprotected sex resulting from the AIDS epidemic.[5]

- In 2000, Nunavut had significantly higher rates of live births to teen mothers for all age groups. Quebec had the lowest rate of live births for teenage mothers less than 18 years of age, and British Columbia had the lowest rate of live births for teenage mothers 18 to 19 years of age (Figure 1.15).

- Since 1991, the proportion of live births to teenage mothers has declined in all three age groups (Figure 1.16). In 2000, live births to mothers 18 to 19 years of age accounted for 4.2% of all live births (Figure 1.17) — a marginal decline from 4.4% in 1991 (Figure 1.16). In 2000, live births to females less than 18 years of age accounted for approximately 2% of all live births in Canada. In 2000, Nunavut had the overall highest proportion of live births to teenage mothers (Figure 1.17). *Tabular information is presented in Appendix F.*

Data Limitations

Canadian data on maternal age were obtained from birth registrations. In a small fraction of records maternal age was unstated. Late registered births, stillbirths, ectopic pregnancies and aborted pregnancies are not included in the above statistics. Therefore, these rates do not reflect the total number of pregnancies to teenagers. Ontario data have been excluded because of data quality concerns; they are presented in *Appendix G*.

FIGURE 1.14 **Age-specific live birth rate, females ≤ 14, 15-17 and 18-19 years,** *Canada (excluding Ontario),* 1991-2000

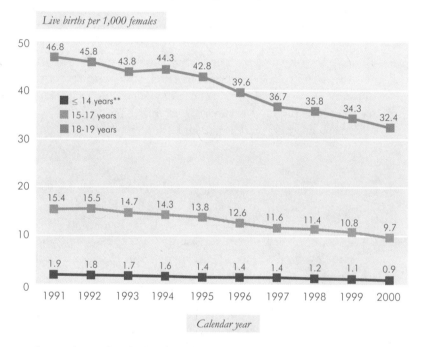

Live births per 1,000 females

- ≤ 14 years**
- 15-17 years
- 18-19 years

Sources: Statistics Canada. Canadian Vital Statistics System, 1991-2000 (unlinked live birth files).
Statistics Canada. *Annual Demographics Statistics, 2001*. Demography Division,
Catalogue No. 91-213-XPB, Annual, Ottawa, 2002.

*Data for Ontario were excluded because of data quality concerns; they are presented in *Appendix G*.
**Rates based on female population 14 years of age.

FIGURE 1.15 **Age-specific live birth rate, females ≤ 19 years, by province/territory,** *Canada (excluding Ontario),* 2000*

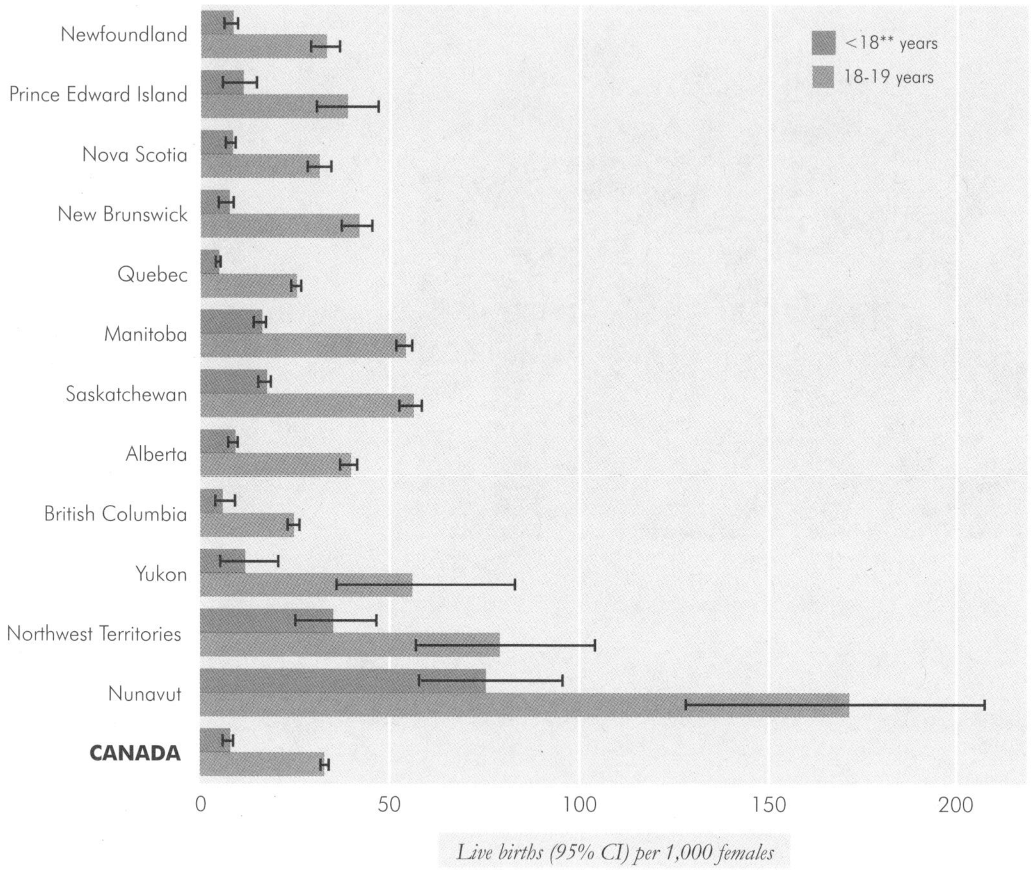
Newfoundland
Prince Edward Island
Nova Scotia
New Brunswick
Quebec
Manitoba
Saskatchewan
Alberta
British Columbia
Yukon
Northwest Territories
Nunavut
CANADA
<18** years
18-19 years
0
50
100
150
200
Live births (95% CI) per 1,000 females

Sources: Statistics Canada. Canadian Vital Statistics System, 2000 (unlinked live birth file).
Statistics Canada. *Annual Demographics Statistics, 2001*. Demography Division, Catalogue No. 91-213-XPB, Annual, Ottawa, 2002.

*Data for Ontario were excluded because of data quality concerns; they are presented in *Appendix G*.

**Age groups < 14 years and 15-17 years have been collapsed because of small numbers. Rates based on female population 14-17 years of age.

CI — confidence interval.

FIGURE 1.16 **Proportion of live births to teenage mothers,**
Canada (excluding Ontario),* 1991-2000

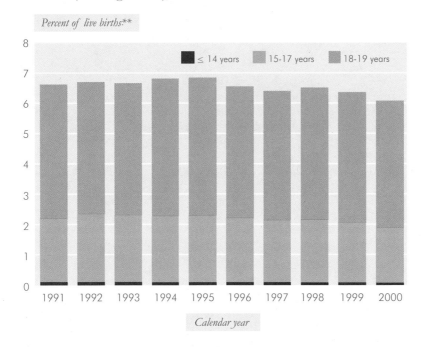

Percent of live births**

≤ 14 years 15-17 years 18-19 years

Calendar year

Source: Statistics Canada. Canadian Vital Statistics System, 1991-2000 (unlinked live birth files).
*Data for Ontario were excluded because of data quality concerns; they are presented in *Appendix G*.
**Excludes live births with unknown maternal age.

FIGURE 1.17 **Proportion of live births to teenage mothers, by province/territory,**
Canada (excluding Ontario),* 2000

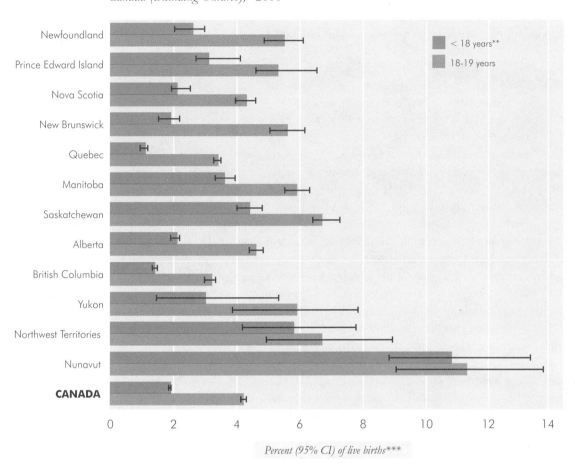

Legend:
- < 18 years**
- 18-19 years

Percent (95% CI) of live births***

Source: Statistics Canada. Canadian Vital Statistics System 2000 (unlinked live birth file).
*Data for Ontario were excluded because of data quality concerns; they are presented in *Appendix G*.
**Age groups ≤ 14 years and 15-17 years have been collapsed because of small numbers.
***Excludes live births with unknown maternal age.
CI — confidence interval.

References

1. Huizinga D, Loeber R, Thornberry TP. Longitudinal study of delinquency, drug use, sexual activity and pregnancy among children and youth in three cities. *Public Health Rep* 1993;108(S1):90-6.

2. Berenson AB, San Miguel VV, Wilinkson GS. Prevalence of physical and sexual assault in pregnant adolescents. *J Adolesc Health* 1992;13:466-9.

3. Fraser AM, Brockert JE, Ward RH. Association of young maternal age with adverse reproductive outcomes. *N Engl J Med* 1995;332:1113-7.

4. Miller HS, Lesser KB, Reed KL. Adolescence and very low birth weight infants: a disproportionate association. *Obstet Gynecol* 1996;87:83-8.

5. Dryburgh H. Teenage pregnancy. *Health Rep* 2000;12(1):9-19.

6. Singh S, Darroch JE. Adolescent pregnancy and childbearing: levels and trends in developed countries. *Family Planning Perspectives* 2000;32(1):14-23

Rate of Live Births to Older Mothers

Author:
Jennifer Crain

The age-specific live birth rate among older mothers is defined as the number of live births to women aged 30-34, 35-39, 40-44 or 45 years and older per 1,000 females aged 30-34, 35-39, 40-44, and 45-49 years, respectively (in a given place and time). A related indicator is the proportion of live births to older mothers, which refers to the number of live births to mothers aged 30-34, 35-39, 40-44 or 45 years and older expressed as a percentage of all live births (in a given place and time).

The proportion of women who are delaying childbearing to later in life has increased markedly in Canada in recent years. There is some evidence that this may be associated with adverse outcomes for both mother and infant. For example, as a woman's age increases, her risk of having a baby with Down syndrome also increases.[1,2] Furthermore, antepartum complications associated with delayed childbearing include increased risks of spontaneous abortion, gestational diabetes, hypertension, pre-eclampsia, placenta previa and prenatal hospital admission.[3] Labour and delivery complications shown to increase with advanced maternal age include malpresentation, fetal distress, prolonged labour, operative deliveries and postpartum hemorrhage.[3-5]

Studies have shown that babies of older mothers are at increased risk of preterm birth, multiple birth, low birth weight and admission to newborn intensive care.[6] Some recent evidence suggests, however, that older women with prudent health behaviours (e.g., smoking abstinence) who receive good quality obstetric care are not at increased risk of complications such as preterm birth and small-for-gestational age infants.[3,5]

Rates of live births to older mothers were calculated using vital statistics data.

Results

- Between 1991 and 2000, the live birth rate among older mothers increased. Among women aged 35 to 39 years, the age-specific live birth rate increased steadily from 25.6 per 1,000 females in 1991 to 30.6 per 1,000 females in 2000 (Figure 1.18). Similar increases in rates were observed in other older age groups. For example, among women aged 40 to 44 years, the rate increased from 3.5 per 1,000 females in 1991 to 5.1 per 1,000 females in 2000 (Figure 1.19).

- In 2000, rates of live births to older mothers were highest in the Yukon for females 35-39 years of age, and highest in Nunavut for women 30-34 years of age (Figure 1.20).

- The proportion of live births to older mothers has also been steadily increasing over the past decade. In 1991, 25.6% of all live births in Canada were to women aged 30 to 34 years, 7.6% were to women aged 35 to 39 years, and 1.0% of live births were to women ≥ 40 years (Figure 1.21). In 2000, these national percentages were 27.4%, 12.4% and 2.1%, respectively (Figure 1.21). British Columbia reported the highest proportion of live births to mothers 30-34 and ≥ 40 years of age in 2000, while the Yukon reported the highest proportion for mothers 35-39 years of age (Figure 1.22). *Tabular information is presented in Appendix F.*

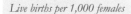

FIGURE 1.18 **Age-specific live birth rate, females 30-39 years,**
Canada (excluding Ontario),* 1991-2000

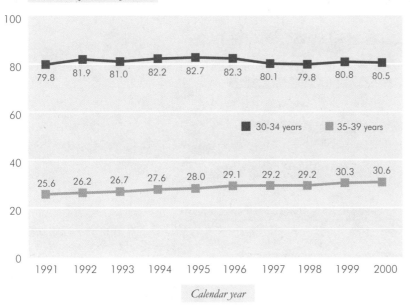

Sources: Statistics Canada. Canadian Vital Statistics System, 1991-2000 (unlinked live birth files).
Statistics Canada. *Annual Demographics Statistics*, 2001. Demography Division,
Catalogue No. 91-213-XPB, Annual, Ottawa, 2002.
*Data for Ontario were excluded because of data quality concerns; they are presented in *Appendix G.*

FIGURE 1.19 **Age-specific live birth rate, females ≥ 40 years,**
Canada (excluding Ontario),* 1991-2000

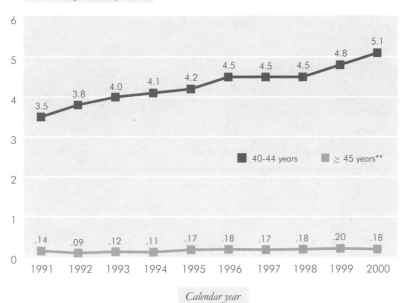

Sources: Statistics Canada. Canadian Vital Statistics System, 1991-2000 (unlinked live birth files).
Statistics Canada. *Annual Demographics Statistics, 2001.* Demography Division,
Catalogue No. 91-213-XPB, Annual, Ottawa, 2002.
*Data for Ontario were excluded because of data quality concerns; they are presented in *Appendix G.*
**Rates based on female population 45-49 years of age.

FIGURE 1.20 **Age-specific live birth rate, females ≥ 30 years, by province/territory,** *Canada (excluding Ontario),* 2000*

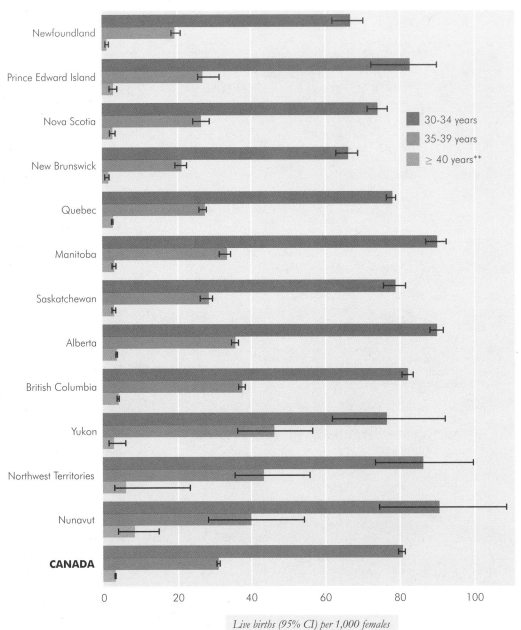

Live births (95% CI) per 1,000 females

Sources: Statistics Canada. Canadian Vital Statistics System, 2000 (unlinked live birth file).
Statistics Canada. *Annual Demographics Statistics*, 2001. Demography Division,
Catalogue No. 91-213-XPB, Annual, Ottawa, 2002.

*Data for Ontario were excluded because of data quality concerns; they are presented in *Appendix G*.

**Age groups 40-44 years and ≥ 45 years have been collapsed because of small numbers. Rates based on
female population 40-49 years of age.

CI — confidence interval.

FIGURE 1.21 **Proportion of live births to older mothers,**
Canada (excluding Ontario), 1991-2000*

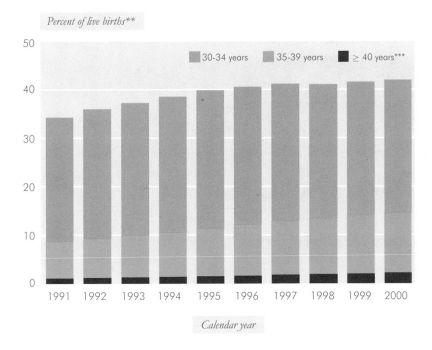

Source: Statistics Canada. Canadian Vital Statistics System, 1991-2000 (unlinked live birth files).
*Data for Ontario were excluded because of data quality concerns; they are presented in *Appendix G*.
**Excludes live births with unknown maternal age.
***Age groups 40-44 years and ≥ 45 years have been collapsed because of small numbers.

FIGURE 1.22 **Proportion of live births to older mothers, by province/territory,** *Canada (excluding Ontario),* 2000*

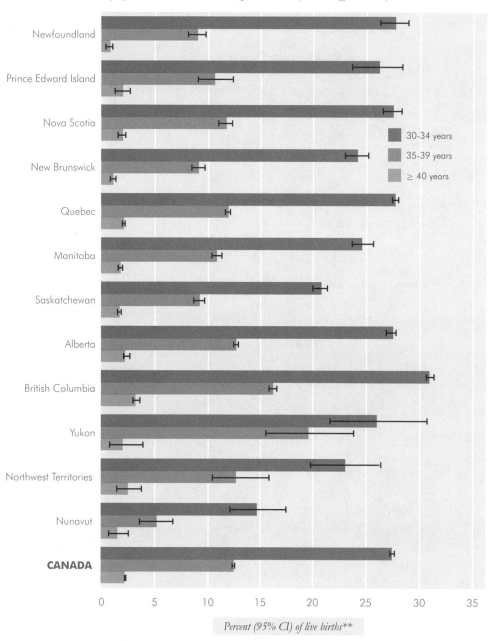

*Percent (95% CI) of live births***

Source: Statistics Canada. Canadian Vital Statistics System, 2000 (unlinked live birth file).
*Data for Ontario were excluded because of data quality concerns; they are presented in *Appendix G.*
**Excludes live births with unknown maternal age.
CI — confidence interval.

Data Limitations

Canadian data on maternal age were obtained from birth registrations. Maternal age was unstated in a small fraction of records. Late registered births, stillbirths, ectopic pregnancies and pregnancies that end in abortion are not included in the above statistics. Therefore, these rates are not necessarily representative of the rate of pregnancies to older mothers. Ontario data have been excluded from the figures because of data quality concerns; they are presented in *Appendix G.*

References

1. Health Canada. *Congenital Anomalies in Canada — A Perinatal Health Report, 2002.* Ottawa: Minister of Public Works and Government Services Canada, 2002 (Catalogue No. H39-641/2002E). URL: <http://www.hc-sc.gc.ca/pphb-dgspsp/rhs-ssg/index.html>.

2. Harper PS. *Practical Genetic Counselling,* 5th Edition. Boston: Butterworth Heinemann, 1998:61.

3. Berkowitz GS, Skovron ML, Lapinski RH, Berkowitz RL. Delayed childbearing and the outcome of pregnancy. *N Engl J Med* 1990;322:659-64.

4. Leyland AH, Boddy FA. Maternal age and outcome of pregnancy. *N Engl J Med* 1990; 323:413-4.

5. Prysak M, Lorenz RP, Kisly A. Pregnancy outcome in nulliparous women 35 years and older. *Obstet Gynecol* 1995;85:65-70.

6. Tough SC, Newburn-Cook C, Johnston DW, Svenson LW, Rose S, Belik J. Delayed childbearing and its impact on population rate changes in low birth weight, multiple birth, and preterm delivery. *Pediatrics* 2002;109:399-403.

Health Services

Rate of Labour Induction

Author:
I.D. Rusen,
MD, MSc, FRCPC

The labour induction rate is defined as the number of delivering women whose labour was induced by medical or surgical means (before the onset of labour) expressed as a proportion of all women giving birth (in a given place and time).

Labour can be induced medically using a variety of pharmacological techniques, including oxytocin and prostaglandins.[1] Labour can also be induced surgically by the artificial rupture of membranes (AROM), referred to as amniotomy.[1] Induction of labour is an obstetric intervention associated with increased complications compared with spontaneous labour. These include an increased incidence of chorioamnionitis and an increased rate of cesarean delivery.[1] In certain situations, the risks of continuing pregnancy for either mother or fetus will outweigh the risks associated with induction. Indications for labour induction include pre-labour rupture of membranes, maternal hypertension, non-reassuring fetal status and postterm gestation.[1] In the United States,[2] the induction rate doubled between 1990 and 1998, attributable to both clinically indicated and elective inductions.

Labour induction rates were calculated using hospitalization data.

Results

- Between 1991-1992 and 2000-2001, the rate of medical induction of labour in Canada increased steadily from 12.9% to 19.7%. (Figure 2.1). These results are consistent with a rate of 10% to 25% previously estimated by the Society of Obstetricians and Gynaecologists of Canada (SOGC).[3] The SOGC has also reported an increasing trend.[4]

- The rate of induction by AROM ranged from 6.3% of deliveries in 1991-1992 to 8.1% of deliveries in 1997-1998 and 7.7% of deliveries in 2000-2001 (Figure 2.1).

- The total induction rate (medical and/or surgical inductions) for Canada (excluding Nova Scotia, Quebec and Manitoba) in 2000-2001 was 22.0%, an increase from 16.5% in 1991-1992.

- Rates of medical induction of labour varied substantially among Canadian provinces and territories, from a low of 3.0% among women delivering in Nunavut to a high of 23.5% among those delivering in Alberta. Rates of induction by AROM also varied across the country, from a low of 0.0% in Nunavut and Yukon to a high of 13.8% among women delivering in Prince Edward Island (Figure 2.2). *Tabular information is presented in Appendix F.*

Data Limitations

The data on labour induction in Canada are limited by the validity of the procedure coding used to estimate induction rates. A recent medical chart re-abstraction study conducted to evaluate the quality of CIHI hospital discharge data suggests that information on medical induction of labour may not be reliably captured.[5] Furthermore, coding for surgical induction of labour may not be used consistently in all provinces and territories. Additional limitations in estimating the labour induction rates relate to errors in identifying whether the labour was induced or whether existing labour was augmented. Augmentation is defined as the use of medical or surgical means to enhance labour that has already begun spontaneously.

FIGURE 2.1 **Rate of labour induction,** *Canada, 1991-1992 to 2000-2001*

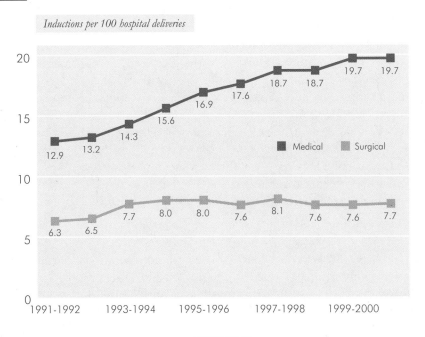

Inductions per 100 hospital deliveries

Fiscal year

Sources: Canadian Institute for Health Information. Discharge Abstract Database (DAD), 1991-1992 to 2000-2001.
Population Health Research Unit, Dalhousie University, Nova Scotia. ASD, 1991-1992 to 2000-2001.
Ministère de la Santé et des Services sociaux (Québec). Banque de données sur les hospitalisations du système MED-ÉCHO, 1991-1992 to 2000-2001.
Manitoba Health, Health Information Management. Manitoba Hospital Abstract System, 1991-1992 to 2000-2001.

FIGURE 2.2 **Rate of labour induction, by province/territory,**
Canada, 2000-2001

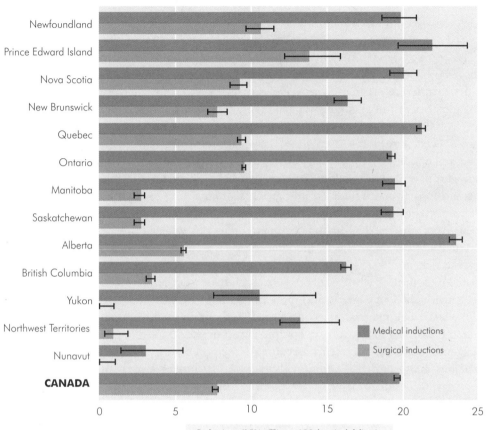

Inductions (95% CI) per 100 hospital deliveries

Sources: Canadian Institute for Health Information. Discharge Abstract Database (DAD), 2000-2001.
Population Health Research Unit, Dalhousie University, Nova Scotia. ASD, 2000-2001.
Ministère de la Santé et des Services sociaux (Québec). Banque de données sur les hospitalisations du système MED-ÉCHO, 2000-2001.
Manitoba Health, Health Information Management. Manitoba Hospital Abstract System, 2000-2001.
CI — confidence interval.

References

1. Cunningham FG, MacDonald PC, Grant NF, Leveno KJ, Gilstrap LC, Hankins GDV, et al. (Eds.). *Williams Obstetrics*, 21st Edition. Toronto: McGraw-Hill, 2001.

2. Zhang J, Yancey MK, Henderson CE. U.S. national trends in labor induction, 1989-1998. *J Reprod Med* 2002;47:120-4.

3. Society of Obstetricians and Gynaecologists of Canada. *Induction of Labour, SOGC Clinical Practice Guidelines for Obstetrics, Number 23*. Ottawa: SOGC, 1996.

4. Society of Obstetricians and Gynaecologists of Canada. *Induction of Labour at Term, SOGC Clinical Practice Guidelines for Obstetrics, Number 107*. Ottawa: SOGC, 2001.

5. Wen SW, Brown A, Mitchell S, Kramer MS, for the Canadian Perinatal Surveillance System. An evaluation of the validity of obstetric/neonatal discharge abstract data by re-abstraction of medical charts (unpublished manuscript), 2002.

Rate of Cesarean Delivery

Author:
Shiliang Liu,
MB, PhD

The cesarean delivery (CD) rate is defined as the number of deliveries by cesarean expressed as a percentage of the total number of deliveries (in a given place and time). The primary cesarean delivery rate is the number of cesarean deliveries to women who have not previously had a cesarean delivery expressed as a percentage of all deliveries to women who have not had a cesarean delivery previously. This rate includes primiparas (i.e., women giving birth for the first time) and multiparas (i.e., women who have given birth one or more times previously). The repeat cesarean delivery rate is the number of cesarean deliveries to women who have had a cesarean delivery previously expressed as a percentage of all deliveries to women who have had a previous cesarean delivery. Older maternal age is a risk factor for cesarean delivery. As well, primiparous women are more likely to require cesarean delivery than women having their second or third child who have not had a cesarean delivery previously. Previous cesarean delivery, dystocia, breech presentation and fetal distress have been recognized as the most important indications for cesarean delivery.[1]

The proportion of women who delivered by cesarean increased from approximately 5% to nearly 20% in Canada and the United States between the late 1960s and the early 1980s.[2] The factors that contributed to the increased cesarean delivery rate during the last decades are not completely understood. While the seemingly high rates continue to be of concern because of the potentially increased risks to the mother and baby[1] and the additional costs due to longer length of hospital stay associated with cesarean delivery, the rate remained at a level of 18% to 19% for approximately 10 years, and increased in more recent years in spite of efforts to lower it.[1-4] The main strategies to lower the cesarean delivery rate in Canada have been the establishment of clinical guidelines for cesarean delivery and efforts to encourage women who have had a previous cesarean delivery to attempt a vaginal delivery (or VBAC, vaginal birth after cesarean).[5-10] Cesarean delivery rates were calculated using hospitalization data.

Results

- The cesarean delivery rate decreased from 18.2% of deliveries in 1991-1992 to 17.5% in 1994-1995, then increased steadily to 21.2% in 2000-2001 (Table 2.1). The recent increase is largely due to a pronounced increase in the primary cesarean delivery rate among women of all age groups (Table 2.1 and Figure 2.3).

- The proportion of women who have had a previous cesarean delivery increased from 9.5% to 10.2% between 1991-1992 and 2000-2001 (Table 2.1). The repeat cesarean delivery rate dropped from 73.2% in 1991-1992 to 64.7% in 1995-1996, and then rose steadily to 70.1% in 2000-2001.

- Data from Statistics Canada for 1991 to 2000 indicate an increase in the percentage of first births among women aged 25 years and older (Table 2.2). Increases in the percentage of first births to women in older age groups may partially explain the increase in the primary cesarean delivery rate.

- In 2000-2001, cesarean delivery rates varied substantially among Canadian provinces and territories, from a low of 8.1% in Nunavut to a high of 25.8% in New Brunswick (Figure 2.4). *Tabular information is presented in Appendix F.*

Data Limitations

Because women having their first birth (particularly women having their first birth at a later age) are at increased risk of cesarean delivery and because of a continuing trend for women to delay first births, it is preferable to adjust for both of these factors when considering trends over time. Simultaneous adjustment for both age of mother and parity could not be made, as the latter is not recorded in the Discharge Abstract Database. Another possible limitation is that the denominator used in the calculation of the above cesarean delivery rates includes hospital deliveries only. While the number of births that occur outside of hospital is small, temporal variation in this number could contribute to variation in cesarean delivery rates, though any effect is probably small.

TABLE 2.1 **Rate of cesarean delivery (CD) and proportion of women who have had a previous CD,** *Canada, 1991-1992 to 2000-2001*

Fiscal year	CD per 100 hospital deliveries	Primary CD per 100 hospital deliveries	Percentage of delivering women with a previous CD	Repeat CD rate (%)
1991-1992	18.2	12.4	9.5	73.2
1992-1993	17.9	12.3	9.7	69.7
1993-1994	17.8	12.4	9.7	67.9
1994-1995	17.5	12.4	9.6	66.0
1995-1996	17.6	12.6	9.7	64.7
1996-1997	18.2	13.1	9.9	64.9
1997-1998	18.5	13.4	9.9	64.9
1998-1999	19.0	13.8	10.0	65.3
1999-2000	19.7	14.5	10.0	66.9
2000-2001	21.2	15.6	10.2	70.1

Sources: Canadian Institute for Health Information. Discharge Abstract Database (DAD), 1991-1992 to 2000-2001.
Population Health Research Unit, Dalhousie University, Nova Scotia. ASD, 1991-1992 to 2000-2001.
Ministère de la Santé et des Services sociaux (Québec). Banque de données sur les hospitalisations du système MED-ÉCHO, 1991-1992 to 2000-2001.
Manitoba Health, Health Information Management. Manitoba Hospital Abstract System, 1991-1992 to 2000-2001.

TABLE 2.2 **Proportion of live births* that were first births,** by maternal age,** *Canada (excluding Ontario),*** 1991-2000*

Year	Maternal age (years)		
	< 25	**25-34**	**≥ 35**
1991	62.8	36.6	23.2
1992	61.7	36.6	22.8
1993	61.6	36.8	23.7
1994	61.8	36.7	24.1
1995	62.1	37.3	24.7
1996	61.9	37.7	24.8
1997	61.8	38.0	25.5
1998	59.8	36.9	25.0
1999	59.8	37.3	25.5
2000	60.3	38.6	25.7

Source: Statistics Canada. Canadian Vital Statistics System, 1991-2000 (unlinked live birth files).
*Excludes live births with unknown maternal age.
**Live births to women who have not had a previous live birth or stillbirth.
***Data for Ontario were excluded because of data quality concerns; they are presented in *Appendix G.*

FIGURE 2.3 **Rate of primary cesarean delivery (CD), by maternal age,** *Canada, 1991-1992 to 2000-2001*

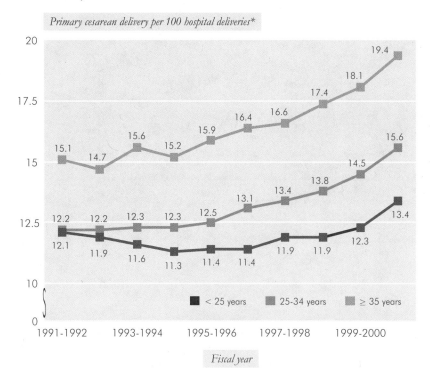

Primary cesarean delivery per 100 hospital deliveries*

- ■ < 25 years
- ■ 25-34 years
- ■ ≥ 35 years

Fiscal year

Sources: Canadian Institute for Health Information. Discharge Abstract Database (DAD), 1991-1992 to 2000-2001.
Population Health Research Unit, Dalhousie University, Nova Scotia. ASD, 1991-1992 to 2000-2001.
Ministère de la Santé et des Services sociaux (Québec). Banque de données sur les hospitalisations du système MED-ÉCHO, 1991-1992 to 2000-2001.
Manitoba Health, Health Information Management. Manitoba Hospital Abstract System, 1991-1992 to 2000-2001.
*Excludes hospital deliveries with unknown maternal age.

FIGURE 2.4 **Rate of cesarean delivery (CD), by province/territory,**
Canada, 2000-2001

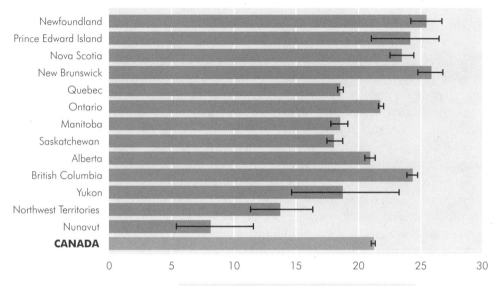

Cesarean deliveries (95% CI) per 100 hospital deliveries

Sources: Canadian Institute for Health Information. Discharge Abstract Database (DAD), 2000-2001.
          Population Health Research Unit, Dalhousie University, Nova Scotia. ASD, 2000-2001.
          Ministère de la Santé et des Services sociaux (Québec). Banque de données sur les hospitalisations
            du système MED-ÉCHO, 2000-2001.
          Manitoba Health, Health Information Management. Manitoba Hospital Abstract System, 2000-2001.
CI — confidence interval.

References

1. American College of Obstetricians and Gynecologists Women's Health Care Physicians, Task Force on Cesarean Delivery Rates. *Evaluation of Cesarean Delivery.* Washington, DC: American College of Obstetricians and Gynecologists, 2000.

2. Notzon FC, Placek PJ, Taffel SM. Comparisons of national cesarean-section rates. *N Engl J Med* 1987;316:386-9.

3. Canadian Institute for Health Information. *Health Indicators 2002.* Ottawa: CIHI, 2002 (No. 2: Catalogue No. 82-221-XIE).

4. Nair C. Trends in cesarean deliveries in Canada. *Health Rep* 1991;3:203-19.

5. Helewa M. Cesarean sections in Canada: what constitutes an appropriate rate? *J Soc Obstet Gynaecol Can* 1995;17:237-46.

6. Society of Obstetricians and Gynaecologists of Canada. *Dystocia. Society of Obstetricians and Gynaecologists of Canada Policy Statement.* Ottawa: SOGC, 1995.

7. Society of Obstetricians and Gynaecologists of Canada. *Vaginal Birth after Previous Cesarean Birth. Society of Obstetricians and Gynaecologists of Canada Policy Statement.* Ottawa: SOGC, 1997.

8. Society of Obstetricians and Gynaecologists of Canada. *The Canadian Consensus Conference on Breech Management at Term. Society of Obstetricians and Gynaecologists of Canada Policy Statement.* Ottawa: SOGC, 1994.

9. Society of Obstetricians and Gynaecologists of Canada. *Fetal Health Surveillance in Labour, Parts 1 through 4. Society of Obstetricians and Gynaecologists of Canada Policy Statement.* Ottawa: SOGC, 1995.

10. Society of Obstetricians and Gynaecologists of Canada. *Fetal Health Surveillance in Labour, Conclusion. Society of Obstetricians and Gynaecologists of Canada Policy Statement.* Ottawa: SOGC, 1996.

Rate of Operative Vaginal Delivery

Author:
Ruth Kohut,
RN, MSc

The rate of operative vaginal delivery is defined as the number of hospital vaginal deliveries assisted by means of forceps or vacuum extraction expressed as a proportion of all hospital vaginal deliveries (in a given place and time).

Operative vaginal delivery is an alternative procedure when spontaneous vaginal delivery needs to be facilitated for fetal or maternal concerns. Choice of forceps or vacuum extraction has been based largely on tradition and training.[1] Results from randomized trials have shown lower rates of cesarean delivery and use of regional and general anesthesia, as well as reduced maternal morbidity among vaginal deliveries using vacuum extraction than vaginal deliveries using forceps.[2-4] However, these randomized trials were too small to assess rare and important outcomes such as intracranial hemorrhage and mortality in infants. Some studies have suggested an increased risk of neonatal scalp trauma and intracranial injury associated with vacuum-assisted delivery, but the absolute risk of infant morbidity is considered to be low and may be due, in part, to an underlying abnormality of labour rather than a direct result of the operative procedure.[5,6] Further studies are required to determine the potential risk for neonatal outcomes following operative vaginal delivery.

Rates of operative vaginal delivery were calculated using hospitalization data.

Results

- In 2000-2001 in Canada, the overall rate of operative vaginal delivery was 16.3%. The overall rate has remained relatively constant, fluctuating between 17.4% and 16.3% over the past decade (Figure 2.5). Deliveries in which both forceps and vacuum extraction were used account for the discrepancy between the overall rate and the sum of the individual forceps use and vacuum extraction rates.
- In 2000-2001, the rate of forceps delivery was 6.2%. This rate has declined considerably over the past decade.
- In 2000-2001, the rate of vacuum extraction was 10.6%. In contrast to forceps delivery, the reported rates of vacuum extraction delivery increased in the early 1990s, stabilizing between 10% and 11% in recent years.
- Operative vaginal delivery rates varied considerably among Canadian provinces and territories (Figures 2.6, 2.7 and 2.8). These regional differences may reflect variations in clinical practice or preference. *Tabular information is presented in Appendix F.*

Data Limitations

Use of operative instruments to assist vaginal delivery is considered a minor procedure. Coding of these procedures may therefore be incomplete, resulting in an underestimation of rates.

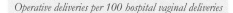

Health Services

FIGURE 2.5 **Rate of operative vaginal delivery,** *Canada, 1991-1992 to 2000-2001*

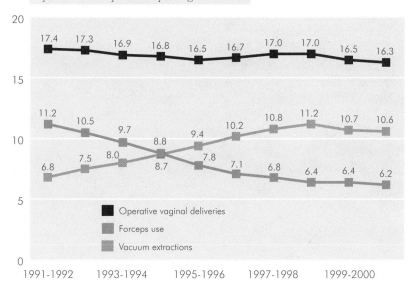

Operative deliveries per 100 hospital vaginal deliveries

Legend:
- Operative vaginal deliveries
- Forceps use
- Vacuum extractions

Fiscal year

Sources: Canadian Institute for Health Information. Discharge Abstract Database, 1991-1992 to 2000-2001.
Population Health Research Unit, Dalhousie University, Nova Scotia. ASD, 1991-1992 to 2000-2001.
Ministère de la Santé et des Services sociaux (Québec). Banque de données sur les hospitalisations du système MED-ÉCHO, 1991-1992 to 2000-2001.
Manitoba Health, Health Information Management. Manitoba Hospital Abstract System, 1991-1992 to 2000-2001.

FIGURE 2.6 **Rate of operative vaginal delivery, by province/territory,** *Canada, 2000-2001*

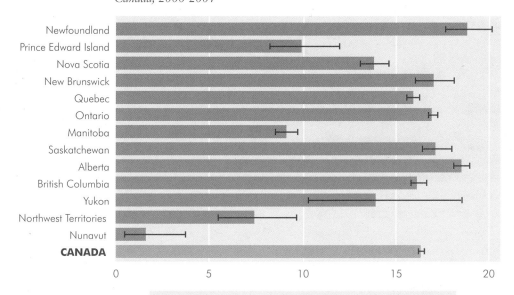

Operative vaginal deliveries (95% CI) per 100 hospital vaginal deliveries

Sources: Canadian Institute for Health Information. Discharge Abstract Database (DAD), 2000-2001.
Population Health Research Unit, Dalhousie University, Nova Scotia. ASD, 2000-2001.
Ministère de la Santé et des Services sociaux (Québec). Banque de données sur les hospitalisations du système MED-ÉCHO, 2000-2001.
Manitoba Health, Health Information Management. Manitoba Hospital Abstract System, 2000-2001.
CI — confidence interval.

FIGURE 2.7 **Rate of vaginal delivery by forceps, by province/territory,**
Canada, 2000-2001

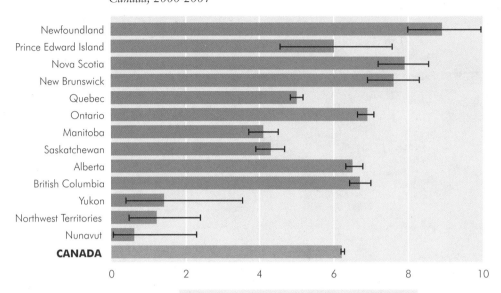

Forceps use (95% CI) per 100 hospital vaginal deliveries

Sources: Canadian Institute for Health Information. Discharge Abstract Database (DAD), 2000-2001.
Population Health Research Unit, Dalhousie University, Nova Scotia. ASD, 2000-2001.
Ministère de la Santé et des Services sociaux (Québec). Banque de données sur les hospitalisations du système MED-ÉCHO, 2000-2001.
Manitoba Health, Health Information Management. Manitoba Hospital Abstract System, 2000-2001.
CI — confidence interval.

FIGURE 2.8 **Rate of vaginal delivery by vacuum extraction, by province/territory,** *Canada, 2000-2001*

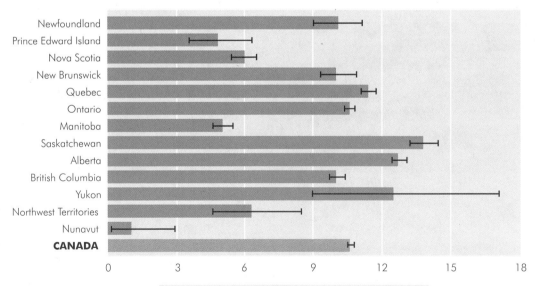

Vacuum extractions (95% CI) per 100 hospital vaginal deliveries

Sources: Canadian Institute for Health Information. Discharge Abstract Database (DAD), 2000-2001.
Population Health Research Unit, Dalhousie University, Nova Scotia. ASD, 2000-2001.
Ministère de la Santé et des Services sociaux (Québec). Banque de données sur les hospitalisations système MED-ÉCHO, 2000-2001.
Manitoba Health, Health Information Management. Manitoba Hospital Abstract System, 2000-2001.
CI — confidence interval.

References

1. Editorial. Vacuum versus forceps. *Lancet* 1984;i:144.

2. Johanson RB, Rice C, Doyle M, Arthur J, Anyanwu L, Ibrahim J, et al. A randomized prospective study comparing the new vacuum extractor policy with forceps delivery. *Br J Obstet Gynaecol* 1993;100:524-30.

3. Johanson RB, Mendon V. Vacuum extraction versus forceps for assisted vaginal delivery (Cochrane Review). In: *The Cochrane Library*, Issue 2, 2002. Oxford: Update Software.

4. Kabiru WN, Jamieson D, Graves W, Lindsay M. Trends in operative vaginal delivery rates and associated maternal complication rates in an inner-city hospital. *Am J Obstet Gynecol* 2001;184:1112-4.

5. Towner D, Castro MA, Eby-Wilkens E, Gilbert WM. Effect of mode of delivery in nulliparous women on neonatal intracranial injury. *N Engl J Med* 1999;341:1709-14.

6. Wen SW, Liu S, Kramer MS, Marcoux S, Ohlsson A, Sauve R, et al. Comparison of maternal and infant outcomes between vacuum extraction and forceps deliveries. *Am J Epidemiol* 2001;153:103-7.

Rate of Trauma to the Perineum

Author:
Ruth Kohut,
RN, MSc

The rate of trauma to the perineum is defined as the number of women who had an episiotomy or a delivery resulting in a first-, second-, third- or fourth-degree laceration (tear) of the perineum expressed as a proportion of all women who had a hospital vaginal delivery (in a given place and time).

Minimizing trauma to the perineum is important in reducing postpartum discomfort and the risk of long-term pelvic floor damage. Randomized studies have not supported the liberal use of episiotomy to prevent extended lacerations or secondary long-term genitourinary complications.[1,2] Consequently, the Society of Obstetricians and Gynaecologists of Canada has recommended that episiotomy should be used only to expedite delivery in the case of fetal compromise or maternal distress and lack of progress.[3] Although there has been a downward trend in the routine use of episiotomy in Canada and the United States,[4] episiotomy continues to be one of the most common surgical procedures, particularly for primiparous women. Continued surveillance is necessary to monitor obstetric practices and procedures that affect the rate of trauma to the perineum.

Rates of trauma to the perineum were calculated using hospitalization data.

Results

- In 2000-2001, the episiotomy rate in Canada was 23.8 per 100 hospital vaginal deliveries. The rate of episiotomy has dropped 51% since 1991-1992 (Figure 2.9). This decline was likely due to recommendations against routine episiotomy rather than a change in indications of fetal or maternal risk.

- Conversely, there has been an increasing trend in the combined rate of first- and second-degree lacerations since 1991-1992. However, the rate of the more serious third- and fourth-degree lacerations has remained relatively constant (Figure 2.9).

- Considerable variations existed in the use of episiotomy in the provinces and territories of Canada in 2000-2001 (Figure 2.10). The regional differences may be due, in part, to dissimilar reporting practices and to variations in clinical practice or preference. *Tabular information is presented in Appendix F.*

Data Limitations

There are no standards for the case definition and classification of perineal trauma in Canada. This is an important limitation in the surveillance of trauma to the perineum. A change in reporting practices may account for the trends in perineal trauma. For example, greater reporting of first- and second-degree lacerations may have resulted from greater attention being paid to the occurrence of these events because of the decreasing use of episiotomy. Under-reporting of episiotomy may occur as a result of data collection and coding practices.[5]

FIGURE 2.9 **Rate of trauma to the perineum by episiotomy and perineal laceration,** *Canada, 1991-1992 to 2000-2001*

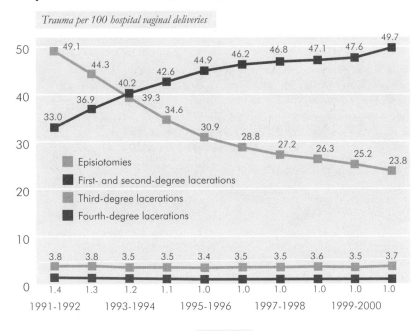

Trauma per 100 hospital vaginal deliveries

Legend:
- Episiotomies
- First- and second-degree lacerations
- Third-degree lacerations
- Fourth-degree lacerations

Fiscal year

Sources: Canadian Institute for Health Information. Discharge Abstract Database (DAD), 1991-1992 to 2000-2001.
Population Health Research Unit, Dalhousie University, Nova Scotia. ASD, 1991-1992 to 2000-2001.
Ministère de la Santé et des Services sociaux (Québec). Banque de données sur les hospitalisations du système MED-ÉCHO, 1991-1992 to 2000-2001.
Manitoba Health, Health Information Management. Manitoba Hospital Abstract System, 1991-1992 to 2000-2001.

FIGURE 2.10 **Rate of episiotomy, by province/territory,** *Canada, 2000-2001*

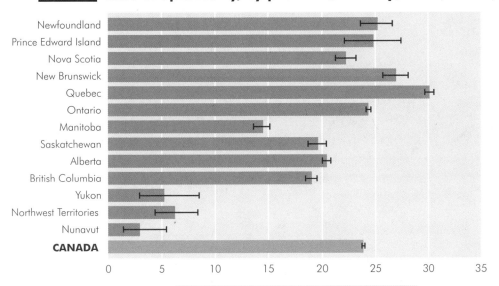

Episiotomies (95% CI) per 100 hospital vaginal deliveries

Sources: Canadian Institute for Health Information. Discharge Abstract Database (DAD), 2000-2001.
Population Health Research Unit, Dalhousie University, Nova Scotia. ASD, 2000-2001.
Ministère de la Santé et des Services sociaux (Québec). Banque de données sur les hospitalisations du système MED-ÉCHO, 2000-2001.
Manitoba Health, Health Information Management. Manitoba Hospital Abstract System, 2000-2001
CI — confidence interval.

References

1. Carroli G, Belizan J, Stamp G. Episiotomy policies in vaginal births. In: Neilson JP, Crowther CA, Hofmeyer GJ (Eds.), *The Cochrane Collaboration: Pregnancy and Childbirth Database*. Hochett ED, 1998, Disk Issue I. URL: <http://www.members.tripod.com/~gineco/EPISIOTO.HTM>.

2. Klein MC, Gauthier RJ, Robbins JM, Kaczorowski J, Jorgensen SH, Franco ED, et al. Relationship of episiotomy to perineal trauma and morbidity, sexual dysfunction, and pelvic floor relaxation. *Am J Obstet Gynecol* 1994;171:591-8.

3. Society of Obstetricians and Gynaecologists of Canada. *Clinical Practice Guidelines: Healthy Beginnings: Guidelines for Care during Pregnancy and Childbirth*. Ottawa: SOGC, 1998. URL: <http://www.sogc.org/sogcnet/sogc%5Fdocs/common/guide/pdfs/healthybegeng.pdf>.

4. Weeks JD, Kozak LJ. Trends in the use of episiotomy in the United States: 1980-1998. *Birth* 2001;28:152-60.

5. Graham ID, Fowler-Graham D. Episiotomy counts: trends and prevalence in Canada, 1981-1982 to 1993-1994. *Birth* 1997;24:141-7.

Rate of Early Maternal Discharge from Hospital after Childbirth

Author:
Shiliang Liu,
MB, PhD

The rate of early maternal discharge from hospital after childbirth is defined as the number of women discharged from hospital early (for example, within two days after vaginal birth or within four days after cesarean birth) expressed as a proportion of all women discharged from hospital after childbirth (in a given place and time).

Early discharge of healthy mothers with their babies has become routine, partly because of a need to curtail hospital costs.[1-3] Studies have attempted to assess the association between early maternal discharge and the quality, efficiency and accessibility of hospital services for childbirth. However, the length of time that mothers should stay in hospital for childbirth remains controversial because early postpartum discharge may pose risks to the health of mothers and their infants.[2-5] Nevertheless, most studies evaluating early postpartum discharge in terms of major maternal outcomes have not shown it to be associated with significant adverse effects on mothers.[1,3,6,7]

Rates of early maternal discharge were calculated using hospitalization data. Results are presented separately for vaginal and cesarean births.

Results

- The proportion of mothers who stayed in hospital for less than two days for a vaginal birth increased significantly from 3.7% in 1991-1992 to 21.5% in 1998-1999, then showed a slight decline in 1999-2000 (to 20.5%) and in 2000-2001 (to 19.8%) (Figure 2.11). On the other hand, the proportion of mothers who stayed in hospital for less than four days for a cesarean birth increased steadily, from 2.7% in 1991-1992 to 35.7% in 2000-2001.

- Between 1991-1992 and 2000-2001, the average maternal length of hospital stay for childbirth declined significantly from 3.6 to 2.4 days for vaginal births and from 6.3 to 4.4 days for cesarean births (Table 2.3).

- In 2000-2001, women delivering in Nunavut and Alberta were discharged from hospital after childbirth sooner than women delivering in other provinces or territories (Figure 2.12, Table 2.4). *Tabular information is presented in Appendix F.*

Data Limitations

Information regarding the time of birth is not available on the mother's file in the hospital discharge database. As a result, the maternal length of hospital stay reported includes the time between admission and childbirth, and childbirth and discharge.

FIGURE 2.11 **Rate of short maternal length of stay (LOS) in hospital for childbirth,** *Canada, 1991-1992 to 2000-2001*

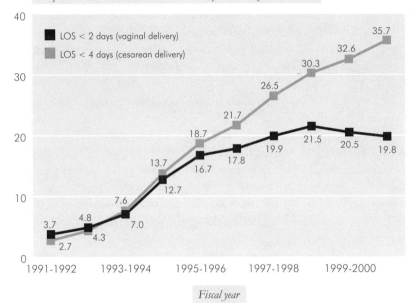

Hospital deliveries with short maternal LOS per 100 hospital deliveries

- LOS < 2 days (vaginal delivery)
- LOS < 4 days (cesarean delivery)

Fiscal year

Sources: Canadian Institute for Health Information. Discharge Abstract Database, (DAD) 1991-1992 to 2000-2001.
Population Health Research Unit, Dalhousie University, Nova Scotia. ASD, 1991-1992 to 2000-2001.
Ministère de la Santé et des Services sociaux (Québec). Banque de données sur les hospitalisations du système MED-ÉCHO, 1991-1992 to 2000-2001.
Manitoba Health, Health Information Management. Manitoba Hospital Abstract System, 1991-1992 to 2000-2001.

TABLE 2.3 **Average maternal length of stay (LOS) in hospital for childbirth,** *Canada, 1991-1992 to 2000-2001*

Year	Mean LOS in days (SD)	
	Vaginal delivery	Cesarean delivery
1991-1992	3.6 (1.8)	6.3 (2.7)
1992-1993	3.3 (1.7)	6.0 (2.7)
1993-1994	3.1 (1.7)	5.6 (2.6)
1994-1995	2.8 (1.6)	5.3 (2.6)
1995-1996	2.6 (1.6)	5.0 (2.5)
1996-1997	2.5 (1.5)	4.8 (2.5)
1997-1998	2.4 (1.5)	4.6 (2.5)
1998-1999	2.4 (1.5)	4.5 (2.5)
1999-2000	2.4 (1.5)	4.5 (2.4)
2000-2001	2.4 (1.5)	4.4 (2.4)

Sources: Canadian Institute for Health Information. Discharge Abstract Database (DAD), 2000-2001.
Population Health Research Unit, Dalhousie University, Nova Scotia. ASD, 2000-2001.
Ministère de la Santé et des Services sociaux (Québec). Banque de données sur les hospitalisations du système MED-ÉCHO, 2000-2001.
Manitoba Health, Health Information Management. Manitoba Hospital Abstract System, 2000-2001.
SD — standard deviation.

FIGURE 2.12 **Rate of short maternal length of stay (LOS) in hospital for childbirth, by province/territory,** *Canada, 2000-2001*

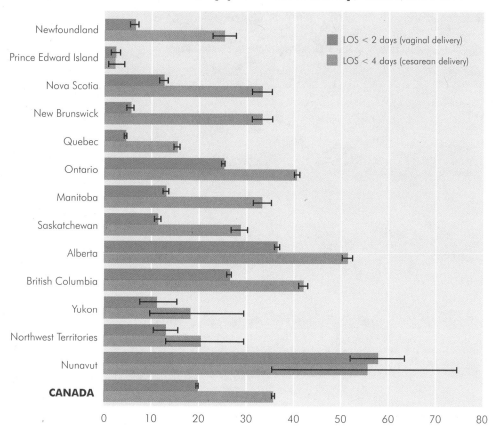

Hospital deliveries with short maternal LOS (95% CI) per 100 hospital deliveries

Sources: Canadian Institute for Health Information. Discharge Abstract Database (DAD), 2000-2001.
Population Health Research Unit, Dalhousie University, Nova Scotia. ASD, 2000-2001.
Ministère de la Santé et des Services sociaux (Québec). Banque de données sur les hospitalisations du système MED-ÉCHO, 2000-2001.
Manitoba Health, Health Information Management. Manitoba Hospital Abstract System, 2000-2001.
CI — confidence interval.

TABLE 2.4 **Average maternal length of stay (LOS) in hospital for childbirth, by province/territory,** *Canada, 2000-2001*

Province/territory	Mean LOS in days (SD)	
	Vaginal deliveries	Cesarean deliveries
Newfoundland	3.4 (2.3)	5.5 (3.6)
Prince Edward Island	3.1 (1.6)	5.5 (2.3)
Nova Scotia	2.9 (2.0)	4.7 (2.9)
New Brunswick	2.8 (1.6)	4.6 (2.5)
Quebec	2.7 (1.4)	4.8 (2.3)
Ontario	2.2 (1.4)	4.2 (2.3)
Manitoba	2.6 (1.4)	4.6 (2.7)
Saskatchewan	2.8 (1.6)	4.6 (2.4)
Alberta	2.0 (1.4)	4.0 (2.5)
British Columbia	2.3 (1.6)	4.2 (2.4)
Yukon	3.1 (1.4)	4.7 (1.6)
Northwest Territories	2.7 (1.4)	4.9 (2.0)
Nunavut	1.6 (0.9)	3.9 (2.9)
CANADA	2.4 (1.5)	4.4 (2.4)

Sources: Canadian Institute for Health Information. Discharge Abstract Database (DAD), 2000-2001.
Population Health Research Unit, Dalhousie University, Nova Scotia. ASD, 2000-2001.
Ministère de la Santé et des Services sociaux (Québec). Banque de données sur les hospitalisations du système MED-ÉCHO, 2000-2001.
Manitoba Health, Health Information Management. Manitoba Hospital Abstract System, 2000-2001.
SD — standard deviation.

References

1. Centers for Disease Control and Prevention. Trends in length of stay for hospital deliveries: United States, 1970-1992. *MMWR* 1995;44:335-7.

2. Britton JR. Postpartum early hospital discharge and follow-up practices in Canada and the United States. *Birth* 1998;25:161-8.

3. Dalby DM, Williams JI, Hodnett E, Rush J. Postpartum safety and satisfaction following early discharge. *Can J Public Health* 1996;87:90-4.

4. Gloor JE, Kissoon N, Joubert GI. Appropriateness of hospitalization in a Canadian pediatric hospital. *Pediatrics* 1993;91:70-4.

5. Wen SW, Liu S, Marcoux S, Fowler D. Trends and variations in length of hospital stay for childbirth in Canada. *Can Med Assoc J* 1998;158:875-80.

6. Meikle SF, Lyons E, Hulac P, Orleans M. Rehospitalizations and outpatient contacts of mothers and neonates after hospital discharge after vaginal delivery. *Am J Obstet Gynecol* 1998;179:166-71.

7. Liu S, Heaman M, Kramer MS, Demissie K, Wen SW, Marcoux S, for the Maternal Health Study Group of the Canadian Perinatal Surveillance System. Length of hospital stay, obstetric conditions at childbirth, and maternal readmission: a population-based cohort study. *Am J Obstet Gynecol* 2002;87:681-7.

Rate of Early Neonatal Discharge from Hospital after Birth

Author:
Shiliang Liu,
MB, PhD

The rate of early neonatal discharge from hospital after birth is defined as the number of newborns discharged from hospital early (for example, within 24 or 48 hours of birth) expressed as a proportion of all newborns discharged from hospital after birth (in a given place and time).

Appropriate early discharge of newborns, taking into account their health status, may increase the efficiency of hospital services and may also benefit newborns and their families.[1] In most circumstances, early discharge programs are safe for normal newborns, especially if community follow-up services are provided. However, the question of how long a newborn should stay in hospital after birth remains controversial. The potential risks and benefits of early discharge policies for newborns have not yet been adequately examined using randomized clinical trials.[1-3] Recent studies have shown an increased neonatal morbidity among newborns with a very short length of stay at birth.[3-5]

Rates of early neonatal discharge were calculated using hospitalization data. They are presented separately for newborns weighing 1,000-2,499 g and for those weighing $\geq$ 2,500 g.

Results

- The proportion of newborns weighing 1,000-2,499 g who stayed in hospital for less than two days after birth increased in the early 1990s, peaked at 12.4% in 1995-1996 and declined subsequently to 9.0% in 2000-2001 (Figure 2.13). The rate of early discharge among newborns weighing $\geq$ 2,500 g increased dramatically, from 4.3% in 1991-1992 to 24.5% in 1998-1999, then declined to 22.3% in 2000-2001.

- Among newborns weighing 1,000-2,499 g at birth, the average length of hospital stay at birth decreased from 8.5 days in 1991-1992 to 7.7 days in 1995-1996, and then increased to 8.5 days in 2000-2001 (Table 2.5). For newborns weighing $\geq$ 2,500 g, the average length of hospital stay after birth decreased steadily, from 3.5 days in 1991-1992 to 2.4 days in 2000-2001.

- In 2000-2001, Nunavut had the largest proportion of low birth weight newborns (62.5%) and Alberta had the largest proportion of normal birth weight newborns (42.2%) discharged within two days of birth (Figure 2.14). Also, low birth weight (1,000-2,499 g) newborns in the Yukon and Nunavut had the shortest average neonatal length of stay (LOS), at 4.6 and 5.5 days, respectively. The Northwest Territories had the shortest average LOS for newborns weighing $\geq$ 2,500 g (1.4 days, Table 2.6). *Tabular information is presented in Appendix F.*

Data Limitations

The time of birth is not recorded in the Discharge Abstract Database (DAD) and other hospital discharge databases. Therefore it is not possible to obtain the exact duration of hospital stay, which would be of interest, especially with respect to infants discharged on the first day after birth. Also, it is not possible to obtain length of stay analyses stratified by gestational age for Canada because the DAD does not as yet include information on gestational age.

FIGURE 2.13 **Rate of early neonatal discharge from hospital after birth,**
Canada, 1991-1992 to 2000-2001

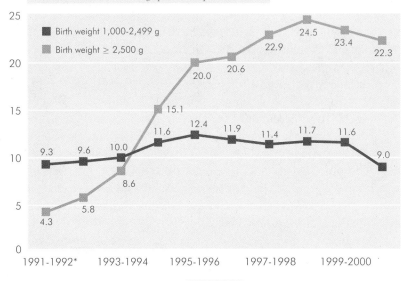

Newborns with LOS < 2 days per 100 hospital live births

■ Birth weight 1,000-2,499 g
■ Birth weight ≥ 2,500 g

Fiscal year

Sources: Canadian Institute of Health Information. Discharge Abstract Database (DAD), 1991-1992 to 2000-2001.
Population Health Research Unit, Dalhousie University, Nova Scotia. ASD, 1992-1993 to 2000-2001.
Ministère de la Santé et des Services sociaux (Québec). Banque de données sur les hospitalisations du
système MED-ÉCHO, 1991-1992 to 2000-2001.
Manitoba Health, Health Information Management. Manitoba Hospital Abstract System, 1991-1992 to 2000-2001.
*Complete data for Nova Scotia were not available for 1991-1992 and were not included in the estimates for that year.
LOS — length of stay.

TABLE 2.5 **Average neonatal length of stay (LOS) in hospital after birth,**
Canada, 1991-1992 to 2000-2001

Year	Mean LOS (SD) in days	
	Birth weight 1,000-2,499 g	Birth weight ≥ 2,500 g
1991-1992*	8.5 (6.6)	3.5 (1.8)
1992-1993	8.2 (6.7)	3.2 (1.7)
1993-1994	8.1 (6.8)	2.9 (1.7)
1994-1995	7.8 (6.8)	2.6 (1.6)
1995-1996	7.7 (6.8)	2.5 (1.6)
1996-1997	7.8 (6.8)	2.4 (1.6)
1997-1998	7.9 (6.8)	2.3 (1.6)
1998-1999	7.9 (6.8)	2.3 (1.6)
1999-2000	8.0 (6.8)	2.3 (1.6)
2000-2001	8.5 (6.8)	2.4 (1.7)

Sources: Canadian Institute for Health Information. Discharge Abstract Database (DAD), 1991-1992 to 2000-2001.
Population Health Research Unit, Dalhousie University, Nova Scotia. ASD, 1992-1993 to 2000-2001.
Ministère de la Santé et des Services sociaux (Québec). Banque de données sur les hospitalisations du système
MED-ÉCHO, 1991-1992 to 2000-2001.
Manitoba Health, Health Information Management. Manitoba Hospital Abstract System, 1991-1992 to 2000-2001.
*Complete data for Nova Scotia were not available for 1991-1992 and were not included in the estimates for that year.
SD — standard deviation.

FIGURE 2.14 **Rate of early neonatal discharge from hospital after birth, by province/territory,** *Canada, 2000-2001*

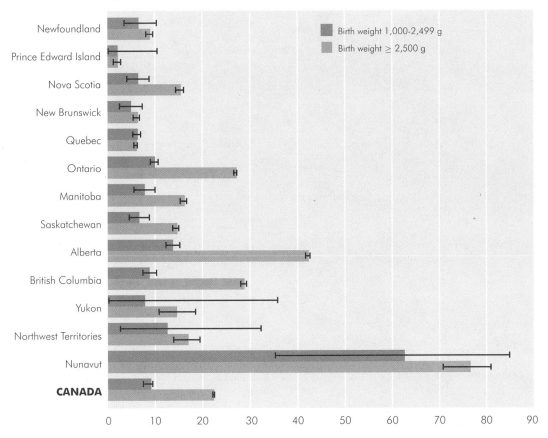

Newborns (95% CI) with LOS < 2 days per 100 hospital live births

Sources: Canadian Institute for Health Information. Discharge Abstract Database (DAD), 2000-2001.
Population Health Research Unit, Dalhousie University, Nova Scotia. ASD, 2000-2001.
Ministère de la Santé et des Services sociaux (Québec). Banque de données sur les hospitalisations du système MED-ÉCHO, 2000-2001.
Manitoba Health, Health Information Management, Manitoba Hospital Abstract System, 2000-2001.
CI — confidence interval.
LOS — length of stay.

TABLE 2.6 **Average neonatal length of stay (LOS) in hospital after birth, by province/territory,** *Canada, 2000-2001*

Province/territory	Mean LOS (SD) in days	
	Birth weight 1,000-2,499 g	Birth weight ≥ 2,500 g
Newfoundland	9.7 (6.8)	3.0 (1.7)
Prince Edward Island	11.5 (7.2)	3.4 (2.0)
Nova Scotia	10.5 (7.2)	2.9 (1.9)
New Brunswick	12.2 (7.3)	3.0 (2.1)
Quebec	9.3 (7.0)	2.8 (1.6)
Ontario	8.1 (6.7)	2.3 (1.6)
Manitoba	9.6 (7.0)	2.6 (1.9)
Saskatchewan	9.5 (7.2)	2.7 (1.8)
Alberta	7.6 (6.5)	2.1 (1.6)
British Columbia	9.0 (6.7)	2.4 (1.7)
Yukon	4.6 (3.3)	3.0 (1.8)
Northwest Territories	5.8 (5.9)	1.4 (1.2)
Nunavut	5.5 (8.3)	2.6 (1.7)
CANADA	8.5 (6.8)	2.4 (1.7)

Sources: Canadian Institute for Health Information. Discharge Abstract Database (DAD), 2000-2001.
Population Health Research Unit, Dalhousie University, Nova Scotia. ASD, 2000-2001.
Ministère de la Santé et des Services sociaux (Québec). Banque de données sur les hospitalisations du système MED-ÉCHO, 2000-2001.
Manitoba Health, Health Information Management, Manitoba Hospital Abstract System, 2000-2001.
SD — standard deviation.

References

1. Braverman P, Egerter S, Pearl M, Marchi K, Miller C. Problems associated with early discharge of newborn infants. Early discharge of newborns and mothers: a critical review of the literature. *Pediatrics* 1995;96:716-26.

2. Liu LL, Clemens CJ, Shay DK, Davis RL, Novack AH. The safety of newborn early discharge. The Washington State experience. *JAMA* 1997;278:293-8.

3. Lee KS, Perlman M, Ballantyne M, Elliott I, To T. The association between duration of neonatal hospital stay and readmission rate. *J Pediatr* 1995;127:758-66.

4. Liu S, Wen SW, McMillan D, Trouton K, Fowler D, McCourt C. Increased neonatal readmission rate associated with decreased length of hospital stay at birth in Canada. *Can J Public Health* 2000;91:46-50.

5. Wen SW, Liu S, Fowler D. Trends and variations in neonatal length of in-hospital stay in Canada. *Can J Public Health* 1998;89:115-9.

B

Maternal, Fetal and Infant Health Outcomes

Maternal Health Outcomes

Maternal Mortality Ratio

Author:
Sharon Bartholomew,
MHSc

The maternal mortality ratio (MMR) is defined as the number of maternal deaths per 100,000 live births (in a given place and time).

A country's MMR is considered an important indicator of the general health of the population and the availability and quality of medical care, as well as the status of women.[1] At approximately three maternal deaths reported for every 100,000 live births, Canada has one of the lowest MMRs in the world, reflecting our universal access to high quality medical care, our relatively healthy population, and the generally favourable economic and social status of Canadian women.

In Canada, for deaths occurring from January 1, 1979, to December 31, 1999, underlying causes of death were coded according to the Ninth Revision of the *International Classification of Diseases* (ICD-9).[2] Maternal deaths are those in which the underlying cause of death has been assigned a numerical code between 630 and 676 under Chapter 11 (Complications of Pregnancy, Childbirth and the Puerperium) of ICD-9.

The definition of maternal death under ICD-9 is as follows: The death of a woman while pregnant or within 42 days of the termination of the pregnancy, irrespective of the duration and the site of the pregnancy, from any cause related to or aggravated by the pregnancy or its management but not from accidental or incidental causes.

Maternal deaths are considered to be either:

a. **Direct obstetric deaths** — that is, deaths resulting from obstetric complications of the pregnant state (pregnancy, labour and puerperium); from interventions, omissions or incorrect treatment; or from a chain of events resulting from any of the above; or

b. **Indirect obstetric deaths** — that is, deaths that were not due to direct obstetric causes but, rather, resulted from previous existing disease or disease that developed during pregnancy and was aggravated by the physiologic effects of pregnancy. A definition of "indirect obstetric death" first appeared in the Ninth Revision of the ICD system; deaths considered to be indirect obstetric deaths have, therefore, been included in counts of maternal deaths in Canada only since ICD-9 was adopted for use in this country in 1979.

Some deaths of pregnant women are due to causes such as motor vehicle collisions, poisonings or violence, which do not appear related to the pregnancy. These are not included in the MMR. MMRs were calculated using vital statistics data.

Results

- Overall, the MMR decreased from 6.1 per 100,000 live births in 1979-1981 to 2.5 per 100,000 live births in 1997-1999 (Figure 3.1).

- Direct obstetric deaths are the most common causes of maternal death in Canada. In fact, few maternal deaths attributable to indirect causes were reported between 1979 and 1999. Figure 3.1 shows that the trend for direct deaths follows the same curve as that for direct and indirect deaths combined.

- Pulmonary embolism, hypertension and postpartum hemorrhage were the most common causes of direct maternal death in 1979-1984. With the exception of pulmonary embolism, the ratios for these causes have fluctuated over time but have generally shown a downward trend. Maternal deaths due to pulmonary embolism still remain relatively high in comparison with other causes of death (Table 3.1). *Tabular information is presented in Appendix F.*

FIGURE 3.1 **Maternal mortality ratio (MMR),** *Canada (excluding Ontario),* 1979-1981 to 1997-1999***

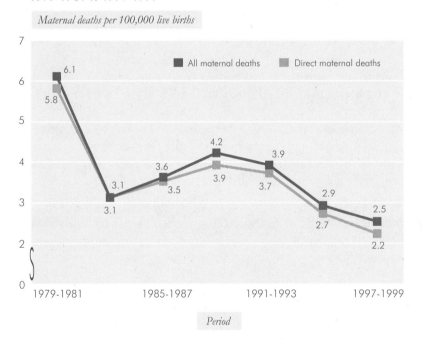

Maternal deaths per 100,000 live births

Period

Sources: Years 1979-1990.[3-11]
     Years 1991-1999: Statistics Canada. Canadian Vital Statistics System, 1991-1999 (unlinked live birth and death files).
*Data for Ontario were excluded because of data quality concerns; they are presented in *Appendix G.*
**Maternal deaths are coded using ICD-10 from 2000 onwards and will be presented in subsequent reports.

TABLE 3.1 **Direct maternal deaths by cause,** *Canada (excluding Ontario),* 1979-1984, 1985-1990, 1991-1996 and 1997-1999*

Cause (ICD-9 code)	1979-1984		1985-1990		1991-1996		1997-1999**	
	Number of deaths	Deaths (95% CI) per 1,000,000 live births	Number of deaths	Deaths (95% CI) per 1,000,000 live births	Number of deaths	Deaths (95% CI) per 1,000,000 live births	Number of deaths	Deaths (95% CI) per 1,000,000 live births
Ectopic and molar pregnancy (630-633)	5	3.4 (1.3-7.7)	4	2.7 (1.0-7.0)	4	2.8 (1.0-7.1)	1	1.6 (0.4-8.7)
Other pregnancy with abortive outcome (634-639)	0	0.0 (0.0-2.4)	3	2.1 (0.3-6.4)	2	1.4 (0.4-4.7)	1	1.6 (0.4-8.7)
Antepartum hemorrhage, abruptio placentae and placenta previa (641)	5	3.4 (1.3-7.7)	4	2.7 (1.0-7.0)	7	4.9 (2.1-10.1)	1	1.6 (0.4-8.7)
Hypertension complicating pregnancy, childbirth and the puerperium (642)	9	6.1 (2.7-11.3)	13	8.9 (4.7-15.1)	7	4.9 (2.1-10.1)	1	1.6 (0.4-8.7)
Other complications of pregnancy, NEC (640,643,644,645,646)	3	2.0 (0.3-6.3)	1	0.7 (0.3-4.0)	1	0.7 (0.4-4.0)	1	1.6 (0.4-8.7)
Normal delivery, and other indications for care in pregnancy, labour and delivery (650-659)	1	0.7 (0.3-4.0)	1	0.7 (0.3-4.0)	1	0.7 (0.4-4.0)	0	0.0 (0.0-6.2)
Postpartum hemorrhage (666)	6	4.1 (1.3-8.3)	5	3.4 (1.3-7.7)	2	1.4 (0.4-4.7)	1	1.6 (0.4-8.7)
Complications occurring mainly in the course of labour and delivery, NEC (660-665,667-669)	14	9.5 (5.0-15.7)	2	1.4 (0.3-4.7)	5	3.5 (1.3-7.8)	1	1.6 (0.4-8.7)
Major puerperal infection (670)	3	2.0 (0.3-6.3)	3	2.1 (0.3-6.4)	0	0.0 (0.0-2.4)	1	1.6 (0.4-8.7)
Venous complications in pregnancy and the puerperium (671)	3	2.0 (0.3-6.3)	2	1.4 (0.3-4.7)	2	1.4 (0.4-4.7)	0	0.0 (0.0-6.2)
Obstetrical pulmonary embolism (673)	10	6.8 (3.0-12.0)	5	3.4 (1.3-7.7)	13	9.1 (4.8-15.3)	4	6.3 (2.0-16.4)
Cerebrovascular disorders in the puerperium (674.0)	4	2.7 (1.0-7.0)	3	2.1 (0.3-6.4)	0	0.0 (0.0-2.4)	0	0.0 (0.0-6.2)
Other and unspecified complication of the puerperium, NEC (674.1-674.9)	3	2.0 (0.3-6.3)	8	5.5 (2.4-10.7)	2	1.4 (0.4-4.7)	2	3.2 (0.4-11.3)

Sources: Years 1979-1990.[3-11]
 Years 1991-1999: Statistics Canada. Canadian Vital Statistics System, 1991-1999 (unlinked live birth and death files).
*Data for Ontario were excluded because of data quality concerns; they are presented in *Appendix G*.
**Maternal deaths are presented coded using ICD-10 from 2000 onward and will be presented in subsequent reports.
CI — confidence interval.
NEC — not elsewhere classified.

Data Limitations

A recent study by the Canadian Perinatal Surveillance System (CPSS) using 1987-1992 linked birth-death data and death registrations found an under-reporting of maternal deaths from cerebrovascular disorders, pulmonary embolism and indirect causes of death.[12] Two thirds of the direct obstetric deaths that were unreported were associated with cerebrovascular disorders or pulmonary embolism. It has been suggested that classification of deaths from cerebrovascular disorders under ICD-9 is unclear.[13] In ICD-10 these deaths are to be classified as indirect. When the authors excluded deaths due to cerebrovascular disorders, they found that direct deaths were under-reported by approximately 20%, which is within the range of major classification errors reported for death certification in general.[14] Nonetheless, these results do suggest that Canadian MMRs are higher than those presented here.

Other countries have also found maternal mortality to be under-reported by their vital records systems, leading the World Health Organization (WHO) to routinely adjust MMRs. For countries with accurate death registration and good cause of death data, the MMR is adjusted by a factor of 1.5 unless a nationally reported adjustment factor is available. This adjustment allows under-reporting to be taken into account when comparing country-specific rates.[15]

It is important to note that the deaths reported here are only those related to pregnancy. At this time it is not possible to report on reproductive deaths, such as those related to the use of contraceptives or reproductive technologies. Ontario data have been excluded because of data quality concerns; they are presented in *Appendix G*.

References

1. World Health Organization/UNICEF. *Revised 1990 Estimates of Maternal Mortality: A New Approach by WHO and UNICEF*. Geneva: WHO, 1996.

2. World Health Organization. *Manual of the International Statistical Classification of Diseases, Injuries, and Causes of Death*, 9th Revision, Vol. 1. Geneva: WHO, 1977.

3. Statistics Canada. *Causes of Death*, 1979, 1980, 1981, 1982, 1983, 1984, 1985, 1986. Ottawa: Statistics Canada, Health Statistics Division (Catalogue No. 84-203-XPB (annual)).

4. Statistics Canada. Causes of death, 1987. *Health Rep* 1989;(11S):1(1) (Catalogue No. 82-003S).

5. Statistics Canada. Causes of death, 1988. *Health Rep* 1990;(11S):2(1) (Catalogue No. 82-003S).

6. Statistics Canada. Causes of Death, 1989. *Health Rep* 1991;(11S):3(1) (Catalogue No. 82-003S11).

7. Statistics Canada. Causes of Death, 1990. *Health Rep* 1992;(11S):4(1) (Catalogue No. 82-003S11).

8. Statistics Canada. *Vital Statistics: Volume 1 Births and Deaths*, 1979, 1980, 1981, 1982, 1983, 1984, 1985, 1986. Ottawa: Statistics Canada, Health Statistics Division (Catalogue No. 84-204 (annual)).

9. Statistics Canada. Births 1987-1988. *Health Rep* 1990;(14S):2(1) (Catalogue No. 82-003S).

10. Statistics Canada. Births 1989. *Health Rep* 1991;(14S):3(1) (Catalogue No. 82-003S14).

11. Statistics Canada. Births 1990. *Health Rep* 1992;(14S):4(1) (Catalogue No. 82-003S14).

12. Turner LA, Cyr M, Kinch RA, Liston R, Kramer MS, Fair M, et al. for the Maternal Mortality and Morbidity Study Group of the Canadian Perinatal Surveillance System. Under-reporting of maternal mortality in Canada: a question of definition. *Chronic Dis Can* 2002;23:22-30.

13. Bouvier-Colle MH, Varnoux N, Costes P, Hatton F. Reasons for the underreporting of maternal mortality in France, as indicated by a survey of all deaths among women of childbearing age. *J Epidemiol* 1991;20:717-21.

14. Myers KA, Farquhar DRE. Improving the accuracy of death certification. *Can Med Assoc J* 1998;158:1317-23.

15. World Health Organization/UNICEF. *Maternal Mortality in 1995: Estimates Developed by WHO, UNICEF, UNFPA*. Geneva: WHO, 2001.

Severe Maternal Morbidity Ratio

Author:
Shi Wu Wen,
MB, PhD

The severe maternal morbidity ratio is defined as the number of women who experience severe (life-threatening) maternal morbidity per 100,000 live births (in a given place and time). Severe maternal morbidity can also be reported per 100,000 deliveries, which is the method used in this report.

While maternal death is the most serious health consequence of pregnancy, it reflects only a small proportion of pregnancy complications. Experts have suggested that surveillance of health hazards associated with childbearing should include life threatening events that do not result in death.[1-3] The Canadian Perinatal Surveillance System (CPSS) has developed a list of conditions associated with pregnancy and childbirth that are potentially life threatening and that are likely to be captured on hospital discharge summaries.[4] These conditions are amniotic fluid embolism, obstetric pulmonary embolism, eclampsia, septic shock, anesthesia complications, cerebrovascular disorders, hemorrhage (antepartum or postpartum) requiring either transfusion or hysterectomy, and rupture of the uterus.

This section highlights amniotic fluid embolism and postpartum hemorrhage requiring hysterectomy. In future CPSS perinatal health reports, other life-threatening conditions related to pregnancy and childbearing will be included.

Amniotic fluid embolism is defined as the entry of amniotic fluid into maternal blood circulation, resulting in severe disturbance of cardiorespiratory function and coagulopathy.[5] These rare events — with a reported incidence ranging between 11 and 30 per 100,000 deliveries — have been associated with a high case fatality rate (as high as 80%) as well as a high risk of neurological impairment among survivors.[5,6] There are no known predisposing risk factors,[7] nor is there understanding of how to prevent this condition.[8]

Postpartum hemorrhage is a common complication related to childbirth, with varying degrees of severity. Information on the severity of postpartum hemorrhage is poorly captured in large perinatal databases. In order to focus on the most severe form of postpartum hemorrhage, analysis was restricted to those cases that required a hysterectomy.

Rates of amniotic fluid embolism and postpartum hemorrhage requiring hysterectomy were calculated using hospitalization data.

Results

- Amniotic fluid embolism occurs very rarely in Canada. The overall incidence for the years 1991-1992 through 2000-2001 was 5.4 per 100,000 deliveries (Table 3.2). No clear temporal trend was observed in the incidence or case fatality rate of amniotic fluid embolism.

- The overall incidence of postpartum hemorrhage requiring hysterectomy in Canada for the years 1991-1992 through 2000-2001 was 34.1 per 100,000 deliveries (Table 3.3).

- The rate of postpartum hemorrhage requiring hysterectomy increased substantially between 1991-1992 (23.3 per 100,000) and 2000-2001 (44.2 per 100,000). This increase may be partly attributed to the increased rate of vaginal birth after cesarean delivery (VBAC)[5] and partly to the change in the algorithm used in defining obstetric deliveries (see page 128), which may have included some more severe cases. The case fatality rate of postpartum hemorrhage requiring hysterectomy fluctuated between 1991-1992 and 2000-2001. *Tabular information is presented in Appendix F.*

TABLE 3.2 **Incidence and case fatality rate of amniotic fluid embolism,** *Canada, 1991-1992 to 2000-2001*

Fiscal year	Incidence per 100,000 deliveries	Case fatality rate* per 100 cases
1991-1992	3.3	7.7
1992-1993	7.7	23.3
1993-1994	4.2	12.5
1994-1995	4.7	11.1
1995-1996	6.7	16.0
1996-1997	6.4	21.7
1997-1998	7.5	7.7
1998-1999	5.6	0.0
1999-2000	3.3	0.0
2000-2001	4.9	6.3
TOTAL	5.4	12.2

Sources: Canadian Institute for Health Information. Discharge Abstract Database (DAD), 1991-1992 to 2000-2001.
 Population Health Research Unit, Dalhousie University, Nova Scotia. ASD, 1991-1992 to 2000-2001.
 Ministère de la Santé et des Services sociaux (Québec). Banque de données sur les hospitalisations du système MED-ÉCHO, 1991-1992 to 2000-2001.
 Manitoba Health, Health Information Management. Manitoba Hospital Abstract System, 1991-1992 to 2000-2001.
*The overall case fatality rate of 12.2% and the case fatality rates for each year are low in comparison with case fatality rates of approximately 80% reported in hospital-based studies. This suggests that amniotic fluid embolism may be over-reported in hospitalization data, perhaps because of a tendency to diagnose less serious events as amniotic fluid embolisms.[5]

TABLE 3.3 **Incidence and case fatality rate of postpartum hemorrhage requiring hysterectomy,** *Canada, 1991-1992 to 2000-2001*

Fiscal year	Incidence per 100,000 deliveries	Case fatality rate per 100 cases
1991-1992	23.3	1.1
1992-1993	26.9	2.9
1993-1994	28.4	1.8
1994-1995	29.3	2.7
1995-1996	34.9	1.5
1996-1997	34.9	1.6
1997-1998	37.1	0.8
1998-1999	39.4	2.3
1999-2000	46.9	0.0
2000-2001	44.2	0.7
TOTAL	34.1	1.5

Sources: Canadian Institute for Health Information. Discharge Abstract Database (DAD), 1991-1992 to 2000-2001.
 Population Health Research Unit, Dalhousie University, Nova Scotia. ASD, 1991-1992 to 2000-2001.
 Ministère de la Santé et des Services sociaux (Québec). Banque de données sur les hospitalisations du système MED-ÉCHO, 1991-1992 to 2000-2001.
 Manitoba Health, Health Information Management. Manitoba Hospital Abstract System, 1991-1992 to 2000-2001.

Data Limitations

There is no single criterion upon which a diagnosis of amniotic fluid embolism can be made validly; definitive diagnoses are made at autopsy.[7] Although the accuracy of diagnoses of amniotic fluid embolism cannot be determined with the data source used here, the low case fatality rates suggest that amniotic fluid embolism may be over-reported in hospitalization data. Other diagnoses are known to be mistaken for amniotic fluid embolism.[6] The reported incidence and mortality rates are based on hospital deliveries only. Amniotic fluid embolism may also occur in association with pregnancy termination. For postpartum hemorrhage, using a combination of diagnosis (ICD-9) and procedure (CCP — Canadian Classification of Diagnostic, Therapeutic and Surgical Procedures) codes to define severe postpartum hemorrhage will add validity to the coding of this condition. The number of maternal deaths due to postpartum hemorrhage (based on Statistics Canada's death registration system) differs from the number of case fatalities among women with postpartum hemorrhage requiring hysterectomy (based on hospitalization data). The former codes a single cause of death, whereas the latter codes up to 16 hospitalization diagnoses.

References

1. Mantel GD, Buchmann E, Rees H, Pattinson RC. Severe acute maternal morbidity: a pilot study of a definition for a near-miss. *Br J Obstet Gynaecol* 1998;105:985-90.

2. Baskett TF, Sternadel J. Maternal intensive care and near-miss mortality in obstetrics. *Br J Obstet Gynaecol* 1998;105:981-4.

3. Harmer M. Maternal mortality — is it still relevant? *Anesthesia* 1997;52:99-100.

4. Health Canada. *Perinatal Health Indicators for Canada: A Resource Manual*. Ottawa: Minister of Public Works and Government Services Canada, 2000 (Catalogue No. H49-135/2000E). URL: <http://www.hc-sc.gc.ca/pphb-dgspsp/rhs-ssg/index.html>.

5. Morgan M. Amniotic fluid embolism. *Anesthesia* 1979;34:20-32.

6. Burrows A, Khoo SK. The amniotic fluid embolism syndrome: 10 years experience at a major teaching hospital. *Aust NZ J Obstet-Gynaecol* 1995;35:245-50.

7. Clark SL, Hankins GD, Dudley DA, Dildy GA, Porter TF. Amniotic fluid embolism: analysis of the national registry. *Am J Obstet Gynecol* 1995;172:1158-69.

8. Clark SL. New concepts of amniotic fluid embolism: a review. *Obstet Gynecol Surv* 1990;45:360-8.

Induced Abortion Ratio

Author:

I.D. Rusen,
MD, MSc, FRCPC

The induced abortion ratio is defined as the number of induced abortions per 100 live births (in a given place and time). A related indicator is the age-specific induced abortion rate, defined as the number of induced abortions for women in a specified age category per 1,000 women in the same age category.

Access to abortion services is now viewed as an indicator of society's attitude toward women and their right to reproductive choice. In 1969, a law was passed to regulate abortion under the *Criminal Code* of Canada. This law permitted a qualified medical practitioner to perform an abortion, if prior approval had been obtained by a Therapeutic Abortion Committee. A 1988 Supreme Court of Canada decision found this process to be unconstitutional. The 1969 law was rendered unenforceable and abortion was effectively decriminalized.[1]

The Canadian Institute for Health Information is responsible for the collection of national abortion statistics, which are then reported by Statistics Canada. Induced abortion statistics for this report were obtained from Statistics Canada. Induced abortion data include data on abortions performed in clinic and hospital settings.

Results

- In 2000, the induced abortion ratio was 32.9 per 100 live births in Canada (excluding Ontario) (Figure 3.2). With the exception of a small decrease in 1999, the induced abortion ratio has been increasing since 1992. The Canadian induced abortion rate (excluding Ontario) was 15.6 per 1,000 females aged 15 to 44, which was slightly higher than the rate of 15.5 in 1999 but a decrease from the 1998 rate of 16.0 per 1,000.

- In 2000, provincial and territorial induced abortion ratios ranged from 11.0 per 100 live births in Prince Edward Island to 43.2 per 100 live births in Quebec, and the induced abortion rates per 1,000 women of reproductive age ranged from 5.2 to 28.2 in Prince Edward Island and Nunavut, respectively (Figure 3.3). These variations may be attributable to differences in the availability of abortion services, ease of travel to the United States for abortion services and other local factors.[2]

- In 2000, Canadian women (excluding Ontario) aged 20 to 24 years had the highest induced abortion rate, at 32.4 per 1,000 women. Females less than 15 years of age and women aged 40 to 44 had the lowest induced abortion rates, at 2.3 and 2.7 per 1,000 women, respectively (Figure 3.4).

- The proportion of induced abortions performed in clinic settings has increased during the last decade. In 1990, 12.3% of induced abortions in Canada (excluding Ontario residents) were performed in clinic settings; by 2000, this proportion had increased to 36.4%. This increase probably reflects an increase in the availability of clinic-based abortion services over time. *Tabular information is presented in Appendix F.*

Data Limitations

Medically or pharmacologically induced abortions performed in physicians' offices are not systematically reported in abortion statistics. They may become a major under-reporting issue as the use of these procedures increases with time. Additional sources of under-reporting include abortions provided in physicians' offices that have not been designated as abortion facilities, as well as some abortions provided to Canadian women in the United States. Ontario data have been excluded from the figures because of data quality concerns and a recent change in reporting practices; they are presented in *Appendix G*.

FIGURE 3.2 **Ratio and rate of induced abortion,*** *Canada (excluding Ontario),*** 1992-2000*

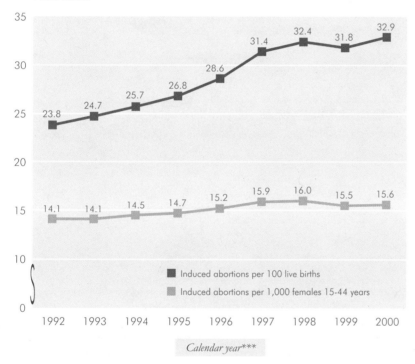

■ Induced abortions per 100 live births

■ Induced abortions per 1,000 females 15-44 years

*Calendar year****

Sources: Canadian Institute for Health Information and Statistics Canada. Therapeutic Abortion Survey.
(Custom tabulation, Health Statistics Division, Statistics Canada, 2003.)
Statistics Canada. CANSIM II, table 051-0001 — Canadian population estimates, 1992-2000.
Statistics Canada. Canadian Vital Statistics System, 1992-2000 (unlinked live birth files).
*Includes cases of unknown area of residence and abortions performed on Canadian residents in selected U.S. states.
Includes cases with age not specified as well as abortions to females ≤ 14 years of age and ≥ 45 years of age.
Rate based on female population 15-44 years of age. Excludes abortions performed in Canada on non-Canadian residents.
**Data for Ontario were excluded because of data quality concerns; they are presented in *Appendix G*.
***1991 data are not presented because data on province of residence for clinic abortions were not available before 1992.

FIGURE 3.3 **Ratio and rate of induced abortion,* by province/territory,**
Canada (excluding Ontario),** 2000

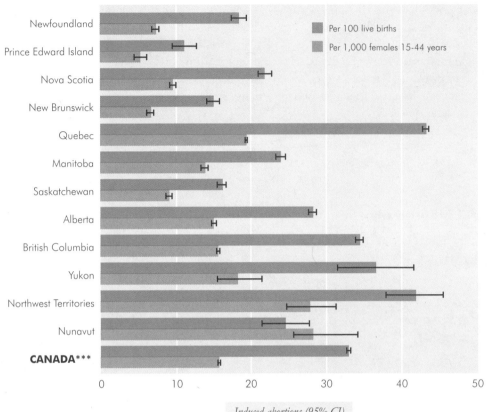

Induced abortions (95% CI)

Sources: Canadian Institute for Health Information and Statistics Canada. Therapeutic Abortion Survey.
(Custom tabulation, Health Statistics Division, Statistics Canada, 2003.)
Statistics Canada. CANSIM II, table 051-0001—Canadian population estimates, 2000.
Statistics Canada. Canadian Vital Statistics System, 2000 (unlinked live birth file).
*Includes cases with age not specified as well as abortions to females ≤ 14 years of age and ≥ 45 years of age.
Rate based on female population 15-44 years of age. Excludes abortions performed in Canada on non-Canadian residents.
**Data for Ontario were excluded because of data quality concerns; they are presented in *Appendix G*.
***Includes cases of unknown area of residence and abortions performed on Canadian residents in selected U.S. states.
CI — confidence interval.

FIGURE 3.4 **Age-specific induced abortion rate,*** *Canada (excluding Ontario),** 2000*

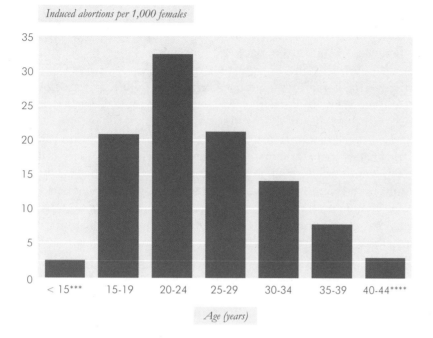

Induced abortions per 1,000 females

Age (years)

Sources: Canadian Institute for Health Information and Statistics Canada. Therapeutic Abortion Survey.
(Custom tabulation, Health Statistics Division, Statistics Canada, 2003.)
Statistics Canada. CANSIM II, table 051-0001 — Canadian population estimates, 2000.

*Includes cases of unknown area of residence. Excludes abortions performed in Canada on non-Canadian residents and abortions performed on Canadian residents in the United States.

**Data for Ontario were excluded because of data quality concerns.

***Rate based on female population 14 years of age.

****Includes induced abortions to women ≥ 45 years of age. Rate based on female population 40-44 years of age.

References

1. *R. v. Morgentaler,* [1988] 1 S.C.R. 30.

2. Statistics Canada. *Statistical Report on the Health of Canadians.* Ottawa: Statistics Canada, 1999 (Catalogue No. 82-570-XPE).

Rate of Ectopic Pregnancy

Author:
I.D. Rusen,
MD, MSc, FRCPC

The ectopic pregnancy rate is defined as the number of ectopic pregnancies per 1,000 reported pregnancies (in a given place and time).

Ectopic pregnancy, defined as the implantation of the blastocyst anywhere other than in the endometrial lining of the uterine cavity,[1] is a significant cause of maternal morbidity and mortality. In industrialized countries, ectopic pregnancy is the leading cause of maternal death during the first trimester of pregnancy, accounting for up to 10% of all maternal deaths.[2] Some countries have reported an increasing ectopic pregnancy rate; potential explanations include an increased prevalence of sexually transmitted tubal infections, an increase in the use of contraception that prevents intrauterine but not extrauterine pregnancies, and better and earlier diagnostic techniques.[1] However, a decrease in the rate of ectopic pregnancies in Sweden has been attributed to declining rates of genital chlamydia.[3] A declining rate of ectopic pregnancies has also been reported from New South Wales, Australia, during the 1990s.[4]

Ectopic pregnancy rates were calculated using hospitalization data. In this analysis, reported pregnancies include all hospital deliveries, hospital-based induced abortion and ectopic pregnancies. Spontaneous abortions and clinic-based induced abortions are not included in the denominator. This analysis also includes day surgery records, which were not included in previous reports.

Results

- In 2000-2001, the ectopic pregnancy rate in Canada was 13.8 per 1,000 reported pregnancies. The rate has been decreasing since 1992-1993 (Figure 3.5).

- The 2000-2001 provincial/territorial ectopic pregnancy rates ranged from 9.0 per 1,000 reported pregnancies in Prince Edward Island to 25.7 per 1,000 pregnancies in Nunavut (note the wide confidence intervals for the territories and smaller provinces) (Figure 3.6).

- The ectopic pregnancy rate increased with increasing maternal age (Figure 3.7). This is likely due in part to an increased prevalence of scarring of the fallopian tubes among older women. *Tabular information is presented in Appendix F.*

Data Limitations

An important limitation in the surveillance of ectopic pregnancy in Canada is the reliance on hospital separation data. As pharmacological management of ectopic pregnancy in outpatient settings becomes more common, the enumeration of ectopic pregnancy may be less complete. There may also be variation in the diagnosis of ectopic pregnancy, particularly at very early gestation, and the frequency of subclinical ectopic pregnancy is unknown.[5] The availability of risk factor information in hospital records is limited.

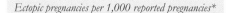

FIGURE 3.5 **Rate of ectopic pregnancy,** *Canada, 1991-1992 to 2000-2001*

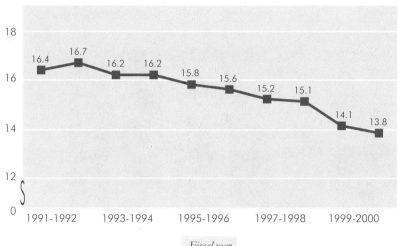

Sources: Canadian Institute of Health Information. Discharge Abstract Database (DAD), 1991-1992 to 2000-2001.
Population Health Research Unit, Dalhousie University, Nova Scotia. ASD, 1991-1992 to 2000-2001.
Ministère de la Santé et des Services sociaux (Québec). Banque de données sur les hospitalisations du système
MED-ÉCHO, 1991-1992 to 2000-2001.
Manitoba Health, Health Information Management. Manitoba Hospital Abstract System, 1991-1992 to 2000-2001.
*Reported pregnancies include all hospital deliveries, hospital-based induced abortions and ectopic pregnancies, but not
spontaneous abortions and clinic-based induced abortions.

FIGURE 3.6 **Rate of ectopic pregnancy, by province/territory,**
Canada, 2000-2001

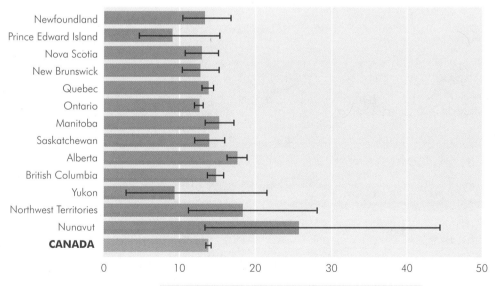

Sources: Canadian Institute of Health Information. Discharge Abstract Database (DAD), 2000-2001.
Population Health Research Unit, Dalhousie University, Nova Scotia. ASD, 2000-2001.
Ministère de la Santé et des Services sociaux (Québec). Banque de données sur les hospitalisations
du système MED-ÉCHO, 2000-2001.
Manitoba Health, Health Information Management. Manitoba Hospital Abstract System, 2000-2001.
*Reported pregnancies include all hospital deliveries, hospital-based induced abortions and ectopic pregnancies,
but not spontaneous abortions and clinic-based induced abortions.
CI — confidence interval.

FIGURE 3.7 **Rate of ectopic pregnancy, by maternal age,** *Canada, 2000-2001*

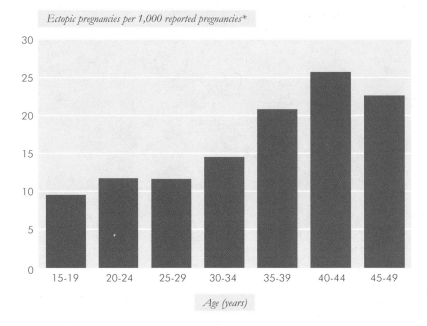

Ectopic pregnancies per 1,000 reported pregnancies*

Age (years)

Sources: Canadian Institute of Health Information. Discharge Abstract Database (DAD), 2000-2001.
Population Health Research Unit, Dalhousie University, Nova Scotia. ASD, 2000-2001.
Ministère de la Santé et des Services sociaux (Québec). Banque de données sur les hospitalisations du système MED-ÉCHO, 2000-2001.
Manitoba Health, Health Information Management. Manitoba Hospital Abstract System, 2000-2001.
*Excludes reported pregnancies with unknown maternal age. Reported pregnancies include all hospital deliveries, hospital-based induced abortions and ectopic pregnancies, but not spontaneous abortions and clinic-based induced abortions.

References

1. Cunningham FG, MacDonald PC, Grant NF, Leveno KJ, Gilstrap LC, Hankins GDV, et al. (Eds.). *Williams Obstetrics*, 21st Edition. Toronto: McGraw-Hill, 2001.

2. Coste J, Job-Spira N, Fernandez H, Papiernik E, Spira A. Risk-factors for ectopic pregnancy: a case-control study in France, with special focus on infectious factors. *Am J Epidemiol* 1991;133:839-49.

3. Egger M, Low N, Smith GD, Lindblom B, Herrmann B. Screening for chlamydial infections and the risk of ectopic pregnancy in a county in Sweden: ecological analysis. *Br Med J* 1998;316:1776-80.

4. Boufous S, Quartararo M, Mohsin M, Parker J. Trends in the incidence of ectopic pregnancy in New South Wales between 1990-1998. *Aust N Z J Obstet Gynaecol* 2001;41:436-8.

5. Orr P, Sherman E, Blanchard J, Fast M, Hammond G, Brunham R. Epidemiology of infection due to *Chlamydia trachomatis* in Manitoba, Canada. *Clin Infect Dis* 1994;19:867-83.

Rate of Maternal Readmission after Discharge following Childbirth

Author:
Shiliang Liu,
MB, PhD

The maternal hospital readmission rate is defined as the number of mothers readmitted to hospital within three months of initial hospital discharge (following childbirth) expressed as a proportion of the total number of women discharged from hospital following childbirth (in a given place and time).

Maternal readmission is an indicator of severe postpartum maternal morbidity. The maternal readmission rate can serve as a proxy for complications related to childbirth.[1,2] Many factors influence maternal readmission rates, including the severity of illness, availability of hospital resources, distance to hospital, hospital admission policies and accessibility of outpatient services. Generally, maternal readmission following childbirth is an under-researched topic, and the impact of maternal readmission on maternal and child health has not been well documented in the scientific literature.[3,4] Recent studies indicate that a short length of hospital stay following a cesarean or assisted vaginal delivery increases the risk of maternal readmission.[5,6]

Readmission rates were calculated using hospitalization data. Maternal readmission cases were identified by linking obstetric delivery records and the subsequent admission records (excluding visits for day surgery). The number of deliveries was based on calendar year. The number of readmissions was calculated for 90 days after initial discharge from hospital. Women who were directly transferred to another hospital after childbirth and women with initial length of hospital stay > 20 days were excluded. Results are presented separately for vaginal and cesarean births.

Results

- Between 1991-1992 and 2000-2001, the three-month maternal readmission rate following vaginal birth remained fairly stable, ranging from 2.0% to 2.3% of deliveries. Readmission rates following cesarean births increased, from 2.6% of deliveries in 1991-1992 to 3.4% of deliveries in 1995-1996, then remained fairly stable thereafter (Figure 3.8).

- In 1998-1999 to 2000-2001 combined, the three-month maternal readmission rate varied by province/territory, both for women with cesarean births and for those with vaginal births (Figure 3.9). These regional differences may be due, in part, to variations in hospital admission and discharge policies.

- For women who gave birth in hospital between 1998-1999 and 2000-2001, the proportion of readmissions attributable to a given primary diagnosis differed for cesarean and vaginal births (Table 3.4). *Tabular information is presented in Appendix F.*

Data Limitations

The identification of maternal readmission was based on record linkage. If a link was not made between the obstetric record and the subsequent admission record, a few cases of maternal readmission after childbirth could be missed.

FIGURE 3.8 **Rate of maternal readmission within three months of discharge from hospital following childbirth,**
Canada (excluding Manitoba),* 1991-1992 to 2000-2001

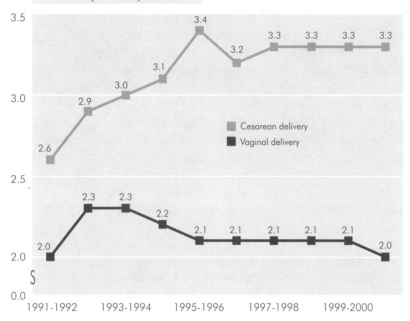

Readmissions per 100 hospital deliveries

Legend:
- Cesarean delivery
- Vaginal delivery

Fiscal year

Sources: Canadian Institute for Health Information. Discharge Abstract Database (DAD), 1991-1992 to 2000-2001.
Population Health Research Unit, Dalhousie University, Nova Scotia. ASD, 1991-1992 to 2000-2001.
Ministère de la Santé et des Services sociaux (Québec). Banque de données sur les hospitalisations du
système MED-ÉCHO, 1991-1992 to 2000-2001.

*Data for Manitoba were not included because the Manitoba Hospital Abstract System does not distinguish readmitted
patients from those transferred from one facility to another.

Please see introductory text for further details on case identification.

FIGURE 3.9 **Rate of maternal readmission within three months of discharge from hospital following childbirth, by province/territory,** *Canada (excluding Manitoba),* 1998-1999 to 2000-2001 combined*

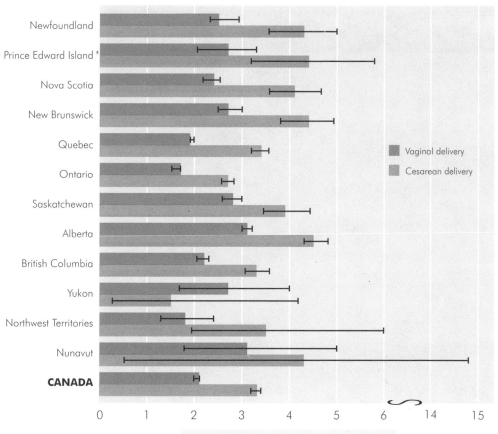

Vaginal delivery
Cesarean delivery

Readmissions (95% CI) per 100 hospital deliveries

Sources: Canadian Institute for Health Information. Discharge Abstract Database (DAD), 2000-2001
Population Health Research Unit, Dalhousie University, Nova Scotia. ASD, 2000-2001.
Ministère de la Santé et des Services sociaux (Québec). Banque de données sur les hospitalisations du système MED-ÉCHO, 2000-2001.
*Data for Manitoba were not included because the Manitoba Hospital Abstract System does not distinguish readmitted patients from those transferred from one facility to another.
Please see introductory text for further details on case identification.
CI — confidence interval.

TABLE 3.4 **Percentage of maternal readmissions according to primary diagnosis within three months of discharge from hospital following childbirth, by delivery mode,** *Canada (excluding Manitoba),* 1998-1999 to 2000-2001 combined*

Primary diagnosis at readmission (ICD-9 code)	Percentage of maternal readmission		
	Total	Cesarean	Vaginal
1. Postpartum hemorrhage (666)	14.4	6.1	17.7
2. Cholelithiasis (574)	13.1	12.0	13.6
3. Major puerperal infection (670)	12.8	12.7	11.9
4. Other and unspecified complications of the puerperium, not elsewhere classified (674)	8.2	21.9	2.9
5. Infection of the breast and nipple associated with childbirth (675)	2.9	2.0	3.3
6. Persons seeking consultation without complaint of sickness (V65)	2.5	1.3	2.9
7. Other current conditions in the mother classifiable elsewhere, but complicating pregnancy, childbirth or the puerperium (648)	2.4	2.6	2.4
8. Complications of pregnancy, not elsewhere classified (646)	2.3	2.3	2.4
9. Symptoms involving abdomen and pelvis (789)	1.7	1.9	1.6
10. Complications of procedures, not elsewhere classified (998)	1.5	3.3	0.8
11. Postpartum care and examination (V24)	0.9	0.7	0.9
12. Venous complications in pregnancy and the puerperium (671)	0.9	1.1	0.7
13. Encounter for contraceptive management (V25)	0.6	0.2	0.8
14. Other diagnoses	36.5	31.9	38.2
TOTAL (%)	100.0	100.0	100.0

Sources: Canadian Institute for Health Information. Discharge Abstract Database (DAD), 2000-2001.
Population Health Research Unit, Dalhousie University, Nova Scotia. ASD, 2000-2001.
Ministère de la Santé et des Services sociaux (Québec). Banque de données sur les hospitalisations du système MED-ÉCHO, 2000-2001.
*Data for Manitoba were not included because the Manitoba Hospital Abstract System does not distinguish readmitted patients from those transferred from one facility to another.
Please see introductory text for further details on case identification.

References

1. Meikle SF, Lyons E, Hulac P, Orleans M. Rehospitalizations and outpatient contacts of mothers and neonates after hospital discharge after vaginal delivery. *Am J Obstet Gynecol* 1998;179:166-71.

2. Glazener CM, Abdalla M, Stroud P, Naji S, Templeton A, Russell IT. Postnatal maternal morbidity: extent, causes, prevention and treatment. *Br J Obstet Gynaecol* 1995;102:282-7.

3. Grimes DA. The morbidity and mortality of pregnancy: still risky business. *Am J Obstet Gynecol* 1994;170:1489-94.

4. Danel I, Johnson C, Berg C, Flowers L, Atrash H. Length of maternal hospital stay for uncomplicated deliveries, 1988-1995: the impact of maternal and hospital characteristics. *Matern Child Health J* 1997;1:237-42.

5. Lydon-Rochelle M, Holt VL, Martin DP, Easterling TR. Association between method of delivery and maternal rehospitalization. *JAMA* 2000;283:2411-6.

6. Liu S, Heaman M, Kramer MS, Demissie K, Wen SW, Marcoux S, for the Maternal Health Study Group of the Canadian Perinatal Surveillance System. Length of hospital stay, obstetric conditions at childbirth, and maternal readmission: a population-based cohort study. *Am J Obstet Gynecol* 2002;87:681-7.

Fetal and Infant Health Outcomes

Preterm Birth Rate

Author:
Shi Wu Wen,
MB, PhD

The preterm birth rate is defined as the number of live births with a gestational age at birth of < 37 completed weeks (< 259 days) expressed as a proportion of all live births (in a given place and time).

Preterm birth is the single most important cause of perinatal mortality and morbidity in industrialized countries: 60% to 80% of deaths of infants without congenital anomalies are related to preterm birth.[1,2] Preterm birth is also associated with cerebral palsy and other long-term health sequelae.[3] One to two percent of all infants are delivered before 32 weeks of gestation, and they account for nearly 50% of all long-term neurological morbidity and about 60% of perinatal mortality.[1] Even mild and moderate preterm birth puts infants at increased risk of death during infancy.[4]

The preterm birth rate has been increasing in many industrialized countries.[1, 5-9] Known risk factors for preterm birth include black race, single marital status, younger or older maternal age, previous preterm delivery, smoking, low pre-pregnancy weight, low or high weight gain,[10] and multiple pregnancy.[7,8] More recently, infection[1] and stress[11] have been identified as potentially important risk factors for preterm birth.

Preterm birth rates were calculated using vital statistics data.

Results

- The preterm birth rate has been increasing in recent years (Figure 4.1); in 2000, it was 7.6 per 100 live births, as compared with 6.6 per 100 live births in 1991. Potential explanations for this trend include increases in obstetric intervention, changes in the frequency and gestational age of multiple births, greater likelihood of extremely early-gestation births (20-27 weeks) being registered as live births, and increases in the use of ultrasound-based estimates of gestational age.[5-7]

- Rates of preterm birth are much higher among twins and higher order multiple births (Figure 4.2). However, in 2000, singleton births were still responsible for over 80% of all preterm births.

- In 2000, provincial/territorial preterm birth rates ranged from 5.8% in Prince Edward Island to 10.4% in Nunavut (Figure 4.3). *Tabular information is presented in Appendix F.*

Data Limitations

An important limitation in the surveillance and research on preterm birth is the potential for error in determining gestational age, particularly when menstrual dates are used[12] without ultrasound confirmation of gestational age. This error may be due to inaccurate maternal reporting of the last menstrual period, the interpretation of post-conception bleeding as normal menses, irregular menstrual cycles or intervening unrecognized pregnancy losses.[13] Ontario data have been excluded from the figures because of data quality concerns; they are presented in *Appendix G*.

FIGURE 4.1   **Rate of preterm birth,** *Canada (excluding Ontario),* 1991-2000*

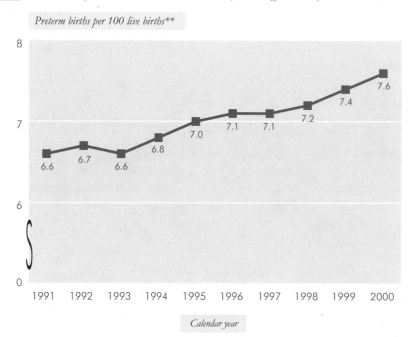

*Preterm births per 100 live births***

Source: Statistics Canada, Canadian Vital Statistics System, 1991-2000 (unlinked live birth files).
*Data for Ontario were excluded because of data quality concerns; they are presented in *Appendix G*.
**Excludes live births with unknown gestational age.

FIGURE 4.2 **Rate of preterm birth among singleton and multiple births,**
Canada (excluding Ontario), 2000*

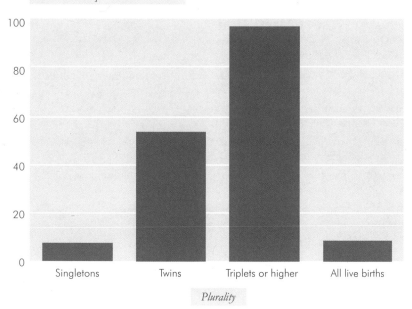

*Preterm births per 100 live births***

Plurality

Source: Statistics Canada, Canadian Vital Statistics System, 2000 (unlinked live birth file).
*Data for Ontario were excluded because of data quality concerns; they are presented in *Appendix G.*
**Excludes live births with unknown gestational age.

FIGURE 4.3 **Rate of preterm birth, by province/territory,**
Canada (excluding Ontario), 2000*

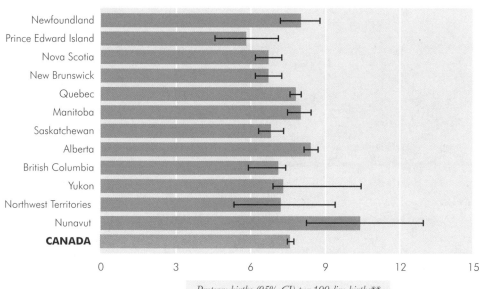

*Preterm births (95% CI) per 100 live births***

Source: Statistics Canada, Canadian Vital Statistics System, 2000 (unlinked live birth file).
*Data for Ontario were excluded because of data quality concerns; they are presented in *Appendix G.*
**Excludes live births with unknown gestational age.
CI — confidence interval.

References

1. Goldenberg RL. The management of preterm labor. *Obstet Gynecol* 2002;100:1020-37.

2. Mesleh RA, Kurdi AM, Sabagh TO, Algwiser RA. Changing trends in perinatal deaths at the Armed Forces hospital, Riyadh, Saudi Arabia. *J Obstet Gynecol* 2001;21:49-55.

3. Hack M, Fanaroff AA. Outcomes of children of extremely low birthweight and gestational age in the 1990s. *Early Hum Dev* 1999;53:193-218.

4. Kramer S, Demissie K, Hong Y, Plat RW, Sauve R, Liston R. The contribution of mild and moderate preterm birth to infant mortality. *JAMA* 2000;284:843-9.

5. Alexander GR, Slay M. Prematurity at birth: trends, racial disparities, and epidemiology. *Ment Retard Dev Disabil Res Rev* 2002;8:215-20.

6. Roberts CL, Algert CS, Morris JM, Henderson-Smart DJ. Trends in twin births in New South Wales, Australia, 1990-1999. *Int J Gynecol Obstet* 2002;78:213-9.

7. Joseph KS, Demissie K, Kramer MS. Trends in obstetric intervention, stillbirth and preterm birth. *Semin Perinatol* 2002;26:250-9.

8. Joseph KS, Kramer MS, Marcoux S, Ohlsson A, Wen SW, Allen A, et al. Determinants of preterm birth rates in Canada from 1981 through 1983 and from 1992 through 1994. *N Engl J Med* 1998;339:1434-9.

9. Kramer MS, Platt R, Yang H, Joseph KS, Wen SW, Morin L, et al. Secular trends in preterm birth: a hospital-based cohort study. *JAMA* 1998;280:1849-54.

10. Wen SW, Goldenberg RL, Cutter GR, Hoffman HJ, Cliver SP. Intrauterine growth retardation and preterm delivery: prenatal risk factors in an indigent population. *Am J Obstet Gynecol* 1990;162:213-8.

11. Mozurkewich E, Luke B, Avni M, Wolf F. Working conditions and adverse pregnancy outcome: a meta-analysis. *Obstet Gynecol* 2000;95:623-35.

12. Kramer MS, McLean FH, Boyd ME, Usher RH. The validity of gestational age estimation by menstrual dating in term, preterm, and postterm gestations. *JAMA* 1988;260:3306-8.

13. Berkowitz GS, Papiernik E. Epidemiology of preterm birth. *Epidemiol Rev* 1993;15:414-43.

Postterm Birth Rate

Author:
Shi Wu Wen,
MB, PhD

The postterm birth rate is defined as the number of live births that occur at a gestational age of 42 or more completed weeks (≥ 294 days) of pregnancy expressed as a proportion of all live births (in a given place and time).

Pregnancies that continue beyond term generally require closer antenatal monitoring because they are associated with increased rates of fetal and infant mortality and neonatal morbidity, and they often end in induction or operative delivery.[1,2] The types of neonatal morbidity that occur include low Apgar scores, fetal distress, meconium staining or aspiration, and admission to the neonatal intensive care unit.[2] Rarely, major congenital anomalies may lead to postterm delivery as a result of alteration of normal fetal adrenal-pituitary function, which interferes with mechanisms that initiate labour.[2] The precise reasons for postterm delivery are most often unknown, but there has been an association with maternal factors such as history of postterm delivery and maternal country of birth.[2] Factors that may lead to adverse fetal or infant outcomes include prolonged labour or unexplained anoxia during labour. The rate of postterm birth varies from 2% to 14% in the published literature.[2]

Controversy exists in the management of postterm pregnancy (intervention versus expectant management). Randomized controlled trials suggest that elective labour induction can reduce perinatal mortality, without an increase in the rate of cesarean delivery.[3,4] Postterm birth rates were calculated using vital statistics data.

Results

- The rate of postterm birth decreased dramatically in Canada, from 4.4% in 1991 to 1.2% in 2000 (Figure 4.4), caused in part by more frequent use of ultrasonography in the estimation of gestational age (which shifts the gestational age distribution to the left), and in part by more frequent labour induction at or over 41 weeks' gestation.

- In 2000, rates of postterm birth varied substantially among Canadian provinces and territories, from 0.5% and 0.6% in Quebec and Newfoundland, to 4.3% in the Yukon (Figure 4.5). These regional variations may be due to differences in the use of ultrasound dating and/or postterm induction. *Tabular information is presented in Appendix F.*

Data Limitations

An important limitation in the surveillance and research on postterm birth is the potential error in determining gestational age, particularly when menstrual dates are used without ultrasound confirmation of gestational age.[5] This error may be due to inaccurate maternal reporting of the last menstrual period, the interpretation of post-conception bleeding as normal menses, irregular menstrual cycles or intervening unrecognized pregnancy losses.[6] Ontario data have been excluded from the figures because of data quality concerns; they are presented in *Appendix G*.

FIGURE 4.4 **Rate of postterm birth,** *Canada (excluding Ontario),* 1991-2000*

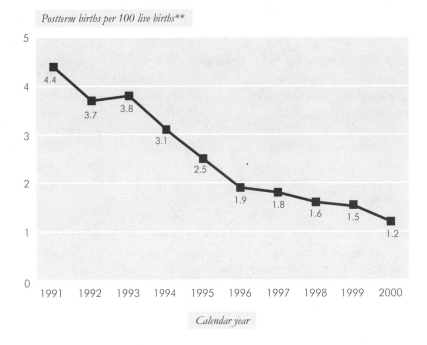

*Postterm births per 100 live births***

1991	4.4
1992	3.7
1993	3.8
1994	3.1
1995	2.5
1996	1.9
1997	1.8
1998	1.6
1999	1.5
2000	1.2

Calendar year

Source: Statistics Canada, Canadian Vital Statistics System, 1991-2000 (unlinked live birth files).
*Data for Ontario are excluded because of data quality concerns; they are presented in *Appendix G.*
**Excludes live births with unknown gestational age.

FIGURE 4.5 **Rate of postterm birth, by province/territory,** *Canada (excluding Ontario),* 2000*

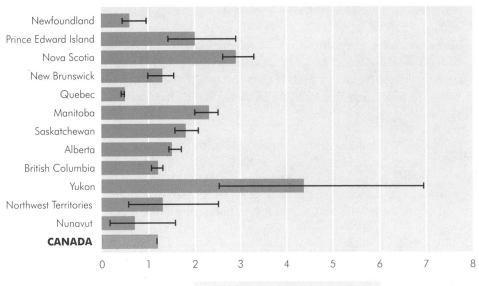

*Postterm births (95% CI) per 100 live births***

Source: Statistics Canada, Canadian Vital Statistics System, 2000 (unlinked live birth file).
*Data for Ontario were excluded because of data quality concerns; they are presented in *Appendix G.*
**Excludes live births with unknown gestational age.
CI — confidence interval.

References

1. Hilder L, Costeloe K, Thilaganathan B. Prolonged pregnancy: evaluating gestation specific risks of fetal and infant mortality. *Br J Obstet Gynaecol* 1998;105:169-73.

2. Shea K, Wilcox A, Little R. Postterm delivery: a challenge for epidemiologic research. *Epidemiology* 1998;9:199-204.

3. Sue-A-Quan AK, Hannah ME, Cohen MM, Foster GA, Liston RM. Effect of labour induction on rates of stillbirth and cesarean section in post-term pregnancies. *Can Med Assoc J* 1999;160:1145-9.

4. Hannah ME, Hannah WJ, Hellmann J, Hewson S, Milner R, Willan A, and the Canadian Multicenter Post-Term Pregnancy Trial Group. Induction of labor as compared with serial antenatal monitoring in post-term pregnancy: a randomized controlled trial. *N Engl J Med* 1992;326:1587-92.

5. Kramer MS, McLean FH, Boyd ME, Usher RH. The validity of gestational age estimation by menstrual dating in term, preterm, and postterm gestations. *JAMA* 1988;260:3306-8.

6. Berkowitz GS, Papiernik E. Epidemiology of preterm birth. *Epidemiol Rev* 1993;15:414-43.

Small-for-Gestational-Age Rate

Author:
Shi Wu Wen,
MB, PhD

The small-for-gestational-age (SGA) rate is defined as the number of live births whose birth weight is below the standard 10th percentile of birth weight for gestational age expressed as a proportion of all live births (in a given place and time). Alternative cut-offs to determine SGA, such as the 3rd percentile of birth weight for gestational age, can also be used.

In industrialized countries, cigarette smoking accounts for about 30% to 40% of fetal growth restriction; "genetically related factors," such as history of fetal growth restriction, maternal race, short maternal stature and fetal sex account for about 20% to 30%; nutritional factors (pre-pregnancy weight, weight gain and low caloric intake) for 10% to 15%; and parity and general maternal morbidity for 5% to 10%.[1]

Fetal growth restriction is associated with increased fetal and infant morbidity and mortality.[2] Because of the difficulty of in-utero measurement of growth, a cross-sectional measure of fetal growth — birth weight for gestational age — has been used in both clinical and public health practice.[2,3] Surveillance of SGA can be helpful in identifying populations at high risk of fetal growth restriction and in planning and evaluating public health programs aimed at reducing the risk.

The SGA rates were calculated using vital statistics data. Because of the limited number and the potentially different fetal growth pattern of multiple births, the analysis was restricted to singleton live births. The SGA cut-off used for these analyses is based on a recently developed Canadian standard.[3]

Results

- From 1991 to 2000, the rate of SGA in Canada decreased (Figure 4.6). This may be due in part to more frequent use of ultrasound-assisted dating (which improves the accuracy of gestational age measurements), as well as increases in maternal anthropometry, reduced cigarette smoking and changes in socio-demographic factors.[4]

- In 2000, the rate of SGA ranged from 5.0% of live births to residents of the Northwest Territories to 8.6% of live births to Alberta residents (Figure 4.7). These regional variations in SGA rates may be due, in part, to ethnic and other socio-economic and demographic differences. Further research is needed to better understand these trends and variations. *Tabular information is presented in Appendix F.*

Data Limitations

An important limitation in the surveillance of SGA births is the potential for error in determining gestational age, particularly when menstrual dates are used.[5] The accuracy of gestational age estimation can be substantially improved by ultrasound-assisted dating early in the second trimester.[5] SGA is a relative measure and varies according to the standard used for calculation. The standard used for this report[3] is a recently developed one that is based on better gestational age information and more sophisticated analytic methods. Ontario data have been excluded from the figures because of data quality concerns; they are presented in *Appendix G.*

FIGURE 4.6 **Rate of small for gestational age (SGA),**
Canada (excluding Ontario),* 1991-2000

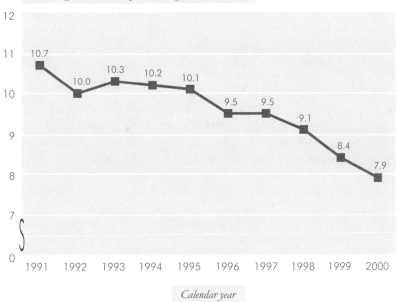

SGA singleton live births per 100 singleton live births**

Calendar year

Source: Statistics Canada. Canadian Vital Statistics System, 1991-2000 (unlinked live birth files).
*Data for Ontario were excluded because of data quality concerns; they are presented in *Appendix G*.
**Excludes live births with unknown gestational age or birth weight, or gestational age < 22 weeks or > 43 weeks.

FIGURE 4.7 **Rate of small for gestational age (SGA),
by province/territory,** *Canada (excluding Ontario),* 2000*

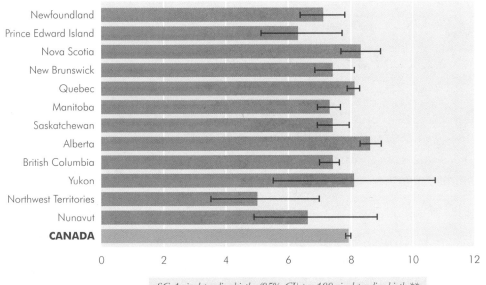

SGA singleton live births (95% CI) per 100 singleton live births**

Source: Statistics Canada. Canadian Vital Statistics System, 2000 (unlinked live birth file).
*Data for Ontario were excluded because of data quality concerns; they are presented in *Appendix G*.
**Excludes live births with unknown gestational age or birth weight, or gestational age < 22 weeks or > 43 weeks.
CI — confidence interval.

References

1. Kramer MS. Determinants of low birth weight: methodological assessment and meta-analysis. *Bull WHO* 1987;65:663-737.

2. Cunningham FG, MacDonald PC, Grant NF, Leveno KJ, Gilstrap LC, Hankins GDV, et al. (Eds.). *Williams Obstetrics*, 21st Edition. Toronto: McGraw-Hill, 2001.

3. Kramer MS, Platt R, Wen SW, Joseph KS, Allen A, Abrahamowicz M, et al. A new and improved population-based Canadian reference for birth weight for gestational age. *Pediatrics* 2001;108(2):E35.

4. Kramer MS, Morin I, Yang H, Platt RW, Usher R, McNamara H, et al. Why are babies getting bigger? Temporal trends in fetal growth and its determinants. *J Pediatr* 2002;141:538-42.

5. Kramer MS, McLean FH, Boyd ME, Usher RH. The validity of gestational age estimation by menstrual dating in term, preterm, and postterm gestations. *JAMA* 1988;260:3306-8.

Large-for-Gestational-Age Rate

Author:
Shi Wu Wen,
MB, PhD

The large-for-gestational-age (LGA) rate is defined as the number of live births of newborns whose birth weight is above the standard 90th percentile of birth weight for gestational age expressed as a proportion of all live births (in a given place and time). Alternative cut-offs to determine LGA can also be used, such as the 97th percentile of birth weight for gestational age.

Information on risk factors for LGA is sparse in the literature. Maternal diabetes is an obvious risk factor for LGA or, specifically, macrosomia.[1] Other factors, including genetic predisposition and maternal diet, may also play a role here. Macrosomia is associated with birth complications.[1] Because of the difficulty of in-utero measurement of growth, a cross-sectional measure of fetal growth — birth weight for gestational age — has been used in both clinical and public health practice.[1,2] Surveillance of LGA can be helpful in identifying populations at high risk of macrosomia, and in planning and evaluating public health programs aimed at reducing the risk of macrosomia. LGA births have been reported to be more common among Canadian Aboriginal women,[3] in particular.

LGA rates were calculated using vital statistics data. Because of the limited number and the potentially different fetal growth pattern of multiple births, the analysis was restricted to singleton live births. The LGA cut-off used for these analyses is based on a recently developed Canadian standard.[2]

Results

- From 1991 to 2000, the rate of LGA increased (Figure 4.8). In addition to more accurate gestational age measurements, this increase may be due, in part, to increases in maternal anthropometry, reduced cigarette smoking and changes in socio-demographic factors.[4]

- In 2000, the rate of LGA ranged from 10.4% of live births in Quebec to 18.1% of live births in the Northwest Territories (Figure 4.9). These regional variations in LGA rates may be partly due to ethnic, socio-economic and demographic differences. Further research is needed to better understand these variations. *Tabular information is presented in Appendix F.*

Data Limitations

An important limitation in the surveillance and research of LGA births is the potential for error in determining gestational age, particularly when menstrual dates are used.[5] The accuracy of gestational age estimation can be substantially improved by ultrasound-assisted dating early in the second trimester.[5] LGA is a relative measure, and varies according to the standard used for its calculation. The standard used for this report[2] is a recently developed one based on better gestational age information and more sophisticated analytic methods. Ontario data have been excluded from the figures because of data quality concerns; they are presented in *Appendix G.*

FIGURE 4.8 **Rate of large for gestational age (LGA),**
Canada (excluding Ontario), 1991-2000*

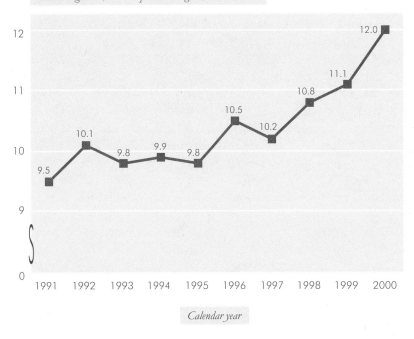

*LGA singleton live births per 100 singleton live births***

Calendar year

Source: Statistics Canada. Canadian Vital Statistics System, 1991-2000 (unlinked live birth files).
*Data for Ontario were excluded because of data quality concerns; they are presented in *Appendix G*.
**Excludes live births with unknown gestational age or birth weight, or gestational age < 22 weeks or > 43 weeks.

FIGURE 4.9 **Rate of large for gestational age (LGA), by province/territory,**
Canada (excluding Ontario), 2000*

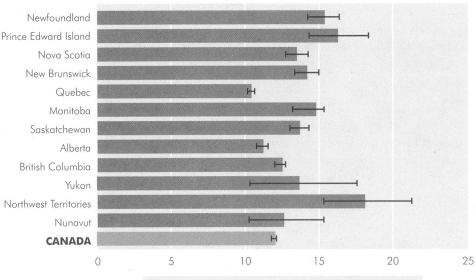

*LGA singleton live births (95% CI) per 100 singleton live births***

Source: Statistics Canada. Canadian Vital Statistics System, 2000 (unlinked live birth file).
*Data for Ontario were excluded because of data quality concerns; they are presented in *Appendix G*.
**Excludes live births with unknown gestational age or birth weight, or gestational age < 22 weeks or > 43 weeks.
CI — confidence interval.

References

1. Cunningham FG, MacDonald PC, Grant NF, Leveno KJ, Gilstrap LC, Hankins GDV, et al. (Eds.). *Williams Obstetrics*, 21st Edition. Toronto: McGraw-Hill, 2001.

2. Kramer MS, Platt R, Wen SW, Joseph KS, Allen A, Abrahamowicz M, et al. A new and improved population-based Canadian reference for birth weight for gestational age. *Pediatrics* 2001;108(2):E35.

3. Thomson M. Heavy birthweight in native Indians of British Columbia. *Can J Public Health* 1990;81:443-6.

4. Kramer MS, Morin I, Yang H, Platt RW, Usher R, McNamara H, et al. Why are babies getting bigger? Temporal trends in fetal growth and its determinants. *J Pediatr* 2002;141:538-42.

5. Kramer MS, McLean FH, Boyd ME, Usher RH. The validity of gestational age estimation by menstrual dating in term, preterm, and postterm gestations. *JAMA* 1988;260:3306-8.

Fetal Mortality Rate

Author:
Shi Wu Wen,
MB, PhD

The crude fetal mortality rate is defined as the number of stillbirths per 1,000 total births (live births and stillbirths), in a given place and time. The fetal mortality rate for ≥ 500 g is based on the exclusion of all stillbirths and live births with a birth weight of < 500 g or, if the birth weight is unknown, those with a gestational age of < 22 weeks. Fetal mortality can be divided into two components: early fetal deaths (between 20 and 27 completed weeks of gestation) and late fetal deaths (at ≥ 28 completed weeks of gestation) (*Appendix D*, page 143).

Fetal deaths account for an increasing proportion of feto-infant mortality in developed countries. Important causes of stillbirth are congenital anomalies, prenatal infections and fetal growth restriction. Other causes include pregnancy-related disorders such as gestational diabetes and pre-eclampsia. However, in a substantial proportion of stillbirths the causes remain unknown. Risk factors identified to date include advanced maternal age, primiparity, maternal smoking during pregnancy and high pre-pregnancy weight.[1-3] Two of these risk factors, advanced maternal age and high pre-pregnancy weight, are increasing in many developed countries. Canadian fetal death rates are low and continue to decline, partly because of the increased use of obstetric intervention.[4,5]

Fetal mortality rates were calculated using vital statistics data.

Results

- Between 1991 and 2000, the crude fetal mortality rate fluctuated between 5.4 per 1,000 total births and 5.9 per 1,000 total births. In 2000, the rate was 5.8 per 1,000 total births (Figure 4.10). The fetal mortality rate for ≥ 500 g ranged from a high of 4.9 per 1,000 total births in 1991 to a low of 4.1 per 1,000 total births in 1998 (Figure 4.10). In 2000, the rate was 4.5 per 1,000 total births.

- In 2000, the crude fetal mortality rate was highest in the Northwest Territories at 11.7 per 1,000 total births (Figure 4.11). Prince Edward Island and Nunavut shared the lowest crude fetal mortality rate, at 4.1 per 1,000 total births. The fetal mortality rate for ≥ 500 g was lowest in Prince Edward Island and Nova Scotia, at 3.5 per 1,000 total births in 2000, and highest in the Northwest Territories, at 8.8 per 1,000 total births. *Tabular information is presented in Appendix F.*

Data Limitations

Vital statistics data may be affected by temporal and regional variations in birth registration practices, particularly for stillbirths and live births at the low end of the birth weight and gestational age distribution.[6] Ontario data have been excluded from the figures because of data quality concerns; they are presented in *Appendix G.*

FIGURE 4.10 **Rate of fetal death,** *Canada (excluding Ontario),* 1991-2000*

Deaths per 1,000 total births

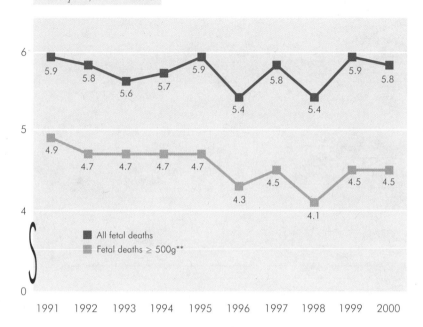

Calendar year

Source: Statistics Canada. Canadian Vital Statistics System, 1991-2000 (unlinked live birth and stillbirth files).
*Data for Ontario were excluded because of data quality concerns; they are presented in *Appendix* G.
**Fetal death rates ≥ 500 g exclude stillbirths and live births with a birth weight < 500 g or, if birth weight
    was unknown, those with a gestational age of < 22 weeks.

FIGURE 4.11 **Rate of fetal death, by province/territory,** *Canada (excluding Ontario),* 2000*

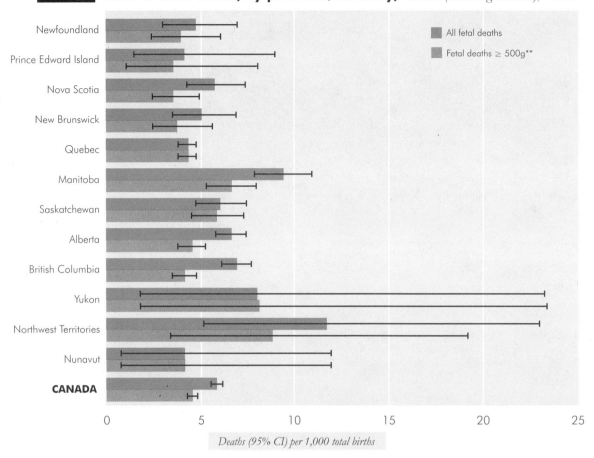

Source: Statistics Canada. Canadian Vital Statistics System, 2000 (unlinked live birth and stillbirth files).

*Data for Ontario were excluded because of data quality concerns; they are presented in *Appendix G*.

**Fetal death rates ≥ 500 g exclude stillbirths and live births with a birth weight < 500 g or, if birth weight was unknown, those with a gestational age of < 22 weeks.

CI — confidence interval.

References

1. Cnattingius S, Stephansson O. The epidemiology of stillbirths. *Semin Perinatol* 2002;26:25-30.

2. Winbo I, Serenius F, Dahlquist G, Källén B. Maternal risk factors for cause-specific stillbirth and neonatal death. *Acta Obstet Gynecol Scand* 2001;80:235-44.

3. Huang GY, Usher RH, Kramer MS, Yang H, Morin L, Fretts RC. Determinants of unexplained antepartum fetal deaths. *Obstet Gynecol* 2000;95:215-21.

4. Sue-A-Quan AK, Hannah ME, Cohen MM, Foster GA, Liston RM. Effect of labour induction on rates of stillbirth and cesarean section in post-term pregnancies. *Can Med Assoc J* 1999;160:1145-9.

5. Joseph KS, Kramer MS, Marcoux S. Ohlsson A, Wen SW, Allen A, et al. Determinants of preterm birth rates in Canada from 1981 through 1983 and from 1992 through 1994. *N Engl J Med* 1998;339:1434-9.

6. Joseph KS, Allen A, Kramer MS, Cyr M, Fair ME, for the Fetal and Infant Mortality Study Group of the Canadian Perinatal Surveillance System. Changes in the registration of stillbirths less than 500 g in Canada, 1985-95. *Paediatr Perinat Epidemiol* 1999;13:278-87.

Infant Mortality Rate and Causes of Death

Author:
Shi Wu Wen,
MB, PhD

The infant mortality rate is defined as the number of deaths of live born babies in the first year after birth per 1,000 live births (in a given place and time). Infant mortality can be divided into three components: early neonatal deaths (0-6 days), late neonatal deaths (7-27 days) and postneonatal deaths (28-364 days) (*Appendix D*, page 143). Infant mortality rates can be refined by the calculation of birth weight-specific and age at death-specific mortality rates, and gestational age-specific and age at death-specific mortality rates. Infant mortality rates can also be refined by calculation of cause-specific mortality rates.

Infant mortality has been considered the single most comprehensive measure of health in a society. In almost all countries, infant mortality has decreased dramatically over the last century with improvements in sanitation, nutrition, infant feeding, and maternal and child health care,[1] although the decline has been slower in recent years.[2] Disparities in the risk of infant death across subpopulations remain, including those in Canada.[3]

Cause-specific infant mortality is presented according to a modified International Collaborative Effort (ICE) classification comprising eight categories: congenital anomaly, asphyxia, immaturity, infection, sudden infant death syndrome (SIDS), other sudden unexplained infant death, external causes and other conditions.[4]

Infant mortality rates were calculated using vital statistics data.

Results

- The infant mortality rate decreased from 6.5 per 1,000 live births in 1991 to 5.1 per 1,000 live births in 2000 (Figure 4.12). The Yukon and Nunavut reported the lowest and highest infant mortality rates, respectively, for 2000 (Figure 4.13).

- The neonatal mortality rate decreased overall from 3.9 per 1,000 live births in 1991 to 3.4 per 1,000 live births in 2000 (Figure 4.12). In 2000, the Yukon reported no neonatal deaths, and the Northwest Territories had the highest neonatal mortality rate at 7.4 per 1,000 live births (Figure 4.14).

- Overall, the postneonatal mortality rate also decreased, from 2.5 per 1,000 neonatal survivors in 1991 to 1.7 per 1,000 neonatal survivors in 2000 (Figure 4.12). In 2000, Nunavut had the highest postneonatal mortality rate at 5.5 per 1,000 neonatal survivors (Figure 4.15); New Brunswick had the lowest rate, at 0.6 per 1,000 neonatal survivors (Figure 4.15).

- In 1999, the leading cause of infant death in Canada was congenital anomalies, accounting for 26.5% of all infant deaths, followed by immaturity and SIDS (Figure 4.16). These include detailed tables on birth weight-specific and gestational age-specific mortality. *Tabular information is presented in Appendix F.*

Data Limitations

Vital statistics data may be affected by regional variations in birth registration, particularly for extremely small, immature newborns.[5,6] Ontario data have been excluded from the figures because of data quality concerns; they are presented in *Appendix G*.

FIGURE 4.12 **Rates of infant, neonatal and postneonatal death,**
Canada (excluding Ontario),* 1991-2000

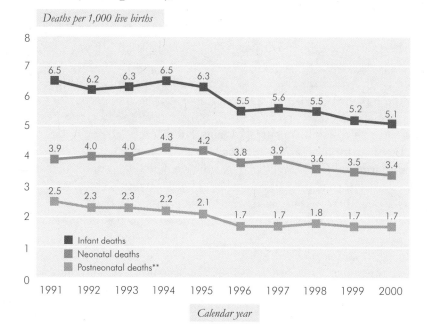

Deaths per 1,000 live births

Infant deaths
Neonatal deaths
Postneonatal deaths**

Calendar year

Source: Statistics Canada. Canadian Vital Statistics System 1991-2000 (period calculation using
unlinked live birth and death files).
*Data for Ontario were excluded because of data quality concerns; they are presented in *Appendix G*.
**Per 1,000 neonatal survivors.

FIGURE 4.13 **Rate of infant death, by province/territory,**
Canada (excluding Ontario),* 2000

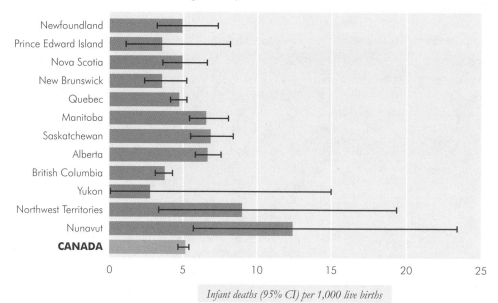

Infant deaths (95% CI) per 1,000 live births

Source: Statistics Canada. Canadian Vital Statistics System, 2000 (period calculation using unlinked live birth and death files).
*Data for Ontario were excluded because of data quality concerns; they are presented in *Appendix G*.
CI — confidence interval.

FIGURE 4.14 **Rate of neonatal death, by province/territory,**
Canada, (excluding Ontario),* 2000

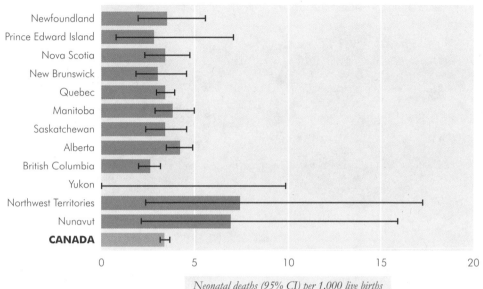

Neonatal deaths (95% CI) per 1,000 live births

Source: Statistics Canada. Canadian Vital Statistics System, 2000 (period calculation using unlinked live birth and death files).
*Data for Ontario were excluded because of data quality concerns; they are presented in *Appendix G*.
CI — confidence interval.

FIGURE 4.15 **Rate of postneonatal death, by province/territory,**
Canada (excluding Ontario),* 2000

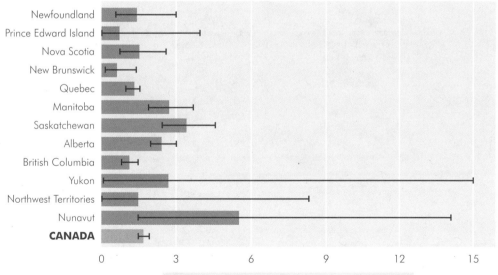

Postneonatal deaths (95% CI) per 1,000 neonatal survivors

Source: Statistics Canada. Canadian Vital Statistics System, 2000 (period calculation using unlinked live birth and death files).
*Data for Ontario were excluded because of data quality concerns; they are presented in *Appendix G*.
CI — confidence interval.

FIGURE 4.16 **Causes of infant death,** *Canada (excluding Ontario),* 1999***

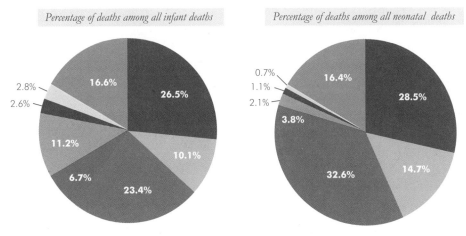

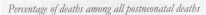

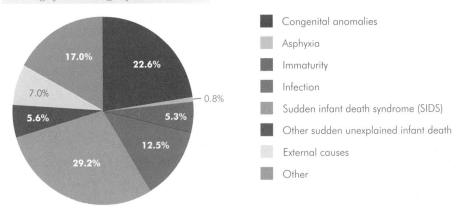

Source: Statistics Canada. Canadian Vital Statistics System, 1999 (period calculation using unlinked death file).
*Data for Ontario were excluded because of data quality concerns; they are presented in *Appendix G.*
**Causes of infant death are presented for 1999 because the ICE classification is based on ICD-9. In 2000, causes of death in the Statistics Canada death file were coded using ICD-10.

References

1. Buehler JW, Kleinman JC, Hodgue CJ, Strauss LT, Smith JC. Birth weight-specific infant mortality, United States, 1960 to 1980. *Public Health Rep* 1987;102:151-61.

2. Kleinman JC. The slowdown in the infant mortality decline. *Paediatr Perinat Epidemiol* 1990;4:373-81.

3. Wilkins R, Houle C, Berthelot JM, Ross N. The changing health status of children in Canada. *Isuma* 2000;1:58-63.

4. Cole S, Hartford RB, Bergsjo P, McCarthy B. International Collaborative Effort (ICE) on birthweight, plurality, perinatal, and infant mortality: a method of grouping underlying causes of infant death to aid international comparisons. *Acta Obstet Gynecol Scand* 1989;68:113-7.

5. Joseph KS, Kramer MS. Recent trends in Canadian infant mortality rates: Effect of changes in registration of live newborns weighing less than 500 grams. *Can Med Assoc J* 1996;155:1047-52.

6. Joseph KS, Allen AC, Kramer MS, Cyr M, Fair ME, for the Fetal and Infant Mortality Study Group of the Canadian Perinatal Surveillance System. Changes in the registration of stillbirths less than 500 g in Canada, 1985-95. *Paediatr Perinat Epidemiol* 1999;13:278-87.

Severe Neonatal Morbidity Rate

Author:
Shiliang Liu,
MB, PhD

The severe neonatal morbidity rate is defined as the number of infants identified as having severe morbidity in the first month of life expressed as a proportion of all live born infants (in a given place and time).

Severe morbid conditions during the neonatal period are important predictors of postneonatal morbidity and disability.[1-3] Classification of these conditions may vary. Certain conditions are more likely to predict long-term disability, including severe respiratory distress syndrome (RDS), sepsis, seizures, severe intraventricular hemorrhage, persistent fetal circulation and multisystem congenital anomalies. These conditions are often associated with each other, e.g., intraventricular hemorrhage is predictive of the development of seizures, and persistent fetal circulation is linked with sepsis and RDS.

This section highlights RDS and sepsis. Future Canadian Perinatal Surveillance System (CPSS) perinatal health reports may discuss other conditions. Rates of RDS and sepsis were calculated using hospitalization data. RDS and neonatal sepsis cases include infants whose conditions were diagnosed during the birth admission only.

Results

- The rate of RDS decreased during the early 1990s, and this was followed by a slight increase in more recent years (Figure 4.17). In 2000-2001, the rate of RDS was 11.6 per 1,000 live births in Canada.

- Between 1991-1992 and 2000-2001, the rate of neonatal sepsis increased significantly, from 16.9 to 24.8 per 1,000 live births in Canada (Figure 4.17).

- Provincial and territorial rates of RDS varied widely in 2000-2001, from 3.0 per 1,000 live births in the Northwest Territories to 13.4 per 1,000 live births in Newfoundland (Figure 4.18). Rates of neonatal sepsis also varied substantially by province and territory in 2000-2001, ranging from 0.0 in the Yukon and the Northwest Territories to 43.4 per 1,000 live births in Ontario. These wide regional variations in rates are very likely due to differences in the case definition and/or coding of RDS and sepsis cases as well as to data completeness. *Tabular information is presented in Appendix F.*

Data Limitations

Limitations in the surveillance of severe neonatal morbidity are primarily related to limitations of the hospitalization databases. In general, the limitations of the databases used will lead to underestimates of severe neonatal morbidity. Specifically, variations in case definitions and coding of particular morbidities may affect reported cases. As well, the information, as coded, does not distinguish between degrees of severity of a particular condition.

FIGURE 4.17 **Rates of respiratory distress syndrome (RDS) and neonatal sepsis,** *Canada, 1991-1992 to 2000-2001*

Cases per 1,000 hospital live births*

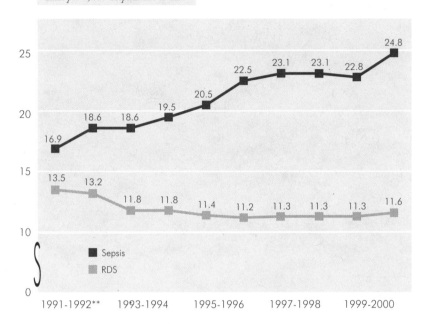

Fiscal year

Sources: Canadian Institute for Health Information. Discharge Abstract Database (DAD), 1991-1992 to 2000-2001.
  Population Health Research Unit, Dalhousie University, Nova Scotia. ASD, 1992-1993 to 2000-2001.
  Ministère de la Santé et des Services sociaux (Québec). Banque de données sur les hospitalisations du système MED-ÉCHO, 1991-1992 to 2000-2001.
  Manitoba Health, Health Information Management. Manitoba Hospital Abstract System, 1991-1992 to 2000-2001.

*Live births with birth weight < 500 g were excluded.

**Complete data for Nova Scotia were not available for 1991-1992 and were not included in the estimates for that year.

FIGURE 4.18 **Rates of respiratory distress syndrome (RDS) and neonatal sepsis, by province/territory,** *Canada, 2000-2001*

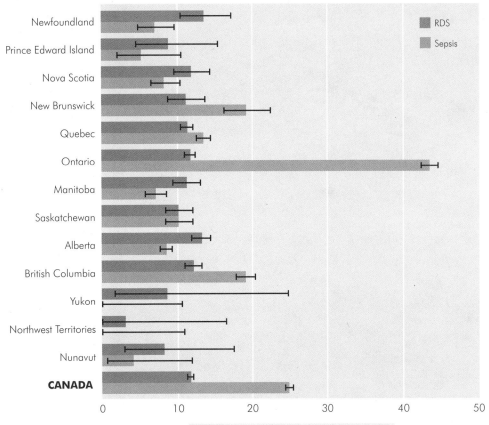

Cases (95% CI) per 1,000 hospital live births*

Sources: Canadian Institute for Health Information. Discharge Abstract Database (DAD), 2000-2001.
Population Health Research Unit, Dalhousie University, Nova Scotia. ASD, 2000-2001.
Ministère de la Santé et des Services sociaux (Québec). Banque de données sur les hospitalisations du système MED-ÉCHO, 2000-2001.
Manitoba Health, Health Information Management. Manitoba Hospital Abstract System, 2000-2001.
*Live births with birth weight < 500 g were excluded.
CI — confidence interval.

References

1. Behrman RE, Shiono PH. Neonatal risk factors. In: Fanhroff AA, Martin RJ (Eds.), *Neonatal-Perinatal Medicine. Diseases of the Fetus and Infant*, 6th Edition, Vol. 1. St. Louis: Mosby Publications, 1997:3-12.

2. Boyer KM, Hayden WR. Sepsis and septic shock. In: Oski FA, DeAngelis CD, McMillan JA, Feigin RA (Eds.), *Principles and Practice of Pediatrics*, 2nd Edition. Philadelphia: J.B. Lippincott Company, 1994:1119-24.

3. Schmidt B, Asztalos EV, Roberts RS, Robertson CM, Sauve RS, Whitfield MF, for the Trial of Indomethacin Prophylaxis in Preterms Investigators. Impact of bronchopulmonary dysplasia, brain injury, and severe retinopathy on the outcome of extremely low-birth-weight infants at 18 months: results from the Trial of Indomethacin Prophylaxis in Preterms. *JAMA* 2003;289:1124-9.

Multiple Birth Rate

Author:
Shi Wu Wen,
MB, PhD

The multiple birth rate is defined as the number of live births and stillbirths following a multiple gestation pregnancy expressed as a proportion of all live births and stillbirths (in a given place and time).

Multiple births are at increased risk of preterm delivery,[1] intrauterine growth restriction and their consequences, which include retinopathy of prematurity, intraventricular hemorrhage and bronchopulmonary dysplasia.[2] An increase in births to older mothers, and increased use of fertility treatments and assisted conception are the main reasons for the recent increase in multiple births.[3,4] It is often difficult to separate the effects of the two factors in the increasing multiple birth rate. Delay in attempting to conceive is an important cause of infertility and therefore associated with infertility treatment. It has been estimated that one quarter to one third of the increase in twin or triplet pregnancies has been caused by an increase in older mothers.[4] In industrialized countries with high rates of multiple births, 30% to 50% of twin pregnancies and at least 75% of triplet pregnancies occur after infertility treatment.[4] The increased use of assisted reproductive technology and the increases in multiple births have had a major impact on the family and on Canadian society. The costs of assisted reproduction include the cost of infertility treatment and health care, and other services associated with the increased risk of preterm birth and its sequelae. There are also substantial indirect costs to the family and society.

Multiple birth rates were calculated using vital statistics data.

Results

- Rates of multiple birth have increased steadily over time, from 2.1 per 100 total births in 1991 to 2.7 per 100 total births in 2000 (Figure 4.19).

- In 2000, rates of multiple birth were similar across the provinces and territories. The Yukon had the highest rate, at 3.5 per 100 total births, and Prince Edward Island had the lowest rate, at 1.7 per 100 total births (Figure 4.20). *Tabular information is presented in Appendix F.*

Data Limitations

Canadian data on multiple births were obtained from birth registrations and may be subject to some transcribing errors. Ontario data have been excluded from the figures because of data quality concerns; they are presented in *Appendix G.*

FIGURE 4.19 **Rate of multiple birth,** *Canada (excluding Ontario),* 1991-2000*

Multiple births per 100 total births

Calendar year

Source: Statistics Canada. Canadian Vital Statistics System, 1991-2000 (unlinked live birth and stillbirth files).
*Data for Ontario were excluded because of data quality concerns; they are presented in *Appendix G.*

FIGURE 4.20 **Rate of multiple birth, by province/territory,** *Canada (excluding Ontario),* 2000*

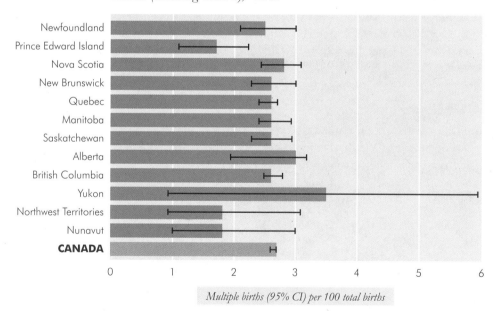

Multiple births (95% CI) per 100 total births

Source: Statistics Canada. Canadian Vital Statistics System, 2000 (unlinked live birth and stillbirth files).
*Data for Ontario were excluded because of data quality concerns; they are presented in *Appendix G.*
CI — confidence interval.

References

1. Newman RB, Ellings JM. Antepartum management of the multiple gestation: the case for specialized care. *Semin Perinatol* 1995;19:387-403.

2. Millar WJ, Wadhera S, Nimrod C. Multiple births: trends and patterns in Canada, 1974-1990. *Health Rep* 1992;4:223-50.

3. Wilcox LS, Kiely JL, Melvin CL, Martin MC. Assisted reproductive technologies: estimates of their contribution to multiple births and newborn hospital days in the United States. *Fertil Steril* 1996;65:361-6.

4. Blondel B, Kaminski M. Trends in the occurrence, determinants, and consequences of multiple births. *Semin Perinatol* 2002;26:239-49.

Prevalence of Congenital Anomalies

Author:
Ruth Kohut,
RN, MSc

The prevalence of congenital anomalies (CAs) is defined as the number of individual live births and stillbirths with at least one congenital anomaly expressed as a proportion of the total number of live births and stillbirths (in a given place and time).

Congenital anomalies, birth defects and congenital malformations are synonymous terms used to describe an abnormality of structure, function or metabolism that is present at birth (even if not diagnosed until later in life).[1] Major congenital anomalies are detected in 2% to 3% of births every year. They are a leading cause of infant deaths and are one of the top 10 causes of potential years of life lost.[2-4] The most prevalent categories of CAs in Canada are musculoskeletal anomalies, congenital heart defects and central nervous system anomalies, such as neural tube defects (NTDs).

This report highlights the birth prevalence of two CAs, Down syndrome (DS) and neural tube defects (NTDs). Down syndrome is highlighted for two reasons. Women of advanced maternal age are at increased risk of DS, and over the past two decades there has been an increasing proportion of births among women in their late 30s and 40s. Second, prenatal screening for DS (ultrasonography and maternal serum screening) has evolved considerably and is commonly offered as a routine component of prenatal care. Neural tube defects are of particular importance because of: 1) the significant impact these serious CAs have on the health and well-being of affected children and their families; and 2) the opportunity for reducing the birth prevalence through the effective primary preventive strategies of periconceptional folic acid supplementation and food fortification with folic acid.[5]

The prevalence of CAs was calculated using data from the Canadian Congenital Anomalies Surveillance System (CCASS).

Results: Down Syndrome

- In 1999 in Canada, the birth prevalence of DS was 14.4 per 10,000 total births (Figure 4.21).

- Excluding Nova Scotia, the birth prevalence of DS from 1991 to 1999 has remained relatively constant, fluctuating between 12.0 and 14.3 per 10,000 total births (Figure 4.21). This may, in part, be due to the opposing effects of two factors — advancing maternal age, and increasing use of prenatal diagnosis and subsequent termination of affected pregnancies.

- For the years 1997 to 1999 combined, the provincial and territorial birth prevalence ranged from 10.9 per 10,000 total births in Alberta to 24.7 per 10,000 births in the Yukon (Figure 4.22). Regional differences may reflect variation in maternal age as well as access to or use of prenatal diagnosis. Availability, access and use of prenatal diagnosis among the provinces and territories and how these relate to the birth prevalence of DS have not been fully explored. *Tabular information is presented in Appendix F.*

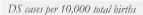

FIGURE 4.21 **Rate of Down syndrome (DS),** *Canada, 1991-1999*

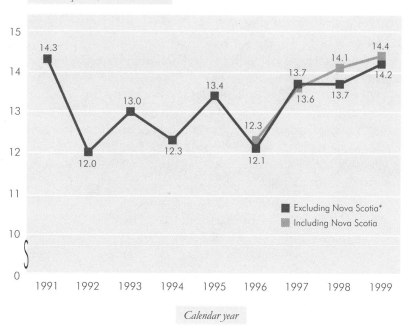

Source: Health Canada. Canadian Congenital Anomalies Surveillance System, 1991-1999.
*Nova Scotia data were not available to CCASS before 1996.

FIGURE 4.22 **Rate of Down syndrome (DS), by province/territory,** *Canada, 1997 to 1999 combined*

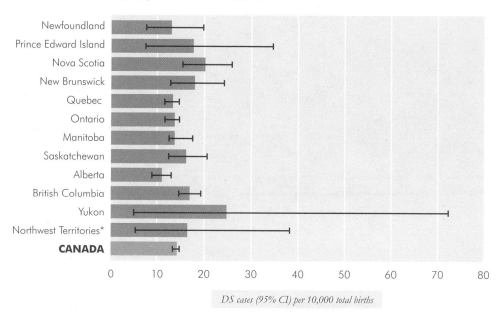

Source: Health Canada. Canadian Congenital Anomalies Surveillance System, 1997-1999.
*Nunavut is included in the Northwest Territories in the data for 1999.
CI — confidence interval.

Results: Neural Tube Defects

- In 1999, the birth prevalence of NTDs in Canada was 5.8 per 10,000 total births (Figure 4.23). The birth prevalence of the two major subcategories of NTDs was 0.9 per 10,000 total births for anencephaly, and 4.0 per 10,000 total births for spina bifida (*Appendix F*, Tables F4.33 and F4.35).

- In the past decade, there has been a significant decline in the birth prevalence of both anencephaly and spina bifida (*Appendix F*, Tables F4.33 and F4.35). The 1991-1999 NTD national trend is depicted in Figure 4.23. Increased use of vitamin supplements and of prenatal diagnosis and termination of affected pregnancies may have contributed to the reduction in NTD birth prevalence. Mandatory folic acid fortification of white flour and enriched pasta and cornmeal began in November 1998 in Canada. Hence, we may begin to see the impact of food fortification on the birth prevalence rates.

- For the three years 1997-1999 combined, the provincial and territorial NTD birth prevalence ranged from 0.0 per 10,000 total births in Prince Edward Island, the Yukon and the Northwest Territories to 9.7 per 10,000 total births in Newfoundland (Figure 4.24). Differences in dietary folate intake and vitamin supplementation, genetic makeup, and access to and use of prenatal testing services may all have contributed to the observed variation. *Tabular information is presented in Appendix F.*

FIGURE 4.23 **Rate of neural tube defects (NTDs),** *Canada, 1991-1999*

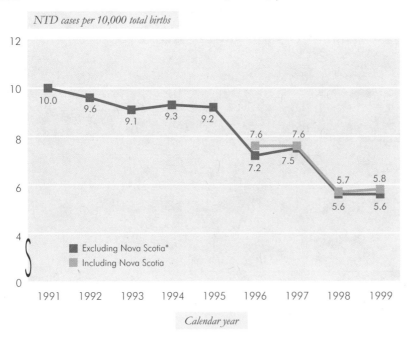

Source: Health Canada. Canadian Congenital Anomalies Surveillance System, 1991-1999.
*Nova Scotia data were not available to CCASS before 1996.

FIGURE 4.24 **Rate of neural tube defects (NTDs), by province/territory,**
Canada, 1997 to 1999 combined

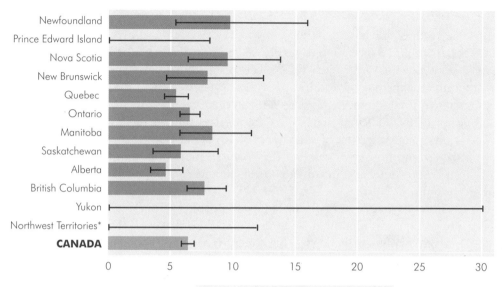

NTD cases (95% CI) per 10,000 total births

Source: Health Canada. Canadian Congenital Anomalies Surveillance System, 1997-1999 combined.
*Nunavut is included in the Northwest Territories in the data for 1999.
CI — confidence interval.

Data Limitations

Concerns about incomplete ascertainment and inconsistent coding as a result of the lack of standardized case definitions and inclusion and exclusion criteria limit most population-based CA surveillance systems. In addition, failure to include pregnancy termination data underestimates the NTD and DS incidence, and limits interpretation of temporal trends and the impact of prenatal diagnosis and termination of affected pregnancies.

References

1. March of Dimes Resource Center. *Birth Defects*. 1998. URL: <http://www.modimes.org>.

2. Perspectives in disease prevention and health promotion. Premature mortality due to congenital anomalies — United States. *MMWR* 1988;37:505-6.

3. Wen SW, Liu S, Joseph KS, Rouleau J, Allen A. Patterns of infant mortality caused by major congenital anomalies. *Teratology* 2000;61:342-6.

4. Liu S, Joseph KS, Kramer MS, Allen AC, Sauve R, Rusen ID, et al. for the Fetal and Infant Health Study Group of the Canadian Perinatal Surveillance System. Relationship of prenatal diagnosis and pregnancy termination to overall infant mortality in Canada. *JAMA* 2002;12:1561-7.

5. Van Allen MI, McCourt C, Lee NS. *Preconception Health: Folic Acid for the Primary Prevention of Neural Tube Defects. A Resource Document for Health Professionals, 2002*. Ottawa: Minister of Public Works and Government Services Canada, 2002.

Rate of Neonatal Hospital Readmission after Discharge following Birth

Author:
Shiliang Liu,
MB, PhD

The neonatal hospital readmission rate is defined as the number of newborns readmitted to hospital within 28 days of birth expressed as a proportion of all newborns discharged from hospital after birth (in a given place and time). This indicator can also be specified as the rate of readmission within seven days after birth.

Newborn readmission rates have been used as an outcome to evaluate the quality of perinatal health care.[1-3] They are related to the length of hospital stay following birth,[4-6] and they are one measure of the impact of hospital maternal and infant discharge policies. In addition, they may reflect hospital, practitioner and community approaches to monitoring and treating neonatal jaundice, and initiation and support of infant feeding.

Neonatal hospital readmission rates were calculated using hospitalization data. Cases of neonatal readmission were identified by internal record linkage of the hospital discharge data, which involves matching live birth records to the subsequent admission records. The number of neonatal readmissions within 28 days after initial discharge from hospital was determined. Newborns who were directly transferred to another hospital after birth or newborns with initial length of hospital stay of > 20 days were excluded. In addition, hospital discharges following day surgery were not counted as readmissions in the analysis.

Results

- Between 1991-1992 and 2000-2001, the neonatal hospital readmission rate (excluding Nova Scotia and Manitoba) increased from 1.9 neonatal readmissions per 100 hospital live births to 3.2 per 100 hospital live births (Figure 4.25). Although many factors may contribute to neonatal readmission, the practice of early discharge of newborns without adequate application of guidelines[6] may be responsible for recent increases in neonatal readmission.

- In 2000-2001, neonatal readmission rates (excluding Manitoba) varied across Canadian provinces and territories (Figure 4.26). The readmission rate was highest in Nunavut (9.3 per 100 live births) and lowest in Prince Edward Island (1.5 per 100 live births). The provinces and territories with higher neonatal readmission rates also tended to have shorter average length of hospital stay at birth and earlier age at readmission.[7]

- The most common reasons for neonatal readmission were neonatal jaundice, feeding problems, sepsis, dehydration and inadequate weight gain (Figure 4.27). The principal causes for neonatal readmission changed considerably over time. For example, neonatal jaundice accounted for 27.9% of readmissions in 1991-1992, as compared with 38.8% in 2000-2001. *Tabular information is presented in Appendix F.*

Data Limitations

Concerns with regard to the accuracy and completeness of the record linkage may arise as a result of newborn transfers and home births. As well, differences in health status at birth, initial length of hospital stay and other issues may confound the association between length of hospital stay at birth and neonatal readmission.

FIGURE 4.25 **Rate of neonatal hospital readmission after discharge following birth,** *Canada (excluding Manitoba),* 1991-1992 to 2000-2001*

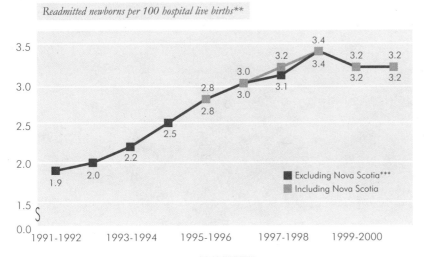

Sources: Canadian Institute for Health Information, Discharge Abstract Database (DAD), 1991-1992 to 2000-2001.
Population Health Research Unit, Dalhousie University, Nova Scotia. ASD, 1995-1996 to 2000-2001.
Ministère de la Santé et des Services sociaux (Québec). Banque de données sur les hospitalisations du système MED-ÉCHO, 1991-1992 to 2000-2001.
*Data for Manitoba were not included because the Manitoba Hospital Abstract System does not distinguish readmitted patients from those transferred from one facility to another.
**Live births with birth weight < 1,000 g were excluded.
***Complete data for Nova Scotia were not available for 1991-1992 to 1994-1995.
Please see introductory text for further details on case identification.

FIGURE 4.26 **Rate of neonatal hospital readmission after discharge following birth, by province/territory,** *Canada (excluding Manitoba),* 2000-2001*

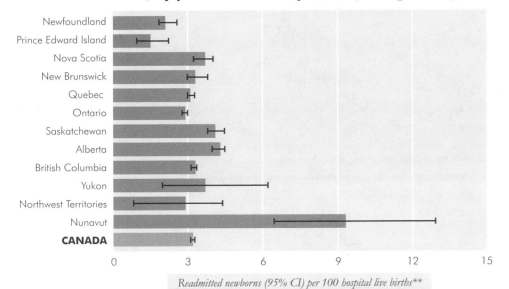

Sources: Canadian Institute for Health Information, Discharge Abstract Database (DAD), 2000-2001.
Population Health Research Unit, Dalhousie University, Nova Scotia. ASD, 2000-2001.
Ministère de la Santé et des Services sociaux (Québec). Banque de données sur les hospitalisations du système MED-ÉCHO, 2000-2001.
*Data for Manitoba were not included because the Manitoba Hospital Abstract System does not distinguish readmitted patients from those transferred from one facility to another.
**Live births with birth weight < 1,000 g were excluded.
Please see introductory text for further details on case identification.

FIGURE 4.27 **Principal diagnosis for readmitted newborns,**
Canada (excluding Manitoba),* 1991-1992 and 2000-2001

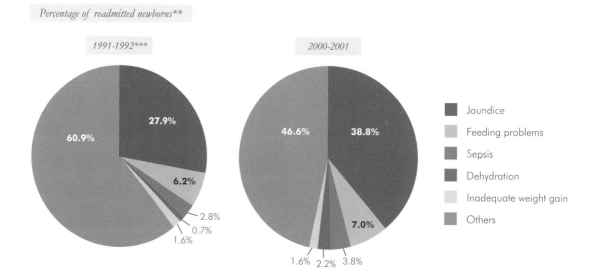

Sources: Canadian Institute for Health Information, Discharge Abstract Database (DAD), 1991-1992 and 2000-2001.
    Population Health Research Unit, Dalhousie University, Nova Scotia. ASD, 2000-2001.
    Ministère de la Santé et des Services sociaux (Québec). Banque de données sur les hospitalisations du système
    MED-ÉCHO, 1991-1992 and 2000-2001.
* Data for Manitoba were not included because the Manitoba Hospital Abstract System does not distinguish readmitted
    patients from those transferred from one facility to another.
**Live births with birth weight < 1,000 g were excluded.
***Complete data for Nova Scotia were not available for 1991-1992, and were not included in the estimates for that year.
Please see introductory text for further details on case identification.

References

1. Braverman P, Egerter S, Pearl M, Marchi K, Miller C. Problems associated with early discharge of newborn infants. Early discharge of newborns and mothers: a critical review of the literature. *Pediatrics* 1995;96:716-26.

2. Liu LL, Clemens CJ, Shay DK, Davis RL, Novack AH. The safety of newborn early discharge. The Washington State experience. *JAMA* 1997;278:293-8.

3. Britton JR, Britton HL, Beebe SA. Early discharge of the term newborn: a continued dilemma. *Pediatrics* 1994;94:291-5.

4. Lee KS, Perlman M, Ballantyne M, Elliott I, To T. Association between duration of neonatal hospital stay and readmission rate. *J Pediatr* 1995;127:758-66.

5. Lee KS, Perlman M. The impact of early obstetric discharge on newborn health care. *Curr Opin Pediatr* 1996;8:96-101.

6. Canadian Paediatric Society and Society of Obstetricians and Gynaecologists of Canada. Facilitating discharge home following a normal term birth. *Paediatr Child Health* 1996;1:165-8.

7. Liu S, Wen SW, McMillan D, Trouton K, Fowler D, McCourt C. Increased neonatal readmission rate associated with decreased length of hospital stay at birth in Canada. *Can J Public Health* 2000;91:46-50.

Bibliography

Alexander GR, Slay M. Prematurity at birth: trends, racial disparities, and epidemiology. *Ment Retard Dev Disabil Res Rev* 2002;8:215-20.

American Academy of Pediatrics, Work Group on Breastfeeding. Breastfeeding and the use of human milk. *Pediatrics* 1997;100:1035-9.

American College of Obstetricians and Gynecologists. *Operative vaginal delivery.* Technical Bulletin No. 196, August 1994.

American College of Obstetricians and Gynecologists Women's Health Care Physicians, Task Force on Cesarean Delivery Rates. *Evaluation of Cesarean Delivery.* Washington, DC: American College of Obstetricians and Gynecologists, 2000.

Ananth CV, Wen SW. Trends in fetal growth among singleton gestations in the United States and Canada, 1985 through 1998. *Semin Perinatol* 2002;26:260-7.

Baeten JM, Bukusi EA, Lambe M. Pregnancy complications and outcomes among overweight and obese nulliparous women. *Am J Public Health* 2001;91;436-40.

Baskett TF, Sternadel J. Maternal intensive care and near-miss mortality in obstetrics. *Br J Obstet Gynaecol* 1998;105:981-4.

Behrman RE, Shiono PH. Neonatal risk factors. In: Fanhroff AA, Martin RJ (Eds.), *Neonatal-Perinatal Medicine. Diseases of the Fetus and Infant*, 6th Edition, Vol. 1. St. Louis: Mosby Publications, 1997:3-12.

Berenson AB, San Miguel VV, Wilkinson GS. Prevalence of physical and sexual assault in pregnant adolescents. *J Adolesc Health* 1992;13:466-9.

Bergh T, Ericson A, Hillensjö T, Nygren KG, Wennerholm UB. Deliveries and children born after in-vitro fertilisation in Sweden 1982-95: a retrospective cohort study. *Lancet* 1999;354:1579-85.

Berkowitz GS, Papiernik E. Epidemiology of preterm birth. *Epidemiol Rev* 1993; 15:414-43.

Berkowitz GS, Skovron ML, Lapinski RH, Berkowitz RL. Delayed childbearing and the outcome of pregnancy. *N Engl J Med* 1990;322:659-64.

Bettiol H, Rona RJ, Chinn S, Goldani M, Barbieri MA. Factors associated with preterm births in Southeast Brazil: a comparison of two birth cohorts born 15 years apart. *Paediatr Perinat Epidemiol* 2000;14:30-8.

Bienefeld M, Woodward GL, Ardal S. *Under-reporting of Live Births in Ontario: 1991-97.* Central East Health Information Partnership. URL: <http://www.cehip.org/ Library/student%20 projects/missing%20births%20final.PDF>.

Blondel B, Kaminski M. Trends in the occurrence, determinants, and consequences of multiple births. *Semin Perinatol* 2002;26:239-49.

Boufous S, Quartararo M, Mohsin M, Parker J. Trends in the incidence of ectopic pregnancy in New South Wales between 1990-1998. *Aust N Z J Obstet Gynaecol* 2001;41:436-8.

Bibliography

Bouvier-Colle MH, Varnoux N, Costes P, Hatton F. Reasons for the underreporting of maternal mortality in France, as indicated by a survey of all deaths among women of childbearing age. *J Epidemiol* 1991;20:717-21.

Boyer KM, Hayden WR. Sepsis and septic shock. In: Oski FA, DeAngelis CD, McMillan JA, Feigin RA (Eds.), *Principles and Practice of Pediatrics*, 2nd Edition. Philadelphia: J.B. Lippincott Company, 1994:1119-24.

Braverman P, Egerter S, Pearl M, Marchi K, Miller C. Problems associated with early discharge of newborn infants. Early discharge of newborns and mothers: a critical review of the literature. *Pediatrics* 1995;96:716-26.

Britton JR. Postpartum early hospital discharge and follow-up practices in Canada and the United States. *Birth* 1998;25:161-8.

Britton JR, Britton HL, Beebe SA. Early discharge of the term newborn: a continued dilemma. *Pediatrics* 1994;94:291-5.

Brost BC, Goldenberg RL, Mercer BM, Iams JD, Meis PJ, Moawad AH, et al. The Preterm Prediction Study: association of cesarean delivery with increases in maternal weight and body mass index. *Am J Obstet Gynecol* 1997;177:333-41.

Buehler J. Surveillance. In: Rothman KJ, Greenland S (Eds.), *Modern Epidemiology*, 2nd Edition. Philadelphia: Lippincott-Raven, 1998.

Buehler JW, Kleinman JC, Hodgue CJ, Strauss LT, Smith JC. Birth weight-specific infant mortality, United States, 1960 to 1980. *Public Health Rep* 1987;102:151-61.

Burrows A, Khoo SK. The amniotic fluid embolism syndrome: 10 years experience at a major teaching hospital. *Aust NZ J Obstet-Gynaecol* 1995;35:245-50.

Canadian Institute for Health Information. *Health Indicators 2002*. Ottawa: CIHI, 2002 (No. 2: Catalogue No. 82-221-XIE).

Canadian Institute for Health Information. Website. URL: <http://www.cihi.ca>. Accessed March 28, 2003.

Canadian Pediatric Society. Fetal alcohol syndrome. *Paediatr Child Health* 2002;7:161-74.

Canadian Paediatric Society and Society of Obstetricians and Gynaecologists of Canada. Facilitating discharge home following a normal term birth. *Paediatr Child Health* 1996;1:165-58.

Canadian Paediatric Society, Dietitians of Canada and Health Canada. *Nutrition for Healthy Term Infants*. Ottawa: Minister of Public Works and Government Services Canada, 1998.

Carroli G, Belizan J, Stamp G. Episiotomy policies in vaginal births. In: Neilson JP, Crowther CA, Hofmeyer GJ (Eds.), *The Cochrane Collaboration: Pregnancy and Childbirth Database*. Hochett ED, 1998, Disk Issue I. URL: <http://www.members. tripod.com/~gineco/EPISIOTO.HTM>.

Centers for Disease Control and Prevention. Trends in length of stay for hospital deliveries: United States, 1970-1992. *MMWR* 1995;44:335-7.

Chen J, Fair M, Wilkins R, Cyr M, and the Fetal and Infant Mortality Study Group of the Canadian Perinatal Surveillance System. Maternal education and fetal and infant mortality in Quebec. *Health Rep* 1998;10:53-64.

Clark SL. New concepts of amniotic fluid embolism: a review. *Obstet Gynecol Surv* 1990;45:360-8.

Clark SL, Hankins GD, Dudley DA, Dildy GA, Porter TF. Amniotic fluid embolism: analysis of the national registry. *Am J Obstet Gynecol* 1995;172:1158-69.

Bibliography

Claussen B, Cnattingius S, Axelsson O. Preterm and term births of small for gestational age infants: a population-based study of risk factors among nulliparous women. *Br J Obstet Gynaecol* 1998;105:1011-7.

Cnattingius S, Lambe M. Trends in smoking and overweight during pregnancy: prevalence, risks of pregnancy complications and adverse pregnancy outcomes. *Semin Perinatol* 2002;26:286-95.

Cnattingius S, Stephansson O. The epidemiology of stillbirths. *Semin Perinatol* 2002;26:25-30.

Cole S, Hartford RB, Bergsjo P, McCarthy B. International Collaborative Effort (ICE) on birthweight, plurality, perinatal, and infant mortality: a method of grouping underlying causes of infant death to aid international comparisons. *Acta Obstet Gynecol Scand* 1989;68:113-7.

Coste J, Job-Spira N, Fernandez H, Papiernik E, Spira A. Risk-factors for ectopic pregnancy: a case-control study in France, with special focus on infectious factors. *Am J Epidemiol* 1991;133:839-49.

Cragan JD, Roberts HE, Edmonds LD, Koury MJ, Kirby RS, Shaw G, et al. Surveillance for anencephaly and spina bifida and the impact of prenatal diagnosis — United States, 1985-1994. *MMWR* 1995;44:1-13.

Crowley P. Interventions for preventing or improving the outcome of delivery at or beyond term (Cochrane Review). In: *The Cochrane Library*, Issue 1, 2003. Oxford: Update Software.

Cunningham FG, MacDonald PC, Grant NF, Leveno KJ, Gilstrap LC, Hankins GDV, et al. (Eds.). *Williams Obstetrics*, 21st Edition. Toronto: McGraw-Hill, 2001.

D'Ascoli PT, Alexander GR, Petersen DJ, Kogan MD. Parental factors influencing patterns of prenatal care utilization. *J Perinatol* 1997;17:283-7.

Dalby DM, Williams JI, Hodnett E, Rush J. Postpartum safety and satisfaction following early discharge. *Can J Public Health* 1996;87:90-4.

Danel I, Johnson C, Berg C, Flowers L, Atrash H. Length of maternal hospital stay for uncomplicated deliveries, 1988-1995: the impact of maternal and hospital characteristics. *Matern Child Health J* 1997;1:237-42.

Dryburgh H. Teenage pregnancy. *Health Rep* 2000;12(1):9-19.

Dwyer T, Cochrane J. Population trends in Sudden Infant Death Syndrome. *Semin Perinatol* 2002;26:296-305.

Editorial. Vacuum versus forceps. *Lancet* 1984;i:144.

Egger M, Low N, Smith GD, Lindblom B, Herrmann B. Screening for chlamydial infections and the risk of ectopic pregnancy in a county in Sweden: ecological analysis. *Br Med J* 1998;316:1776-80.

EUROCAT Working Group. Prevalence of neural tube defects in 20 regions of Europe and the impact of prenatal diagnosis, 1980-1986. *J Epidemiol Community Health* 1991;45:52-8.

Fair M. The development of national vital statistics in Canada: Part 1 — from 1605 to 1945. *Health Rep* 1994;6:355-68.

Fair M, Cyr M. The Canadian Birth Data Base: a new research tool to study reproductive outcomes. *Health Rep* 1993;5:281-90.

Fair M, Cyr M, Allen AC, Wen SW, Guyon G, MacDonald RC. *Validation Study for a Record Linkage of Births and Infant Deaths in Canada*. Ottawa: Statistics Canada, 1999 (Catalogue No. 84F0013-XIE).

Bibliography

Federal, Provincial and Territorial Advisory Committee on Population Health. *Strategies for Population Health: Investing in the Health of Canadians.* Ottawa: Minister of Supply and Services Canada, 1994.

Forrester MB, Merz RD, Yoon PW. Impact of prenatal diagnosis and elective termination on the prevalence of selected birth defects in Hawaii. *Am J Epidemiol* 1998;148:1201-11.

Fraser AM, Brockert JE, Ward RH. Association of young maternal age with adverse reproductive outcomes. *N Engl J Med* 1995;332:1113-7.

Gladstone J, Levy M, Nulman I, Koren G. Characteristics of pregnant women who engage in binge alcohol consumption. *Can Med Assoc J* 1997;156:789-94.

Glazener CM, Abdalla M, Stroud P, Naji S, Templeton A, Russell IT. Postnatal maternal morbidity: extent, causes, prevention and treatment. *Br J Obstet Gynaecol* 1995;102:282-7.

Gloor JE, Kissoon N, Joubert GI. Appropriateness of hospitalization in a Canadian pediatric hospital. *Pediatrics* 1993;91:70-4.

Goldenberg RL. The management of preterm labor. *Obstet Gynecol* 2002;100:1020-37.

Golding J. Birthweight-specific mortality rates — are they meaningful? *Paediatr Perinatal Epidemiol* 1994;8:256-7.

Graham ID, Fowler-Graham D. Episiotomy counts: trends and prevalence in Canada, 1981-1982 to 1993-1994. *Birth* 1997;24:141-7.

Grimes DA. The morbidity and mortality of pregnancy: still risky business. *Am J Obstet Gynecol* 1994;170:1489-94.

Guilhard P, Blondel B. Trends in risk factors for cesarean sections in France between 1981 and 1995: lessons for reducing the rates in the future. *Br J Obstet Gynecol* 2001;108:48-55.

Hack M, Fanaroff AA. Outcomes of children of extremely low birthweight and gestational age in the 1990s. *Early Hum Dev* 1999;53:193-218.

Hannah ME, Hannah WJ, Hellmann J, Hewson S, Milner R, Willan A, and the Canadian Multicenter Post-Term Pregnancy Trial Group. Induction of labor as compared with serial antenatal monitoring in post-term pregnancy: a randomized controlled trial. *N Engl J Med* 1992;326:1587-92.

Hannah ME, Hannah WJ, Hewson SA, Hodnett ED, Saigal S, Willan AR. Planned caesarean section versus planned vaginal birth for breech presentation at term: a randomized multicentre trial. Term Breech Trial Collabourative Group. *Lancet* 2000;356:1375-83.

Hannah ME, Hannah WJ, Hodnett ED, Chalmer B, Kung R, Willan A, et al. Outcomes at 3 months after planned cesarean vs planned vaginal delivery for breech presentation at term: the international randomized Term Breech Trial. *JAMA* 2002;287:1822-31.

Harmer M. Maternal mortality — is it still relevant? *Anesthesia* 1997;52:99-100.

Harper PS. *Practical Genetic Counselling*, 5th Edition. Boston: Butterworth Heinemann, 1998:61.

Health Canada. *Canadian Perinatal Health Report, 2000.* Ottawa: Minister of Public Works and Government Services Canada, 2000 (Catalogue No. H49-142/2000E). URL: <http://www.hc-sc.gc.ca/pphb-dgspsp/rhs-ssg/index.html>.

Health Canada. *Canadian Perinatal Surveillance System Progress Report.* Ottawa: Minister of Supply and Services Canada, 1995.

Bibliography

Health Canada. *Canadian Perinatal Surveillance System Progress Report 1997-1998*. Ottawa: Minister of Public Works and Government Services Canada, 1998.

Health Canada. *Congenital Anomalies in Canada — A Perinatal Health Report, 2002*. Ottawa: Minister of Public Works and Government Services Canada, 2002 (Catalogue No. H39-641/2002E). URL: <http://www.hc-sc.gc.ca/pphb-dgspsp/rhs-ssg/index.html>.

Health Canada. *Joint Statement: Prevention of Fetal Alcohol Syndrome (FAS), Fetal Alcohol Effects (FAE) in Canada*. Ottawa: Health Canada, October 1996 (Catalogue No. H39-348/1996E).

Health Canada. *Perinatal Health Indicators for Canada: A Resource Manual*. Ottawa: Minister of Public Works and Government Services Canada, 2000 (Catalogue No. H49-135/2000E). URL: <http://www.hc-sc.gc.ca/pphb-dgspsp/rhs-ssg/ index.html>.

Heaman M. Smoking cessation in pregnancy: are we doing enough? [guest editorial]. *J Obstet Gynaecol Can* 2002;24:611-3.

Helewa M. Cesarean sections in Canada: what constitutes an appropriate rate? *J Soc Obstet Gynaecol Can* 1995;17:237-46.

Hicks M, Sauve RS, Lyon AW, Clarke M, Tough S. Alcohol use and abuse in pregnancy: an evaluation of the merits of screening. *Can Child Adolesc Psychiatry Rev* 2003;12:77-80.

Hilder L, Costeloe K, Thilaganathan B. Prolonged pregnancy: evaluating gestation specific risks of fetal and infant mortality. *Br J Obstet Gynaecol* 1998;105:169-73.

Howell EM, Blondel B. International infant mortality rates: Bias from reporting differences. *Am J Pub Health* 1994;84:850-2.

Huang GY, Usher RH, Kramer MS, Yang H, Morin L, Fretts RC. Determinants of unexplained antepartum fetal deaths. *Obstet Gynecol* 2000;95:215-21.

Huizinga D, Loeber R, Thornberry TP. Longitudinal study of delinquency, drug use, sexual activity and pregnancy among children and youth in three cities. *Public Health Rep* 1993;108(S1):90-6.

Johanson RB, Mendon V. Vacuum extraction versus forceps for assisted vaginal delivery (Cochrane Review). In: *The Cochrane Library*, Issue 2, 2002. Oxford: Update Software.

Johanson RB, Rice C, Doyle M, Arthur J, Anyanwu L, Ibrahim J, et al. A randomized prospective study comparing the new vacuum extractor policy with forceps delivery. *Br J Obstet Gynaecol* 1993;100:524-30.

Johnson JWC, Longmate JA, Frentzen B. Excessive maternal weight and pregnancy outcome. *Am J Obstet Gynecol* 1992;167:353-72.

Joseph KS. Core concepts in perinatal epidemiology: incidence of birth, growth-restriction and death. *J Clin Epidemiol* (in press).

Joseph KS. *Preterm Birth in Canada*. Background papers — Preterm Birth Prevention Consensus Conference. Ottawa, 1998.

Joseph KS, Allen AC, Dodds L, Vincer MJ, Armson BA. Causes and consequences of recent increases in preterm birth among twins. *Obstet Gynecol* 2001;98:57-64.

Joseph KS, Allen AC, Kramer MS, Cyr M, Fair ME, for the Fetal and Infant Mortality Study Group of the Canadian Perinatal Surveillance System. Changes in the registration of stillbirths less than 500 g in Canada, 1985-95. *Paediatr Perinat Epidemiol* 1999;13:278-87.

Joseph KS, Demissie K, Kramer MS. Trends in obstetric intervention, stillbirth and preterm birth. *Semin Perinatol.* 2002;26:250-9.

Joseph KS, Kramer MS. Recent trends in infant mortality rates and proportions of low-birth-weight live births in Canada. *Can Med Assoc J* 1997;157:535-41.

Joseph KS, Kramer MS. Recent trends in Canadian infant mortality rates: Effect of changes in registration of live newborns weighing less than 500 grams. *Can Med Assoc J* 1996;155:1047-52.

Joseph KS, Kramer MS, Allen AC, Cyr M, Fair M, Ohlsson A, et al. for the Fetal and Infant Mortality Study Group of the Canadian Perinatal Surveillance System. Gestational age- and birth weight-specific declines in infant mortality in Canada, 1985-94. *Paediatr Perinat Epidemiol* 2000;14:332-9.

Joseph KS, Kramer MS, Marcoux S, Ohlsson A, Wen SW, Allen A, et al. Determinants of preterm birth rates in Canada from 1981 through 1983 and from 1992 through 1994. *N Engl J Med* 1998;339:1434-9.

Joseph KS, Liu S, Demissie K, Wen SW, Platt RW, Ananth CV, et al. for the Fetal and Infant Health Study Group of the Canadian Perinatal Surveillance System. A parsimonious explanation for intersecting perinatal mortality curves: understanding the effect of plurality and of parity. *BMC Pregnancy and Childbirth* 2003;3:3. URL: <www.biomedcentral.com/1471-393/3/3>.

Joseph KS, Young DC, Dodds L, O'Connell CM, Allen VM, Chandra S, et al. Changes in maternal characteristics and obstetric practice and recent increases in primary cesarean delivery. *Obstet Gynecol* 2003;102:791-800.

Kabiru WN, Jamieson D, Graves W, Lindsay M. Trends in operative vaginal delivery rates and associated maternal complication rates in an inner-city hospital. *Am J Obstet Gynecol* 2001;184:1112-4.

Kaiser PS, Kirby RS. Obesity as a risk factor for cesarean in a low-risk population. *Obstet Gynecol* 2001;97:39-43.

Katzmarzyk PT. The Canadian obesity epidemic: an historical perspective. *Obes Res* 2002; 10:666-74.

Klein MC, Gauthier RJ, Robbins JM, Kaczorowski J, Jorgensen SH, Franco ED, et al. Relationship of episiotomy to perineal trauma and morbidity, sexual dysfunction, and pelvic floor relaxation. *Am J Obstet Gynecol* 1994;171:591-8.

Kleinman JC. The slowdown in the infant mortality decline. *Paediatr Perinat Epidemiol* 1990;4:373-81.

Kramer MS. Determinants of low birth weight: methodological assessment and meta-analysis. *Bull WHO* 1987;65:663-737.

Kramer MS, Chalmers B, Hodnett ED, Sevkovskaya Z, Dzikovich I, Shapiro S, et al. Promotion of Breastfeeding Intervention Trial (PROBIT): a randomized trial in the Republic of Belarus. *JAMA* 2001;285:413-20.

Kramer MS, Demissie K, Hong Y, Platt RW, Sauve R, Liston R. The contribution of mild and moderate preterm birth to infant mortality. *JAMA* 2000;284:843-9.

Kramer MS, McLean FH, Boyd ME, Usher RH. The validity of gestational age estimation by menstrual dating in term, preterm, and postterm gestations. *JAMA* 1988;260:3306-8.

Kramer MS, McLean FH, Eason EL, Usher RH. Maternal nutrition and spontaneous preterm birth. *Am J Epidemiol* 1992;136:574-83.

Kramer MS, Morin I, Yang H, Platt RW, Usher R, McNamara H, et al. Why are babies getting bigger? Temporal trends in fetal growth and its determinants. *J Pediatr* 2002;141:538-42.

Bibliography

Kramer MS, Platt R, Wen SW, Joseph KS, Allen A, Abrahamowicz M, et al. A new and improved population-based Canadian reference for birth weight for gestational age. *Pediatrics* 2001;108(2):E35.

Kramer MS, Platt RW, Yang H, Haglund B, Cnattingius S, Bergsjo P. Registration artifacts in international comparisons of infant mortality. *Paediatr Perinat Epidemiol* 2002;16:16-22.

Kramer MS, Platt R, Yang H, Joseph KS, Wen SW, Morin L, et al. Secular trends in preterm birth: a hospital-based cohort study. *JAMA* 1998;280:1849-54.

Lawrence RA, Lawrence RM. *Breastfeeding, a Guide for the Medical Profession*, 5th Edition. St. Louis: Mosby, 1999.

Lee KS, Khoshnood B, Chen L, Wall SN, Cromie WJ, Mittendorf RL. Infant mortality from congenital malformations in the United States, 1970-1997. *Obstet Gynecol* 2001;98:620-7.

Lee KS, Perlman M. The impact of early obstetric discharge on newborn health care. *Curr Opin Pediatr* 1996;8:96-101.

Lee KS, Perlman M, Ballantyne M, Elliott I, To T. The association between duration of neonatal hospital stay and readmission rate. *J Pediatr* 1995;127:758-66.

Leyland AH, Boddy FA. Maternal age and outcome of pregnancy. *N Engl J Med* 1990;323:413-4.

Liu LL, Clemens CJ, Shay DK, Davis RL, Novack AH. The safety of newborn early discharge: The Washington State experience. *JAMA* 1997;278:293-8.

Liu S, Heaman M, Kramer MS, Demissie K, Wen SW, Marcoux S, for the Maternal Health Study Group of the Canadian Perinatal Surveillance System. Length of hospital stay, obstetric conditions at childbirth, and maternal readmission: a population-based cohort study. *Am J Obstet Gynecol* 2002;87:681-7.

Liu S, Joseph KS, Kramer MS, Allen A, Sauve R, Rusen ID, et al. for the Fetal and Infant Health Study Group of the Canadian Perinatal Surveillance System. Relationship of prenatal diagnosis and pregnancy termination to overall infant mortality in Canada. *JAMA* 2002;287:1561-7.

Liu S, Joseph KS, Wen SW, Kramer MS, Marcoux S, Ohlsson A, et al. for the Fetal and Infant Mortality Study Group of the Canadian Perinatal Surveillance System. Secular trends in congenital anomaly-related fetal and infant mortality in Canada, 1985-1996. *Am J Med Genetics* 2001;104:7-13.

Liu S, Wen SW. Development of record linkage of hospital discharge data for the study of neonatal readmission. *Chron Dis Can* 1999;20:77-81.

Liu S, Wen SW, McMillan D, Trouton K, Fowler D, McCourt C. Increased neonatal readmission rate associated with decreased length of hospital stay at birth in Canada. *Can J Public Health* 2000;91:46-50.

Lu GC, Rouse DJ, DuBard M, Cliver S, Kimberlin D, Hauth JC. The effect of the increasing prevalence of maternal obesity on perinatal mortality. *Am J Obstet Gynecol* 2001;185:845-9.

Lumley J, Oliver S, Waters E. Interventions for promoting smoking cessation during pregnancy (Cochrane Review). In: *The Cochrane Library*, Issue 3, 2002. Oxford: Update Software.

Lydon-Rochelle M, Holt VL, Martin DP, Easterling TR. Association between method of delivery and maternal rehospitalization. *JAMA* 2000;283:2411-6.

Mantel GD, Buchmann E, Rees H, Pattinson RC. Severe acute maternal morbidity: a pilot study of a definition for a near-miss. *Br J Obstet Gynaecol* 1998;105:985-90.

March of Dimes Resource Center. *Birth Defects*. 1998. URL: <http://www.modimes.org>.

Matthews TG, Crowley P, Chong A, McKenna P, McGarvey C, O'Regan M. Rising caesarean section rates: a cause for concern? *Brit J Obstet Gynaecol* 2003;110:346-9.

McCarthy B. The risk approach revisited: a critical review of developing country experience and its use in health planning. In: Liljestrand J, Povey WG (Eds.). *Maternal Health Care in an International Perspective. Proceedings of the XXII Berzelius Symposium, 1991 May 27-29, Stockholm, Sweden*. Sweden: Uppsala University, 1992:107-24.

McMahon MJ, Luther ER, Bowes WA Jr, Olshan AF. Comparison of a trial of labour with an elective second cesarean section. *N Engl J Med* 1996;335:689-95.

Meikle SF, Lyons E, Hulac P, Orleans M. Rehospitalizations and outpatient contacts of mothers and neonates after hospital discharge after vaginal delivery. *Am J Obstet Gynecol* 1998;179:166-71.

Mesleh RA, Kurdi AM, Sabagh TO, Algwiser RA. Changing trends in perinatal deaths at the Armed Forces hospital, Riyadh, Saudi Arabia. *J Obstet Gynecol* 2001; 21:49-55.

Millar WJ, Wadhera S, Nimrod C. Multiple births: trends and patterns in Canada, 1974-1990. *Health Rep* 1992;4:223-50.

Miller HS, Lesser KB, Reed KL. Adolescence and very low birth weight infants: a disproportionate association. *Obstet Gynecol* 1996;87:83-8.

Minkoff H, Chervenak FA. Elective primary cesarean delivery. *N Engl J Med* 2003;348:946-50.

Morgan M. Amniotic fluid embolism. *Anesthesia* 1979;34:20-32.

Morris CD, Menashe VD. 25-year mortality after surgical repair of congenital heart defect in childhood. A population-based cohort study. *JAMA* 1991; 266:3447-52.

Mozurkewich E, Luke B, Avni M, Wolf F. Working conditions and adverse pregnancy outcome: a meta-analysis. *Obstet Gynecol* 2000;95:623-35.

Myers KA, Farquhar DRE. Improving the accuracy of death certification. *Can Med Assoc J* 1998;158:1317-23.

Naeye RL. Causes of perinatal excess deaths in prolonged gestations. *Am J Epidemiol* 1978;108:429-33.

Nair C. Trends in cesarean deliveries in Canada. *Health Rep* 1991;3:203-19.

Nault F. Infant mortality and low birth weight, 1975 to 1995. *Health Rep* 1997;9:39-46.

Newman RB, Ellings JM. Antepartum management of the multiple gestation: the case for specialized care. *Semin Perinatol* 1995;19:387-403.

Notzon FC, Placek PJ, Taffel SM. Comparisons of national cesarean-section rates. *N Engl J Med* 1987;316:386-9.

Office of the Surgeon General. Health consequences of tobacco use among women, reproductive outcomes. In: *Women and Smoking*. Rockville, MD: U.S. Department of Health and Human Services, 2001:272-307.

Orr P, Sherman E, Blanchard J, Fast M, Hammond G, Brunham R. Epidemiology of infection due to *Chlamydia trachomatis* in Manitoba, Canada. *Clin Infect Dis* 1994;19:867-83.

Bibliography

Parker JD, Schoendorf KC, Kiely JL. Associations between measures of socio-economic status and low birth weight, small for gestational age, and premature delivery in the United States. *Ann Epidemiol* 1994;4:271-8.

Patrick DL, Cheadle A, Thompson DC, Diehr P, Koepsell T, Kinne S. The validity of self-reported smoking: a review and meta analysis. *Am J Public Health* 1994; 84:1086-93.

Pelletier G. L'hospitalisation pour soins de courte durée au Québec. Statistiques évolutives 1982-1983 à 1997-1998, Québec, MSSS, Direction générale de la planification stratégique et de l'évaluation, no. 36 (Collection Données statistiques et indicateurs), 1999.

Perspectives in disease prevention and health promotion. Premature mortality due to congenital anomalies — United States. *MMWR* 1988;37:505-6.

Polin RA, Saiman L. Nosocomial infections in the neonatal intensive care unit. *NeoReviews* 2003;4:c81-9.

Prysak M, Lorenz RP, Kisly A. Pregnancy outcome in nulliparous women 35 years and older. *Obstet Gynecol* 1995;85:65-70.

R. v. Morgentaler, [1988] 1 S.C.R. 30.

Rayburn WF, Zhang J. Rising rates of labor induction: present concerns and future strategies. *Obstet Gynecol* 2002;100:164-7.

Roberts CL, Algert CS, Morris JM, Henderson-Smart DJ. Trends in twin births in New South Wales, Australia, 1990-1999. *Int J Gynecol Obstet* 2002;78:213-9.

Roberts G, Nanson J. *Best Practices: Fetal Alcohol Syndrome/Fetal Alcohol Effects and the Effects of Other Substance Use During Pregnancy.* Ottawa: Canada's Drug Strategy Division, Health Canada, 2000.

Rortveit G, Daltveit AK, Hannestad YS, Hunskaar S. Urinary incontinence after vaginal delivery or cesarean section. *N Engl J Med* 2003;348:900-7.

Sachs BP, Fretts RC, Gardner R, Hellerstein S, Wampler NS, Wise PH. The impact of extreme prematurity and congenital anomalies on the interpretation of international comparisons of infant mortality. *Obstet Gynecol* 1995;85:941-6.

Schmidt B, Asztalos EV, Roberts RS, Robertson CM, Sauve RS, Whitfield MF, for the Trial of Indomethacin Prophylaxis in Preterms Investigators. Impact of bronchopulmonary dysplasia, brain injury, and severe retinopathy on the outcome of extremely low-birth-weight infants at 18 months: results from the Trial of Indomethacin Prophylaxis in Preterms. *JAMA* 2003;289:1124-9.

Sepkowitz S. International rankings of infant mortality and the United States' vital statistics natality data collection system — failure and success. *Int J Epidemiol* 1995;24:583-8.

Sharma RK. Causal pathways to infant mortality: linking social variables to infant mortality through intermediate variables. *J Health Soc Policy* 1998;9:15-28.

Shea K, Wilcox A, Little R. Postterm delivery: a challenge for epidemiologic research. *Epidemiology* 1998;9:199-204.

Silva AA, Lamy-Filho F, Alves MT, Coimbra LC, Bettiol H, Barbieri MA. Risk factors for low birthweight in north-east Brazil: the role of caesarean section. *Paediatr Perinat Epidemiol* 2001;15:257-64.

Singh S, Darroch JE. Adolescent pregnancy and childbearing: levels and trends in developed countries. *Family Planning Perspectives* 2000;32(1):14-23.

Smith ME, Newcombe HB. Use of the Canadian Mortality Data Base for epidemiologic follow up. *Can J Public Health* 1982;73:39-45.

Society of Obstetricians and Gynaecologists of Canada. *Clinical Practice Guidelines: Healthy Beginnings: Guidelines for Care during Pregnancy and Childbirth.* Ottawa: SOGC, 1998. URL: <http://www.sogc.org/sogcnet/sogc%5Fdocs/common/guide/pdfs/healthybegeng.pdf>.

Society of Obstetricians and Gynaecologists of Canada. *Dystocia. Society of Obstetricians and Gynaecologists of Canada Policy Statement.* Ottawa: SOGC, 1995.

Society of Obstetricians and Gynaecologists of Canada. *Fetal Health Surveillance in Labour, Parts 1 through 4. Society of Obstetricians and Gynaecologists of Canada Policy Statement.* Ottawa: SOGC, 1995.

Society of Obstetricians and Gynaecologists of Canada. *Fetal Health Surveillance in Labour, Conclusion. Society of Obstetricians and Gynaecologists of Canada Policy Statement.* Ottawa: SOGC, 1996.

Society of Obstetricians and Gynaecologists of Canada. *Induction of Labour, SOGC Clinical Practice Guidelines for Obstetrics, Number 23.* Ottawa: SOGC, 1996.

Society of Obstetricians and Gynaecologists of Canada. *Induction of Labour at Term, SOGC Clinical Practice Guidelines for Obstetrics, Number 107.* Ottawa: SOGC, 2001.

Society of Obstetricians and Gynaecologists of Canada. *The Canadian Consensus Conference on Breech Management at Term. Society of Obstetricians and Gynaecologists of Canada Policy Statement.* Ottawa: SOGC, 1994.

Society of Obstetricians and Gynaecologists of Canada. *Vaginal Birth after Previous Cesarean Birth. Society of Obstetricians and Gynaecologists of Canada Policy Statement.* Ottawa: SOGC, 1997.

Statistics Canada. *Births and Deaths 1996, 1997.* Ottawa: Statistics Canada, Health Statistics Division, 1999 (Catalogue No. 84-F0210-XPB).Statistics Canada. Births 1987-1988. *Health Rep* 1990;(14S):2(1) (Catalogue No. 82-003S).

Statistics Canada. Births 1989. *Health Rep* 1991;(14S):3(1) (Catalogue No. 82-003S14).

Statistics Canada. Births 1990. *Health Rep* 1992;(14S):4(1) (Catalogue No. 82-003S14).

Statistics Canada. Causes of death, 1979, 1980, 1981, 1982, 1983, 1984, 1985, 1986. Ottawa: Statistics Canada, Health Statistics Division (Catalogue No. 84-203-XPB (annual)).

Statistics Canada. Causes of death, 1987. *Health Rep* 1989;(11S):1(1) (Catalogue No. 82-003S).

Statistics Canada. Causes of death, 1988. *Health Rep* 1990;(11S):2(1) (Catalogue No. 82-003S).

Statistics Canada. Causes of death, 1989. *Health Rep* 1991;(11S):3(1) (Catalogue No. 82-003S11).

Statistics Canada. Causes of death, 1990. *Health Rep* 1992;(11S):4(1) (Catalogue No. 82-003S11).

Statistics Canada. *Statistical Report on the Health of Canadians.* Ottawa: Statistics Canada, 1999 (Catalogue No. 82-570-XPE).

Statistics Canada. *Vital Statistics: Volume 1 Births and Deaths,* 1979, 1980, 1981, 1982, 1983, 1984, 1985, 1986. Ottawa: Statistics Canada, Health Statistics Division (Catalogue No. 84-204 (annual)).

Statistics Canada, Human Resources Development Canada. *National Longitudinal Survey of Children and Youth, Overview of the Survey Instruments for 1996-97 Data Collection, Cycle 2*. Ottawa: Statistics Canada, 1997 (Catalogue No. 89-F0078-XPE).

Stoler JM, Huntington KS, Peterson CM, Peterson KP, Daniel P, Aboagye KK, et al. The prenatal detection of significant alcohol exposure with maternal blood markers. *J Pediatr* 1998;133:346-52.

Sue-A-Quan AK, Hannah ME, Cohen MM, Foster GA, Liston RM. Effect of labour induction on rates of stillbirth and cesarean section in post-term pregnancies. *Can Med Assoc J* 1999;160:1145-9.

Thomson M. Heavy birthweight in native Indians of British Columbia. *Can J Public Health* 1990;81:443-6.

Tough SC, Newburn-Cook C, Johnston DW, Svenson LW, Rose S, Belik J. Delayed childbearing and its impact on population rate changes in low birth weight, multiple birth, and preterm delivery. *Pediatrics* 2002;109:399-403.

Towner D, Castro MA, Eby-Wilkens E, Gilbert WM. Effect of mode of delivery in nulliparous women on neonatal intracranial injury. *N Engl J Med* 1999;341:1709-14.

Turner LA, Cyr M, Kinch RA, Liston R, Kramer MS, Fair M, et al. for the Maternal Mortality and Morbidity Study Group of the Canadian Perinatal Surveillance System. Under-reporting of maternal mortality in Canada: a question of definition. *Chronic Dis Can* 2002;23:22-30.

Turner LA, Kramer MS, Liu S, for the Maternal Mortality and Morbidity Study Group of the Canadian Perinatal Surveillance System. Cause-specific mortality during and after pregnancy and the definition of maternal death. *Chronic Dis Can* 2002;23:31-6.

United Nations Children's Fund. *The State of the World's Children 2003*. New York: UNICEF, 2002.

Van Allen MI, McCourt C, Lee NS. *Preconception Health: Folic Acid for the Primary Prevention of Neural Tube Defects. A Resource Document for Health Professionals, 2002*. Ottawa: Minister of Public Works and Government Services Canada, 2002.

Weeks JD, Kozak LJ. Trends in the use of episiotomy in the United States: 1980-1998. *Birth* 2001;28:152-60.

Wen SW, Brown A, Mitchell S, Kramer MS, for the Canadian Perinatal Surveillance System. An evaluation of the validity of obstetric/neonatal discharge abstract data by re-abstraction of medical charts (unpublished manuscript), 2002.

Wen SW, Goldenberg RL, Cutter GR, Hoffman HJ, Cliver SP. Intrauterine growth retardation and preterm delivery: prenatal risk factors in an indigent population. *Am J Obstet Gynecol* 1990;162:213-8.

Wen SW, Kramer MS, Platt R, Demissie K, Joseph KS, Liu S, et al. for the Fetal and Infant Health Study Group of the Canadian Perinatal Surveillance System. Secular trends of fetal growth in Canada, 1981 to 1997. *Paediatr Perinat Epidemiol* 2003;17:347-54.

Wen SW, Liu S, Fowler D. Trends and variations in neonatal length of in-hospital stay in Canada. *Can J Public Health* 1998;89:115-9.

Wen SW, Liu S, Joseph KS, Rouleau J, Allen A. Patterns of infant mortality caused by congenital anomalies. *Teratology* 2000;61:342-6.

Wen SW, Liu S, Joseph KS, Trouton K, Allen A. Regional patterns of infant mortality caused by congenital anomalies. *Can J Public Health* 1999;90:316-9.

Bibliography

Wen SW, Liu S, Kramer MS, Marcoux S, Ohlsson A, Sauve R, et al. Comparison of maternal and infant outcomes between vacuum extraction and forceps deliveries. *Am J Epidemiol* 2001;153:103-7.

Wen SW, Liu S, Marcoux S, Fowler D. Trends and variations in length of hospital stay for childbirth in Canada. *Can Med Assoc J* 1998;158:875-80.

Wen SW, Liu S, Marcoux S, Fowler D. Uses and limitations of routine hospital admission/separation records for perinatal surveillance. *Chron Dis Can* 1997;18:113.

Wilcox AJ, Skjœrven R, Buekens P, Kiely J. Birth weight and perinatal mortality: a comparison of the United States and Norway. *JAMA* 1995;272:709-11.

Wilcox LS, Kiely JL, Melvin CL, Martin MC. Assisted reproductive technologies: estimates of their contribution to multiple births and newborn hospital days in the United States. *Fertil Steril* 1996;65:361-6.

Wilkins R, Houle C, Berthelot JM, Ross N. The changing health status of children in Canada. *Isuma* 2000;1:58-63.

Winbo I, Serenius F, Dahlquist G, Källén B. Maternal risk factors for cause-specific stillbirth and neonatal death. *Acta Obstet Gynecol Scand* 2001;80:235-44.

World Health Organization. *International Statistical Classification of Diseases and Related Health Problems*, 10th Revision. Geneva: WHO, 1996.

World Health Organization. *International Statistical Classification of Diseases and Related Health Problems*, 10th Revision, Vol. 2. Instruction manual. Geneva: WHO, 1993:129-34.

World Health Organization. *Manual of the International Classification of Diseases, Injuries and Causes of Death*. Based on the Recommendation of the Ninth Revision Conference, 1975, Geneva.

World Health Organization. *Manual of the International Statistical Classification of Diseases, Injuries, and Causes of Death*, 9th Revision, Vol. 1. Geneva: WHO, 1977.

World Health Organization. *The Optimal Duration of Exclusive Breastfeeding. Report of an Expert Consultation.* Geneva: WHO, 2001.

World Health Organization/UNICEF. *Maternal Mortality in 1995: Estimates Developed by WHO, UNICEF, UNFPA.* Geneva: WHO, 2001.

World Health Organization/UNICEF. *Revised 1990 Estimates of Maternal Mortality: A New Approach by WHO and UNICEF.* Geneva: WHO, 1996.

Yawn BP, Wollan P, McKeon K, Field CS. Temporal changes in rates and reasons for medical induction of term labor, 1980-1996. *Am J Obstet Gynecol* 2001;184:611-9.

Zhang J, Yancey MK, Henderson CE. U.S. national trends in labor induction, 1989-1998. *J Reprod Med* 2002;47:120-4.

C

Appendices

Appendix A

Data Sources and Methods

Data Sources

Author:
Susie Dzakpasu,
MHSc

The principal data sources for this perinatal health report were vital statistics, hospitalization data and the National Longitudinal Survey of Children and Youth (NLSCY). Population estimates and abortion statistics from Statistics Canada were also used.

Vital Statistics

Registration of births and deaths is compulsory under provincial and territorial Vital Statistics Acts or equivalent legislation. While Vital Statistics Acts may vary slightly among the provinces and territories, they follow a model Vital Statistics Act that was developed to promote uniformity of legislation and reporting among the provinces and territories. Every year, the provinces and territories send their live birth, stillbirth and death registration data to Statistics Canada. Statistics Canada compiles these data into national databases of live births, stillbirths and deaths called the Canadian Vital Statistics System.[1-4]

The Canadian Vital Statistics System covers all births and deaths occurring in Canada. Some births and deaths of Canadian residents occurring in the United States are also included, being reported under a reciprocal agreement. However, births and deaths of Canadian residents occurring in countries other than Canada and the United States are not reported.[1] The preparation and maintenance of these national databases require incorporation of late registrations and amendments, as well as elimination of duplicate registrations.

As part of the Canadian Perinatal Surveillance System (CPSS) initiative, Statistics Canada, under contract to the Health Surveillance and Epidemiology Division, has developed a mechanism by which information on live births and infant deaths will be linked from 1985 onwards.[5] With the permission of the provinces and territories, the resulting birth-infant death linked analysis file is an important data source for CPSS analyses. This file has personal identifiers removed.

The birth and death statistics in this report may differ slightly from those previously published by Statistics Canada as a result of updates to the data files received by Health Canada.

Data Quality

Coverage for births and deaths in the Canadian Vital Statistics System is virtually complete. Because of the large number of records, analysis within subpopulations is possible. An additional strength is that the legislation for the collection of vital statistics data is similar across all provinces and territories, as are data forms, definitions and collection methods. Data are also available at the individual level and can therefore be linked to other data sources. Finally, causes of death are coded using an international classification scheme — the International Classification of Diseases, Ninth Revision (ICD-9), for deaths and stillbirths occurring in 1979 to 1999, and the International Classification of Diseases and Related Health Problems, Tenth Revision (ICD-10), for deaths and stillbirths occurring from 2000 onwards.[6,7]

National vital statistics data also have some limitations. Data are not available on as timely a basis as would be desirable. At the time this report was being prepared, the last year of available birth and death data was 2000. Additional limitations include incomplete data for Newfoundland before 1991, and the fact that cause of death information may not always incorporate the results of coroner and medical examiner investigations.

The most serious limitation of national vital statistics data relates to the quality and completeness of data from Ontario. Studies have identified systematic errors in the data on birth weight and gestational age in Ontario during the early and mid-1990s.[8,9] Although the problems that led to these errors have been corrected, and recent data on birth weight and gestational age appear to be free from the previously identified concerns, other concerns persist.[10] In particular, the CPSS project to link information from live birth registrations with information from infant death registrations has been successful in all provinces and territories of Canada except Ontario. Linkage of live birth and infant death information for Ontario has consistently resulted in a substantial rate of unlinked infant deaths, i.e., infant deaths for which a birth registration could not be located. Approximately 25% of infant deaths in Ontario result in such non-links (page 222, Table G18, and page 223, Table G19), as compared with 0% to 3% of infant deaths in other provinces and territories of Canada. Because of these data quality issues, Ontario vital statistics data were excluded from the *Canadian Perinatal Health Report, 2000*. In the present report, Ontario data were analyzed separately and are presented in *Appendix G*.

Hospitalization Data

Five sources of hospitalization data were used: the Discharge Abstract Database (DAD) of the Canadian Institute for Health Information (CIHI), Nova Scotia's Admissions/Separations/Day Surgery databases (ASD), Quebec's Système de maintenance et d'exploitation des données pour l'étude de la clientèle hospitalière (MED-ÉCHO), Manitoba's Hospital Abstract System and the Canadian Congenital Anomalies Surveillance System (CCASS). All hospitalization data are compiled on a fiscal-year basis (April 1-March 31).

Canadian Institute for Health Information's Discharge Abstract Database

CIHI maintains the DAD, which captures hospital separation information — transfer, discharge or death — from the majority of Canada's acute care hospitals. The DAD is an electronic database that includes information on inpatient acute, chronic and rehabilitation care and day surgery, accounting for about 75% of all hospital inpatient discharges in Canada. The information is obtained directly from participating hospitals.[11] The DAD contains considerable data on each hospitalization, including demographic information, length of stay, most responsible diagnosis, secondary and co-morbid diagnoses, and procedures performed during the hospitalization. In the DAD, up to 2000-2001, diagnoses were coded according to the International Classification of Diseases, Ninth Revision (ICD-9), and procedures were coded according to the Canadian Classification of Diagnostic, Therapeutic and Surgical Procedures (CCP). The DAD also categorizes hospitalizations by case mix group (CMG), a classification based on diagnosis and intensity of care required.

Data Quality

The Division of Health Surveillance and Epidemiology investigated and evaluated the DAD, to see whether it could serve the needs of a national perinatal surveillance system.[12,13] The quality of data for delivering mothers and their newborns recorded in the DAD from April 1, 1984, to March 31, 1995, was examined. The number of illogical and out-of-range values was found to be low, the occurrence of maternal and infant diseases estimated from the data was similar to that in the literature, and major medical or obstetric complications recorded in the DAD were good predictors of adverse pregnancy outcomes.[12]

In 2001, CIHI conducted a re-abstraction study to assess the validity of 1999-2000 hospital discharge data. This involved comparison of information in medical charts with information coded in the DAD for a sample of hospitals. The CPSS collaborated with CIHI to expand this study to include specific maternal and newborn diagnoses. The results showed that procedures and straightforward diagnoses recorded in routine hospital discharge abstract data can be used for perinatal health surveillance and research, but improvements in data quality are needed for complicated diagnoses.[14] Accuracy is also likely to be lower for codes other than the primary or most responsible diagnosis.

In addition to the general limitation of potential coding errors, there are several other problems in using the DAD for national perinatal surveillance:

- Out-of-hospital births are not captured.

- Pregnancies with non-birth outcomes (e.g., spontaneous abortions) may not be captured.

- The DAD does not include all hospital admissions/separations in Canada. Quebec data are not included in the DAD, and data for Manitoba and Nova Scotia are not complete for some years. The level of coverage in other provinces may also have changed over time. The issue of level of coverage and the implications for perinatal health data need to be explored further. Indicators that were calculated using hospitalization data therefore incorporated data obtained directly from Quebec, Manitoba and Nova Scotia (see the following sections for brief descriptions of these provincial data sets).

- Currently, the DAD does not capture information on gestational age and parity.

Nova Scotia's Admissions/Separations/Day Surgery Databases

Before 1995, Nova Scotia did not send hospital information to CIHI. Hospital claims were sent to the Department of Health, where they were collated into the Admissions/Separations/Day Surgery databases (ASD). The information in the ASD is equivalent to that in the DAD.

Quebec's Système de maintenance et d'exploitation des données pour l'étude de la clientèle hospitalière (MED-ÉCHO)

Quebec data on hospitalizations were taken from the MED-ÉCHO hospitalization file. For most of the data on hospitalizations, the universe covered relates to acute physical care; this excludes hospitalizations for mental disorders and behavioural disorders, hospitalizations of healthy newborns, day nursing (day surgery since 1995), extended care, hospitalizations of the home-hospital type, hospitalizations of non-resident Quebecers and long-term hospitalizations in acute care units. Data are kept only for the general and specialized-care hospital centres; centres focusing primarily on psychiatry, rehabilitation or sheltering, and extended care are thus excluded.[15] Hospitalizations of Quebec residents in other provinces are obtained from CIHI and added to the data.

Manitoba Health's Perinatal Surveillance Database

Manitoba's perinatal surveillance statistics were based on Manitoba hospital abstract records processed between April 1, 1991, and March 31, 2001 (i.e., fiscal 1991-1992 to 2000-2001). Hospital abstract records were queried to determine the number of abortions (therapeutic or spontaneous), ectopic pregnancies, deliveries and newborn records. The information in Manitoba's hospital abstract records is similar to that in the DAD.

Data Quality

Hospital records from the provincial databases share many of the features and limitations of the data in the DAD. For example, pregnancies resulting in a home birth, an induced abortion at a private clinic or an unreported spontaneous abortion are not captured in these databases.

Canadian Congenital Anomalies Surveillance System (CCASS)

CCASS data are largely culled from the DAD. Additional data sources are also relied upon, particularly to provide coverage of provinces poorly represented by the DAD. The Manitoba hospitalization database is used for Manitoba, and Quebec data are from MED-ÉCHO. Alberta uses its own reporting system, the Alberta Congenital Anomalies Surveillance System (ACASS). The primary sources of data for ACASS are vital statistics, hospital reporting and special communications with genetics clinics, specialty paediatric clinics and laboratories. Data from Quebec, Manitoba and Alberta are sent to CCASS and merged with the data culled from the DAD to create the CCASS database.

Data Quality

CCASS is the only ongoing population-based congenital anomaly surveillance database that is able to estimate the Canadian birth prevalence of specific congenital anomalies. CCASS provides temporal trends at the national level in addition to provincial/territorial and international comparisons.

One of the most significant limitations of CCASS is its inability to monitor the impact of prenatal diagnoses on the birth prevalence of selected congenital anomalies. Affected pregnancies that are terminated before meeting the jurisdictional criteria for a stillbirth are not captured in CCASS data. This directly limits an assessment of primary and secondary preventive strategies. Additional strengths and limitations of CCASS are outlined elsewhere.[16]

National Longitudinal Survey of Children and Youth[17]

The primary objective of the NLSCY is to develop a national database on the characteristics and life experiences of Canadian children as they grow from infancy to adulthood. Statistics Canada conducts the survey and collects cross-sectional information as well as longitudinal data. Data collection began in 1994-1995 and will be repeated every two years to follow the children surveyed in 1994-1995. In subsequent years, a cross-sectional sample will be added for age groups no longer covered by the longitudinal sample.

Data Quality

The survey is designed primarily for analysis at the national, regional and some provincial/territorial levels. Analysis of subpopulations, including analysis for smaller provinces and the territories, is limited by insufficient sample sizes. Attrition may further reduce the sample in subsequent data collection cycles. Perinatal health information is often not detailed enough to be used for in-depth analysis, and it may be subject to incorrect recall because it is collected retrospectively up to three years after the birth of the child. Perinatal health information may also be subject to a small selection bias because it is collected only for children still living at the time the sample is selected.

Methods

Statistical methods were primarily descriptive and consisted of calculation of frequencies, rates, ratios and means. Results based on rare events or on a small sample have been flagged, and caution should be exercised in interpreting them. Records with key information missing were excluded from analysis. Statistics presented for most indicators consist of the following:

1. **Temporal trends at the national level:** The period covered in the temporal trends dates back as far as 1979, depending on the data sources used and the particular indicator. For most indicators using vital statistics, trends begin in 1991 to allow for the inclusion of Newfoundland. For indicators using hospitalization data, trends begin in 1991-1992. For indicators using NLSCY data, trends begin in 1994-1995, when the first cycle of this survey was carried out. If complete provincial data were not available for all years of a temporal trend, data from that province were excluded from the trend. In some cases, when events were rare, data for several years were aggregated.

2. **Interprovincial/territorial comparisons:** For most indicators, interprovincial/ territorial comparisons are presented for the most recent year for which data were available. In some cases, jurisdictional differences are assessed and interpreted using standard deviations or 95% confidence intervals. In the vital statistics and NLSCY data sets, province/territory refers to the province/territory of residence. In the DAD, province/territory refers to the province/territory of the reporting hospital.

The majority of indicators are presented graphically. Data tables corresponding to all figures are presented in *Appendices E and F*. Some results are statified by relevant factors, such as maternal age or birth weight categories. Tables A1-A3 (see following pages) describe specific methods used for each indicator. All indicators were calculated for the time and place specified in the chapter.

TABLE A1 **Methods for each indicator using vital statistics**

Indicator	Method
Rate of live births to teenagers	Age-specific live birth rate (general) = $\dfrac{\text{Number of live births to females in a specific age group}}{\text{Number of females in that age group}} \times 1{,}000$ Age-specific live birth rate (females < 15 years of age) = $\dfrac{\text{Number of live births to females} < 15 \text{ years of age}}{\text{Number of females 14 years of age}} \times 1{,}000$ Proportion of live births to teenage mothers = $\dfrac{\text{Number of live births to females in a specific teen age group}}{\text{Total number of live births}} \times 100$ **Exclusions:** live births to females with unknown age **Age categories:** < 15, 15-17, 18-19
Rate of live births to older mothers	Age-specific live birth rate (general) = $\dfrac{\text{Number of live births to females in a specific age group}}{\text{Number of females in that age group}} \times 1{,}000$ Age-specific live birth rate (females $\geq$ 45 years of age) = $\dfrac{\text{Number of live births to females} \geq 45 \text{ years of age}}{\text{Number of females 45-49 years old}} \times 1{,}000$ Proportion of live births to older mothers = $\dfrac{\text{Number of live births to females in a specific older age group}}{\text{Total number of live births}} \times 100$ **Exclusions:** live births to females with unknown age **Age categories:** 30-34, 35-39, 40-44, 45+
Maternal mortality ratio	$\dfrac{\text{Number of deaths with cause of death code ICD-9 630 to 676}}{\text{Total number of live births}} \times 100{,}000$ Because of the small number of maternal deaths each year, data were aggregated into three-year intervals, beginning in 1979. Statistics Canada publications (corrected for under-registration) estimate Newfoundland vital statistics prior to 1991, as data for Newfoundland before 1991 are incomplete.
Preterm birth rate	$\dfrac{\text{Number of live births with gestational age} < 37 \text{ completed weeks}}{\text{Number of live births}} \times 100$ **Exclusions:** live births with unknown gestational age
Postterm birth rate	$\dfrac{\text{Number of live births with gestational age} > 41 \text{ completed weeks}}{\text{Number of live births}} \times 100$ **Exclusions:** live births with unknown gestational age
Small-for-gestational-age rate	$\dfrac{\text{Number of singleton live births with birth weight below the 10th percentile for gestational age}}{\text{Number of singleton live births}} \times 100$

Appendix A

Indicator	Method
Large-for-gestational-age rate	**Exclusions:** live births with unknown gestational age, live births with gestational age < 22 weeks or gestational age > 43 weeks, live births with unknown birth weight and multiple births $$\frac{\text{Number of singleton live births with birth weight above the 90th percentile for gestational age}}{\text{Number of singleton live births}} \times 100$$
Fetal mortality rate	**Exclusions:** live births with unknown gestational age, live births with gestational age < 22 weeks or gestational age > 43 weeks, live births with unknown birth weight and multiple births Fetal mortality rate = $$\frac{\text{Number of fetal deaths}}{\text{Number of fetal deaths and live births}} \times 1,000$$
Infant mortality rate	**Exclusions:** fetal death rate $\geq$ 500 g excludes stillbirths and live births of < 500 g, and stillbirths and live births of unknown birth weight with a gestational age of less than 22 weeks Infant mortality rate = $$\frac{\text{Number of deaths among infants} < 1 \text{ year (365 days) of age}}{\text{Number of live births}} \times 1,000$$ Neonatal death rate = $$\frac{\text{Number of deaths among infants} < 28 \text{ days of age}}{\text{Number of live births}} \times 1,000$$ Postneonatal death rate = $$\frac{\text{Number of deaths among infants} \geq 28 \text{ days of age}}{\text{Number of live births — number of neonatal deaths}} \times 1,000$$ **ICD-9 codes for categories of causes of infant mortality** Congenital anomalies: 740-759 Asphyxia-related conditions: 761.6, 761.7, 762.0, 762.1, 762.2, 762.4, 762.5, 762.6, 763, 766-768, 770.1, 772.2, 779.0, 779.2 Immaturity-related conditions: 761.3, 761.4, 761.5, 761.8, 761.9, 762.7, 764, 765, 769, 770.2, 770.3, 770.4, 770.5, 770.6, 770.7, 770.8, 770.9, 772.1, 774, 777.5, 777.6, 778.2, 779.6, 779.8 Infections: 001-139, 320-326, 382, 420-422, 460-466, 475-477, 480-491, 510, 511, 513, 540, 541, 566, 567, 570, 590, 591, 770.0, 771, 790 SIDS: 798.0 Other sudden unexplained infant death: 798.1, 798.2, 798.9, 799, E913 External causes: 260-263, 507, E800-E999 (except E913) Other: all remaining codes In the birth-infant death linked files, all live births at < 22 weeks and < 500 g were assumed to have died on the first day of life and were classified as such.
Multiple birth rate	$$\frac{\text{Number of live and stillbirths following a multiple gestation pregnancy}}{\text{Number of live births and stillbirths}} \times 100$$

Methods Specific to Indicators Using Hospitalization Data as Principal Data Source

The majority of analyses using hospitalization data were carried out on two sets of records — obstetric delivery records and newborn records. Obstetric delivery records in the DAD were identified by means of the algorithm described below. The algorithm used all 16 diagnosis fields and all 10 procedure fields in the DAD. Unless otherwise specified, all of these fields were also used in the analysis of each indicator. All obstetric delivery records without a code indicating a cesarean section procedure (CPP code 86.0, 86.1, 86.2, 86.8 or 86.9) were identified as vaginal deliveries.

Algorithm for Identifying Obstetric Records

Part 1

a)   Identify all cases with CMG codes 601 to 604 and 606 to 611.

b)   *Retain* all that have a procedure or diagnosis code for cesarean OR forceps OR vacuum OR episiotomy OR normal delivery OR outcome of delivery.

c)   From the remainder created in step b, *retain* all those that have an ICD-9 diagnosis between 660 and 669.

d)   From the remainder created in step c, first exclude those whose sole diagnosis/ procedure code is 644.0, and from those left over *retain* only those who have an ICD-9 code between 630 and 659, or between 670 and 676, AND main patient service code 51.

e)   Collate those retained in steps b, c and d.

Part 2

a)   Select all records with CMG codes 600 and 605 from DAD files.

b)   Use "main patient service code 51" to define all obstetric deliveries.

c)   Among the remaining, use procedure codes to specify obstetric deliveries. The obstetric procedure codes to be used are 84.0, 84.1-84.3, 84.5-84.9, 85.22, 85.6, 86.0-86.3, 86.8, 86.9.

Part 3

a)   Exclude all those with CMG codes 600 to 611 from DAD files.

b)   From the remaining records in the DAD, *retain* all those that have a procedure or diagnosis code for cesarean OR forceps OR vacuum OR episiotomy OR normal delivery (ICD-9 650) OR outcome of delivery (ICD-9 V27).

c)   From the remainder created in step 3b, *retain* all those with an ICD-9 code between 660 and 669 AND a patient service code of 51.

d)   Collate those retained in steps b and c.

Part 4

Collate all records identified and retained in parts 1, 2 and 3.

The above algorithm identifies slightly more obstetric deliveries than the algorithm used for the analyses reported in *Canadian Perinatal Health Report, 2000* (only Part 1a was used for analyses presented in that report). For example, for the seven-year period 1994-1995 to 2000-2001 (excluding Nova Scotia, Quebec and Manitoba data), 1,732,855 obstetric records were identified from Part 1a (previous algorithm). The additional steps (i.e., from Part 1b to Part 4) have added 5,017 obstetric records (0.29%). As a result of the use of this new algorithm and updates to the DAD data file following the analyses presented in the 2000 report, statistics in this report differ slightly from those published in the previous report.

TABLE A2 **Methods for each indicator using hospitalization data**

Indicator	Method
Labour induction rate	Medical labour induction rate = $\frac{\text{Number of deliveries with CCP code 85.5}}{\text{Number of deliveries}} \times 100$
	Surgical labour induction rate = $\frac{\text{Number of deliveries with CCP code 85.01}}{\text{Number of deliveries}} \times 100$
	Labour induction rate = $\frac{\text{Number of deliveries with CCP code 85.5 or 85.01}}{\text{Number of deliveries}} \times 100$
Cesarean section rate	Cesarean section rate = $\frac{\text{Number of deliveries with CCP code 86.0, 86.1, 86.2, 86.8 or 86.9}}{\text{Number of deliveries}} \times 100$
	Primary cesarean section rate = $\frac{\text{Number of deliveries with CCP code 86.0, 86.1, 86.2, 86.8 or 86.9 that do not have ICD-9 code 654.2 (previous cesarean)}}{\text{Number of deliveries excluding those with an ICD-9 code 654.2}} \times 100$
	Repeat cesarean section rate = $\frac{\text{Number of deliveries with CCP code 86.0, 86.1, 86.2, 86.8 or 86.9 and ICD-9 code 654.2 (previous cesarean)}}{\text{Number of deliveries with ICD-9 code 654.2}} \times 100$
Rate of operative vaginal deliveries	Forceps rate = $\frac{\text{Number of deliveries with CCP code 84.0, 84.1, 84.2 or 84.3}}{\text{Number of vaginal deliveries}} \times 100$
	Vacuum extraction rate = $\frac{\text{Number of deliveries with CCP code 84.7}}{\text{Number of vaginal deliveries}} \times 100$
	Rate of operative vaginal deliveries = $\frac{\text{Number of deliveries with CCP code 84.0, 84.1, 84.2, 84.3 or 84.7}}{\text{Number of vaginal deliveries}} \times 100$
Rate of trauma to the perineum	Rate of first- and second-degree lacerations = $\frac{\text{Number of deliveries with ICD-9 code 664.0 or 664.1}}{\text{Number of vaginal deliveries}} \times 100$

Indicator	Method
Rate of trauma to the perineum (cont.)	Rate of third-degree lacerations = $\frac{\text{Number of deliveries with ICD-9 code 664.2}}{\text{Number of vaginal deliveries}} \times 100$ Rate of fourth-degree lacerations = $\frac{\text{Number of deliveries with ICD-9 code 664.3}}{\text{Number of vaginal deliveries}} \times 100$ Episiotomy rate = $\frac{\text{Number of deliveries with CCP code 84.1, 84.21, 84.31, 84.71 or 85.7}}{\text{Number of vaginal deliveries}} \times 100$
Rate of early maternal discharge from hospital after childbirth	$\frac{\text{Number of vaginal deliveries with length of stay} < 2 \text{ days}}{\text{Number of vaginal deliveries}} \times 100$ $\frac{\text{Number of cesarean deliveries with length of stay} < 4 \text{ days}}{\text{Number of cesarean deliveries}} \times 100$ If the length of stay was > 20 days, it was set to 20 days for the calculation of the mean length of stay.
Rate of early neonatal discharge from hospital after birth	$\frac{\text{Number of newborns with length of stay} < 2 \text{ days}}{\text{Number of live births}} \times 100$ **Birth weight categories:** 1,000-2,499 g, $\geq$ 2,500 g **Exclusions:** newborns with a birth weight < 1,000 g If the length of stay was > 20 days, it was set to 20 days for the calculation of the mean length of stay.
Induced abortion ratio	Induced abortion ratio = $\frac{\text{Number of induced abortions}}{\text{Number of live births}} \times 100$ Induced abortion rate = $\frac{\text{Number of induced abortions}}{\text{Number of females 15-44 years of age}} \times 1,000$ Age-specific induced abortion rate = $\frac{\text{Number of induced abortions in a specific age category}}{\text{Number of females in that age category}} \times 1,000$ Canadian ratio and rate include cases of unknown area of residence and abortions performed on Canadian residents in selected U.S states. Ratios and overall rates include cases with age not specified, as well as abortions to females $\leq$ 14 years of age and $\geq$ 45 years of age. Overall rates are based on female population 15-44 years of age. Excludes abortions performed in Canada on non-Canadian residents. Induced abortion statistics were provided by Statistics Canada through a custom tabulation request.

Indicator	Method
Ectopic pregnancy rate	Number of ectopic pregnancies <u>(ICD-9 code 633.0, 633.1, 633.2, 633.8 or 633.9)</u> x 1,000 Number of ectopic pregnancies, hospital-based induced abortions (ICD-9 code 635) and hospital deliveries **Exclusions:** Clinic-based abortions were excluded because they were reported by calendar year and could not be reconciled with the fiscal year approach used for this indicator. Spontaneous and "unspecified" abortions were also excluded from the total reported pregnancies.
Severe maternal morbidity ratio	Amniotic fluid embolism incidence rate = <u>Number of deliveries with ICD-9 code 673.1</u> x 100,000 Number of deliveries Postpartum hemorrhage with hysterectomy = Number of deliveries with ICD-9 code 666.0, 666.1, 666.2 or 666.3 <u>(postpartum hemorrhage) and CCP codes 802 to 806 (hysterectomy)</u> x 100,000 Number of deliveries
Rate of maternal readmission after discharge following childbirth	Number of women who were readmitted to hospital <u>within 90 days of a hospital admission for childbirth</u> x 100 Number of deliveries Maternal readmission cases were identified by linking obstetric delivery records and readmission records from January 1, 1991, to March 31, 2001. The number of deliveries is based on the calendar year, and the number of readmissions is counted for up to 90 days after the childbirth discharge. **Exclusions:** women who were directly transferred after childbirth, women with initial length of hospital stay > 20 days and day surgery admissions. The primary diagnosis at readmission was based on the principal discharge diagnosis only. **ICD-9 codes for primary diagnosis at readmission:** Cholelithiasis: 574 Complications of pregnancy, not elsewhere classified: 646 Other current conditions in the mother classified elsewhere, but complicating pregnancy, childbirth or the peurperium: 648 Postpartum hemorrhage: 666 Major puerperal infection: 670 Venous complications in pregnancy and the puerperium: 671 Other and unspecified complications of the puerperium, not elsewhere classified: 674 Infections of the breast and nipple associated with childbirth: 675 Symptoms involving abdomen and pelvis: 789 Complications of procedures, not elsewhere classified: 998 Postpartum care and examination: V24 Persons seeking consultation without complaint of sickness: V65 Encounter for contraceptive management: V25

Appendix A

Indicator	Method
Severe neonatal morbidity rate	Rate of respiratory distress syndrome = $\dfrac{\text{Number of newborns with ICD-9 code 769}}{\text{Number of live births}}$ x 1,000 Rate of sepsis = $\dfrac{\text{Number of newborns with ICD-9 code 771.4 or 771.8}}{\text{Number of live births}}$ x 1,000 **Exclusions:** newborns with birth weight < 500 g.
Prevalence of congenital anomalies	Down syndrome rate = $\dfrac{\text{Number of infants with ICD-9 code 758.0}}{\text{Number of live births and stillbirths}}$ x 10,000 Neural tube defect rate = $\dfrac{\text{Number of infants with ICD-9 code 740.0 to 742.0}}{\text{Number of live births and stillbirths}}$ x 10,000 Congenital anomaly cases were identified using the CCASS database.
Rate of neonatal hospital readmission after discharge following birth	$\dfrac{\text{Number of infants who were readmitted to hospital within} \leq 28 \text{ days of birth}}{\text{Number of hospital live births}}$ x 100 Cases of neonatal readmission were identified by linking newborn records and readmission records from March 1, 1991, to March 31, 2001. The frequency of neonatal readmission is counted for 28 days after birth. **Exclusions:** Newborns who were directly transferred after birth, newborns with initial length of hospital stay > 20 days, newborns with birth weight < 1,000 g, newborns discharged on the same day of birth and day surgery admissions. The primary diagnosis at readmission was based on the principal discharge diagnosis only. **ICD-9 codes for primary diagnosis at readmission:** Jaundice: 773.1, 774.2, 774.3, 774.6, 774.7 Feeding problems: 779.3, 783.3 Sepsis: 771.4, 771.8 Dehydration: 276.0, 276.5, 775.5, 778.4 Inadequate weight gain: 783.2, 783.4

Methods Specific to Indicators Using NLSCY Data

Custom tabulations for the first three cycles of the NLSCY (1994-1995, 1996-1997, 1998-1999) were obtained from Statistics Canada. In the NLSCY, questions on maternal smoking during pregnancy, maternal alcohol consumption during pregnancy and breastfeeding were asked of the person most knowledgeable (PMK) about the child, and were asked for children less than three years of age. As the survey is carried out every two years, analysis was restricted to children less than two years of age in order to keep the estimates independent of one another. Analysis was further restricted to records in which the PMK was the biological mother of the child.

Information on maternal smoking during pregnancy, maternal alcohol consumption during pregnancy and breastfeeding was available for 4,138 children less than two years of age in cycle 1, 3,784 children in cycle 2 and 7,584 children in cycle 3. These children represented approximately 654,600, 667,300 and 616,300 children in each cycle, respectively, when weighted. All estimates presented in this report were calculated using sample weights. According to Statistics Canada's data release guidelines, estimates based on a sample size of 30 or more with a coefficient of variation of 16.5% or less were released without a warning. Estimates based on a sample of 30 or more with a coefficient of variation ranging from 16.6% to 33.3% were released with a warning to readers about the low level of precision associated with the estimate. Estimates based on a sample size of less than 30 or with a coefficient of variation in excess of 33.3% were not released.

TABLE A3 **Methods for each indicator using NLSCY data**

Indicator	Method
Rate of maternal smoking during pregnancy	Rate of maternal smoking = $$\frac{\text{Number of children} < 2 \text{ years of age whose mother reported smoking during pregnancy}}{\text{Number of children} < 2 \text{ years of age}} \times 100$$ Rate of prenatal exposure to > 10 cigarettes per day = $$\frac{\text{Number of children} < 2 \text{ years of age whose mother reported smoking} > 10 \text{ cigarettes per day}}{\text{Number of children} < 2 \text{ years of age}} \times 100$$ Rate of exposure during the third trimester = $$\frac{\text{Number of children} < 2 \text{ years of age whose mother reported smoking during the third trimester}}{\text{Number of children} < 2 \text{ years of age}} \times 100$$ Survey questions used: Did you smoke during your pregnancy with ... ? How many cigarettes per day did you smoke during your pregnancy with ... ? At what stage in your pregnancy did you smoke this amount? Maternal age categories: < 20, 20-24, 25-29, 30-34, ≥ 35, all ages
Rate of maternal alcohol consumption during pregnancy	$$\frac{\text{Number of children} < 2 \text{ years of age whose mother reported drinking alcohol during pregnancy}}{\text{Number of children} < 2 \text{ years of age}} \times 100$$

Indicator	Method
Rate of maternal alcohol consumption during pregnancy (cont.)	**Survey questions used:** How frequently did you consume alcohol (e.g., beer, wine, liquor) during your pregnancy with … ? **Maternal age categories:** < 25, 25-29, 30-34, ≥ 35, all ages
Prevalence of breastfeeding	Breastfeeding initiation rate = $$\frac{\text{Number of children} < 2 \text{ years of age whose mother reported breastfeeding (regardless of duration)}}{\text{Number of children} < 2 \text{ years of age}} \times 100$$ Breastfeeding duration rate = $$\frac{\text{Number of children} < 2 \text{ years of age whose mother reported breastfeeding } 3+ \text{ months}}{\text{Number of children} < 2 \text{ years of age whose mother reported breastfeeding}} \times 100$$ Breastfeeding duration rates are based on children in whom breastfeeding was initiated, but who were no longer breastfed at the time of the survey. **Survey questions used:** Are you currently breastfeeding? Did you breastfeed him/her even if only for a short time? For how long? **Maternal age categories:** < 20, 20-24, 25-29, 30-34, ≥ 35, all ages
Proportion of women with a low educational level	$$\frac{\text{Number of children} < 2 \text{ years of age whose mother had a particular level of education}}{\text{Number of children} < 2 \text{ years of age}} \times 100$$ **Survey questions used:** Have you graduated from high school? Have you ever attended university, community college, business school, trace or vocational school, CEGEP or any other postsecondary institution? What is the highest level of education that you have attained?

References

1. Statistics Canada. *Births and Deaths 1996, 1997*. Ottawa: Statistics Canada, Health Statistics Division, 1999 (Catalogue No. 84-F0210-XPB).

2. Fair M. The development of national vital statistics in Canada: Part 1 — from 1605 to 1945. *Health Rep* 1994;6:355-68.

3. Fair M, Cyr M. The Canadian Birth Data Base: a new research tool to study reproductive outcomes. *Health Rep* 1993;5:281-90.

4. Smith ME, Newcombe HB. Use of the Canadian Mortality Data Base for epidemiologic follow up. *Can J Public Health* 1982;73:39-45.

5. Fair M, Cyr M, Allen AC, Wen SW, Guyon G, MacDonald RC. *Validation Study for a Record Linkage of Births and Infant Deaths in Canada*. Ottawa: Statistics Canada, 1999 (Catalogue No. 84F0013-XIE).

6. World Health Organization. *Manual of the International Classification of Diseases, Injuries, and Causes of Death*. Based on the Recommendation of the Ninth Revision Conference, 1975, Geneva.

7. World Health Organization. *International Statistical Classification of Diseases and Related Health Problems*, 10th Revision. Geneva: WHO, 1996.

8. Joseph KS, Kramer MS. Recent trends in infant mortality rates and proportions of low-birth-weight live births in Canada. *Can Med Assoc J* 1997;157:535-41.

9. Joseph KS. *Preterm Birth in Canada*. Background papers — Preterm Birth Prevention Consensus Conference. Ottawa, 1998.

10. Bienefeld M, Woodward GL, Ardal S. *Under-reporting of Live Births in Ontario: 1991-97*. Central East Health Information Partnership. URL: <http://www.cehip.org/Library/student%20 projects/missing%20births%20final.PDF>.

11. Canadian Institute for Health Information. Website. URL: <http://www.cihi.ca>. Accessed March 28, 2003.

12. Wen SW, Liu S, Marcoux S, Fowler D. Uses and limitations of routine hospital admission/separation records for perinatal surveillance. *Chron Dis Can* 1997;18:113.

13. Liu S, Wen SW. Development of record linkage of hospital discharge data for the study of neonatal readmission. *Chron Dis Can* 1999;20:77-81.

14. Wen SW, Brown A, Mitchell S, Kramer MS, for the Canadian Perinatal Surveillance System. An evaluation of the validity of obstetric/neonatal discharge abstract data by re-abstraction of medical charts (unpublished manuscript), 2002.

15. Pelletier G. L'hospitalisation pour soins de courte durée au Québec. Statistiques évolutives 1982-1983 à 1997-1998, Québec, MSSS, Direction générale de la planification stratégique et de l'évaluation, no. 36 (Collection Données statistiques et indicateurs), 1999.

16. Health Canada. *Congenital Anomalies in Canada — A Perinatal Health Report, 2002*. Ottawa: Minister of Public Works and Government Services Canada, 2002 (Catalogue No. H39-641/2002E). URL: <http://www.hc-sc.gc.ca/pphb-dgspsp/rhs-ssg/index.html>.

17. Statistics Canada, Human Resources Development Canada. *National Longitudinal Survey of Children and Youth, Overview of the Survey Instruments for 1996-97 Data Collection, Cycle 2*. Ottawa: Statistics Canada, 1997 (Catalogue No. 89-F0078-XPE).

Appendix B

List of Perinatal Health Indicators

A health indicator is a measurement that, when compared with either a standard or desired level of achievement, provides information regarding a health outcome or important health determinant.[1] The Maternal and Infant Health Section and the CPSS Steering Committee undertook a process to identify the perinatal health indicators that should be monitored by a national perinatal surveillance system.[2] The group considered the importance of the health outcome or determinant, the scientific properties of the indicator, such as its validity in measuring that outcome or determinant, and the feasibility of collecting the data required to construct it. Below is the set of indicators that resulted from this process. The first 43 indicators listed are ranked according to the Steering Committee's assessment of health importance. Nine additional indicators were added to the list after subsequent consultations. This report contains information on 27 of these perinatal health indicators for which we currently have national data.

*Fetal and infant mortality rates were ranked first. Fetal growth comprising SGA and LGA was ranked second.

Appendix B

Appendix B

Additional Perinatal Health Indicators

Rate of Live Births to Older Mothers   22
Prevalence of Folic Acid Use in the Periconceptional Period
Rate of Prenatal Obstetrical Ultrasound Utilization

Rate of Assisted Conception
Prevalence of Group B Streptococcal Infection
Prevalence of Illicit Drug Use during Pregnancy

Prevalence of Postpartum Depression
Rate of Fetal Monitoring
Rate of Client Satisfaction with Services

References

1. Buehler J. Surveillance. In: Rothman KJ, Greenland S (Eds.). *Modern Epidemiology*, 2nd Edition. Philadelphia: Lippincott-Raven, 1998.

2. Health Canada. *Perinatal Health Indicators for Canada: A Resource Manual*. Ottawa: Minister of Public Works and Government Services Canada, 2000 (Catalogue No. H49-135/2000E). URL: <http://www.hc-sc.gc.ca/pphb-dgspsp/rhs-ssg/index.html>.

Appendix C

List of Acronyms

ACASS	Alberta Congenital Anomalies Surveillance System
AROM	artificial rupture of membranes
ASD	Admissions/Separations/Day Surgery databases
CA	congenital anomaly
CANSIM	Canadian Socio-economic Information Management System
CCASS	Canadian Congenital Anomalies Surveillance System
CCP	Canadian Classification of Diagnostic, Therapeutic and Surgical Procedures
CDC	Centers for Disease Control and Prevention
CI	confidence interval
CIHI	Canadian Institute for Health Information
CMG	case mix group
CPS	Canadian Paediatric Society
CPSS	Canadian Perinatal Surveillance System
CD	cesarean delivery
DAD	Discharge Abstract Database
DC	Dietitians of Canada
DS	Down syndrome
FAS	fetal alcohol syndrome
FASD	fetal alcohol spectrum disorder
FIHSG	Fetal and Infant Health Study Group
ICD-9	International Classification of Diseases, Ninth Revision
ICD-10	International Classification of Diseases and Related Health Problems, Tenth Revision
ICE	International Collaborative Effort (on perinatal and infant mortality)
IMR	infant mortality rate

IUGR	intrauterine growth restriction
LGA	large for gestational age
LOS	length of stay
MED-ÉCHO	Système de Maintenance et d'exploitation des données pour l'étude de la clientèle hospitalière
MES	Maternity Experiences Survey
MESG	Maternity Experiences Study Group
MHSG	Maternal Health Study Group
MMR	maternal mortality ratio
NLSCY	National Longitudinal Survey of Children and Youth
NTD	neural tube defect
PMK	person most knowledgeable
RDS	respiratory distress syndrome
SC	Steering Committee (of the CPSS)
SD	standard deviation
SGA	small for gestational age
SIDS	sudden infant death syndrome
SOGC	Society of Obstetricians and Gynaecologists of Canada
UNICEF	United Nations Children's Fund
VBAC	vaginal birth after cesarean
WHO	World Health Organization

Appendix D

Components of Fetal-Infant Mortality

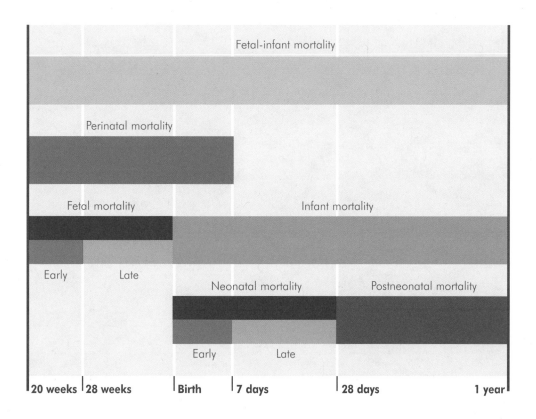

* Adapted from Péron Y, Strohmenger C. *Demographic and Health Indicators: Presentation and Interpretation*. Ottawa: Minister of Supply and Services Canada, 1985 (Catalogue No. 82-543E); and Monnier A. Les méthodes d'analyse de la mortalité infantile. In: *Manuel d'analyse de la mortalité*. Paris: INED, 1985:52-5.

In calculating the fetal-infant mortality rate, perinatal mortality rate and stillbirth rate, the denominator reflects total births (live births and stillbirths), whereas in calculating the infant mortality rate, neonatal mortality rate (early and late) and postneonatal mortality rate, the denominator includes only live births.

Appendix E

Data Tables Accompanying *Perinatal Health in Canada: An Overview*

Data Tables

TABLE E1 **Birth cohort-based infant mortality rates (IMR) among live births ≥ 500 g,**
Canada (excluding Ontario),* 1991-1999

| Year | Number of live births | Number of infant deaths (linked and unlinked) | Birth weight < 500 g** | | Number of unlinked infant deaths | Crude infant mortality rate (95% CI) | | Infant mortality rate ≥ 500 g*** (95% CI) | |
			Number of live births	Number of infant deaths					
1991	250,847	1,603	153	143	39	6.39	(6.08-6.71)	5.82	(5.53-6.13)
1992	247,898	1,585	136	125	36	6.39	(6.08-6.72)	5.89	(5.60-6.20)
1993	240,468	1,494	161	149	31	6.21	(5.90-6.54)	5.60	(5.30-5.90)
1994	238,069	1,515	153	146	36	6.36	(6.05-6.69)	5.75	(5.45-6.07)
1995	231,813	1,414	190	176	13	6.10	(5.79-6.43)	5.34	(5.05-5.65)
1996	226,180	1,226	193	177	15	5.42	(5.12-5.73)	4.64	(4.37-4.93)
1997	215,588	1,192	199	185	22	5.53	(5.22-5.85)	4.68	(4.39-4.97)
1998	209,795	1,168	162	154	12	5.57	(5.25-5.90)	4.84	(4.55-5.14)
1999	206,169	1,082	187	178	7	5.25	(4.94-5.57)	4.39	(4.11-4.68)

Source: Statistics Canada, Canadian Vital Statistics System, 1991-1999 (birth-infant death linked files).
*Data for Ontario were excluded because of data quality concerns.
**Birth weight < 500 g or birth weight missing and gestational age < 22 weeks.
***Infant deaths per 1,000 live births with a birth weight ≥ 500 g. Unlinked infant deaths (i.e., infants whose death registrations could not be linked to their birth registrations) and live births/infant deaths with missing birth weight were also included, except for those with a missing birth weight and a gestational age < 22 weeks.
CI — confidence interval.

TABLE E2 **Birth cohort-based infant mortality rates (IMR) among live births ≥ 1,000 g,**
Canada (excluding Ontario),* 1991-1999

| Year | Number of live births | Number of infant deaths (linked and unlinked) | Birth weight < 1,000 g** | | Number of unlinked infant deaths | Crude infant mortality rate (95% CI) | | Infant mortality rate ≥ 1,000 g*** (95% CI) | |
			Number of live births	Number of infant deaths					
1991	250,847	1,603	937	492	39	6.39	(6.08-6.71)	4.45	(4.19-4.71)
1992	247,898	1,585	886	423	36	6.39	(6.08-6.72)	4.70	(4.44-4.98)
1993	240,468	1,494	907	490	31	6.21	(5.90-6.54)	4.19	(3.94-4.46)
1994	238,069	1,515	992	520	36	6.36	(6.05-6.69)	4.20	(3.94-4.47)
1995	231,813	1,414	937	475	13	6.10	(5.79-6.43)	4.07	(3.81-4.34)
1996	226,180	1,226	966	453	15	5.42	(5.12-5.73)	3.43	(3.20-3.68)
1997	215,588	1,192	995	470	22	5.53	(5.22-5.85)	3.36	(3.12-3.62)
1998	209,795	1,168	909	448	12	5.57	(5.25-5.90)	3.45	(3.20-3.71)
1999	206,169	1,082	904	432	7	5.25	(4.94-5.57)	3.17	(2.93-3.42)

Source: Statistics Canada, Canadian Vital Statistics System, 1991-1999 (birth-infant death linked files).
*Data for Ontario were excluded because of data quality concerns.
**Birth weight < 1,000 g or birth weight missing and gestational age < 28 weeks.
***Infant deaths per 1,000 live births with a birth weight ≥ 1,000 g. Unlinked infant deaths (i.e., infants whose death registrations could not be linked to their birth registrations) and live births/infant deaths with missing birth weight were also included, except for those with a missing birth weight and a gestational age < 28 weeks.
CI — confidence interval.

TABLE E3 | **Birth cohort-based infant mortality rates (IMR) among live births ≥ 500 g and among live births ≥ 1,000 g, by province/territory,** *Canada (excluding Ontario),*
1997-1999 combined

Province/territory	Number of live births	Number of infant deaths (linked and unlinked)	Crude infant mortality rate (95% CI)		Infant mortality rate ≥ 500 g*** (95% CI)		Infant mortality rate ≥ 1,000 g*** (95% CI)	
Newfoundland	15,465	85	5.50	(4.39-6.79)	5.11	(4.05-6.37)	3.51	(2.64-4.58)
Prince Edward Island	4,610	31	6.72	(4.57-9.53)	5.86	(3.87-8.52)	3.71	(2.16-5.93)
Nova Scotia	29,119	128	4.40	(3.67-5.22)	3.92	(3.23-4.70)	2.93	(2.34-3.62)
New Brunswick	23,422	129	5.51	(4.60-6.54)	4.62	(3.79-5.57)	3.26	(2.57-4.08)
Quebec	229,225	1,206	5.26	(4.97-5.57)	4.38	(4.11-4.66)	3.00	(2.78-3.24)
Manitoba	43,431	320	7.37	(6.59-8.22)	5.97	(5.27-6.74)	4.17	(3.58-4.82)
Saskatchewan	38,241	289	7.56	(6.71-8.48)	6.96	(6.15-7.85)	5.23	(4.53-6.01)
Alberta	112,981	631	5.59	(5.16-6.04)	4.79	(4.40-5.21)	3.56	(3.22-3.92)
British Columbia	129,581	555	4.28	(3.94-4.65)	3.60	(3.28-3.94)	2.63	(2.36-2.93)
Yukon	1,253	7	5.59	(2.25-11.48)	5.59	(2.25-11.48)	4.80	(1.77-10.43)
Northwest Territories**	4,212	61	14.48	(11.10-18.57)	13.08	(9.87-16.99)	11.91	(8.85-15.67)
CANADA‡	**631,552**	**3,442**	**5.45**	**(5.27-5.64)**	**4.64**	**(4.47-4.81)**	**3.33**	**(3.19-3.47)**

Source: Statistics Canada, Canadian Vital Statistics System, 1997-1999 (birth-infant death linked files).
*Data for Ontario were excluded because of data quality concerns.
**Nunavut is included in the Northwest Territories in the data for 1999.
***Infant deaths per 1,000 live births with a birth weight ≥ 500 g or with a birth weight ≥ 1,000 g. Unlinked infant deaths (there were 41 infants whose death registrations could not be linked to their birth registrations) and live births/infant deaths with missing birth weight were also included, except for those with a missing birth weight and a gestational age < 22 weeks (infant mortality ≥ 500 g calculation) and those with a missing birth weight and a gestational age < 28 weeks (infant mortality ≥ 1,000 g calculation).
‡Includes 12 live births with missing information on province (birth weight ≥ 1,000 g, no infant deaths).
CI — confidence interval.

TABLE E4 | **Birth cohort-based infant mortality rates (IMR) among live births ≥ 500 g and among live births ≥ 1,000 g, by province/territory,** *Canada (excluding Ontario),* 1999*

Province/territory	Number of live births	Number of infant deaths (linked and unlinked)	Crude infant mortality rate (95% CI)		Infant mortality rate ≥ 500 g*** (95% CI)		Infant mortality rate ≥ 1,000 g*** (95% CI)	
Newfoundland	5,055	27	5.34	(3.52-7.76)	4.75	(3.05-7.06)	2.58	(1.38-4.42)
Prince Edward Island	1,515	9	5.94	(2.72-11.25)	4.63	(1.86-9.51)	2.66	(0.72-6.79)
Nova Scotia	9,575	33	3.45	(2.37-4.84)	2.72	(1.78-3.98)	1.78	(1.04-2.85)
New Brunswick	7,615	33	4.33	(2.99-6.08)	3.55	(2.34-5.16)	2.37	(1.41-3.75)
Quebec	73,596	349	4.74	(4.26-5.27)	3.86	(3.43-4.34)	2.70	(2.34-3.11)
Manitoba	14,315	117	8.17	(6.76-9.79)	6.23	(5.01-7.66)	4.57	(3.53-5.82)
Saskatchewan	12,604	94	7.46	(6.03-9.12)	6.91	(5.54-8.51)	5.26	(4.07-6.69)
Alberta	38,171	242	6.34	(5.57-7.19)	5.51	(4.79-6.30)	4.11	(3.49-4.80)
British Columbia	41,939	158	3.77	(3.20-4.40)	3.15	(2.64-3.73)	2.34	(1.90-2.86)
Yukon	383	1	2.61	(0.0-14.46)	2.61	(0.0-14.46)	2.61	(0.0-14.46)
Northwest Territories**	1,396	19	13.61	(8.21-21.17)	12.20	(7.12-19.45)	10.06	(5.51-16.83)
CANADA‡	**206,169**	**1,082**	**5.25**	**(4.94-5.57)**	**4.39**	**(4.11-4.68)**	**3.17**	**(2.93-3.42)**

Source: Statistics Canada, Canadian Vital Statistics System, 1999 (birth-infant death linked file).
*Data for Ontario were excluded because of data quality concerns.
**Nunavut is included in the Northwest Territories in the data for 1999.
***Infant deaths per 1,000 live births with a birth weight ≥ 500 g or with a birth weight ≥ 1,000 g. Unlinked infant deaths (there were seven infants whose death registrations could not be linked to their birth registrations) and live births/infant deaths with missing birth weight were also included, except for those with a missing birth weight and a gestational age < 22 weeks (infant mortality ≥ 500 g calculation) and those with a missing birth weight and a gestational age < 28 weeks (infant mortality ≥ 1,000 g calculation).
‡Includes seven live births with missing information on province (birth weight ≥ 1,000 g, no infant deaths).
CI — confidence interval.

TABLE E5 · **Birth cohort-based fetal and infant mortality rates among singleton births ≥ 500 g,** *Canada (excluding Newfoundland and Ontario),* 1985-1999

Year	Number of live births	Number of still-births	Number of early neonatal deaths	Number of late neonatal deaths	Number of post-neonatal deaths	Stillbirths per 1,000 total births	Neonatal deaths per 1,000 live births	Perinatal deaths per 1,000 total births	Infant deaths per 1,000 live births	Fetal-infant deaths per 1,000 total births
1985	230,148	1,191	792	176	627	5.1	4.2	8.6	6.9	12.0
1986	226,118	1,170	763	193	633	5.1	4.2	8.5	7.0	12.1
1987	222,275	1,114	678	171	625	5.0	3.8	8.0	6.6	11.6
1988	226,139	1,035	665	153	609	4.6	3.6	7.5	6.3	10.8
1989	234,345	1,170	682	167	581	5.0	3.6	7.9	6.1	11.0
1990	241,412	1,112	650	187	552	4.6	3.5	7.3	5.8	10.3
1991	238,530	1,117	580	150	551	4.7	3.1	7.1	5.4	10.0
1992	235,785	1,067	576	123	539	4.5	3.0	6.9	5.3	9.7
1993	228,924	1,023	522	137	474	4.4	2.9	6.7	4.9	9.4
1994	226,551	1,032	591	144	447	4.5	3.2	7.1	5.2	9.7
1995	220,820	989	509	142	408	4.5	2.9	6.8	4.8	9.2
1996	215,264	922	451	117	321	4.3	2.6	6.4	4.1	8.4
1997	204,957	929	420	114	319	4.5	2.6	6.6	4.2	8.7
1998	199,480	824	399	120	349	4.1	2.6	6.1	4.4	8.4
1999	195,765	852	358	102	326	4.3	2.3	6.2	4.0	8.3

Source: Statistics Canada, Canadian Vital Statistics System, 1985-1999 (birth-infant death linked files).
*Data for Newfoundland were excluded because data were not available nationally prior to 1991. Data for Ontario were excluded because of data quality concerns.

TABLE E6 · **Birth cohort-based fetal and infant mortality rates* among twin births ≥ 500 g,** *Canada (excluding Newfoundland and Ontario),*** 1985-1999

Year	Number of live births	Number of still-births	Number of early neonatal deaths	Number of late neonatal deaths	Number of post-neonatal deaths	Stillbirths per 1,000 total births	Neonatal deaths per 1,000 live births	Perinatal deaths per 1,000 total births	Infant deaths per 1,000 live births	Fetal-infant deaths per 1,000 total births
1985	4,423	75	120	18	42	16.9	28.6	41.2	37.1	53.3
1986	4,263	74	95	15	32	17.9	26.9	40.9	34.5	51.8
1987	4,484	91	93	13	27	17.0	24.8	37.8	31.1	47.6
1988	4,579	66	94	20	25	15.1	24.9	36.3	30.4	45.1
1989	4,677	54	109	13	24	13.8	24.3	34.3	30.1	43.5
1990	4,849	77	90	17	33	12.9	19.9	29.8	26.2	38.8
1991	4,832	57	47	10	33	13.7	18.3	28.7	24.3	37.7
1992	4,877	68	85	17	22	13.2	17.8	27.4	23.3	36.2
1993	4,749	69	76	22	25	14.7	19.1	29.9	23.8	38.2
1994	4,846	79	62	14	22	14.8	18.9	30.1	23.4	37.8
1995	4,826	68	86	12	19	13.6	17.9	28.4	22.4	35.7
1996	4,835	53	69	16	25	13.2	18.5	28.4	22.8	35.7
1997	4,809	72	69	16	18	11.7	17.4	26.1	21.7	33.1
1998	4,971	48	75	10	19	13.5	15.9	26.6	19.7	32.9
1999	4,977	82	52	13	18	12.9	15.1	25.5	18.8	31.5

Source: Statistics Canada, Canadian Vital Statistics System, 1985-1999 (birth-infant death linked files).
*Rates are three-year moving averages, two-year averages for the extreme years.
**Data for Newfoundland were excluded because data were not available nationally prior to 1991. Data for Ontario were excluded because of data quality concerns.

TABLE E7

Birth cohort-based causes of fetal death among singleton births ≥ 500 g,

Canada (excluding Newfoundland and Ontario),* 1985-1988 to 1996-1999

Cause of death (ICD-9 code)	1985-1988		1989-1992		1993-1995		1996-1999	
	Number of stillbirths	Stillbirths per 1,000 total births	Number of stillbirths	Stillbirths per 1,000 total births	Number of stillbirths	Stillbirths per 1,000 total births	Number of stillbirths	Stillbirths per 1,000 total births
Congenital anomalies (740-759)	548	0.60	577	0.60	368	0.54	451	0.55
Short gestation and low birth weight (765)	110	0.12	81	0.08	56	0.08	82	0.10
Maternal complications of pregnancy (761)	195	0.21	194	0.20	123	0.18	171	0.21
Complications of placenta/ cord/membranes (762)	1,757	1.93	1,701	1.78	1,118	1.65	1,128	1.38
Infections — perinatal period (771)	13	0.01	13	0.01	15	0.02	26	0.03
Intrauterine hypoxia and birth asphyxia (768)	330	0.36	262	0.27	223	0.33	214	0.26
Unspecified (779.9)	962	1.06	1,000	1.05	762	1.12	803	0.98
Other	595	0.65	638	0.67	379	0.56	652	0.80
TOTAL	4,510	4.96	4,466	4.68	3,044	4.48	3,527	4.31
Number of total births	909,190		954,538		679,339		818,993	

Source: Statistics Canada, Canadian Vital Statistics System, 1985-1999 (birth-infant death linked files).

*Data for Newfoundland were excluded because data were not available prior to 1991. Data for Ontario were excluded because of data quality concerns.

TABLE E8

Birth cohort-based causes of fetal death among twin births ≥ 500 g,

Canada (excluding Newfoundland and Ontario),* 1985-1988 to 1996-1999

Cause of death (ICD-9 code)	1985-1988		1989-1992		1993-1995		1996-1999	
	Number of stillbirths	Stillbirths per 1,000 total births	Number of stillbirths	Stillbirths per 1,000 total births	Number of stillbirths	Stillbirths per 1,000 total births	Number of stillbirths	Stillbirths per 1,000 total births
Congenital anomalies (740-759)	15	0.83	14	0.72	15	1.02	24	1.21
Short gestation and low birth weight (765)	5	0.28	5	0.26	2	0.14	8	0.40
Maternal complications of pregnancy (761)	62	3.43	81	4.16	61	4.17	66	3.33
Complications of placenta/ cord/membranes (762)	116	6.42	102	5.23	85	5.81	94	4.74
Infections — perinatal period (771)	1	0.06	0	0.00	3	0.20	0	0.00
Intrauterine hypoxia and birth asphyxia (768)	28	1.55	7	0.36	6	0.41	15	0.76
Unspecified (779.9)	53	2.94	34	1.74	27	1.84	28	1.41
Other	26	1.44	13	0.67	17	1.16	21	1.06
TOTAL	306	16.95	256	13.13	216	14.76	256	12.90
Number of total births	18,055		19,491		14,637		19,847	

Source: Statistics Canada, Canadian Vital Statistics System, 1985-1999 (birth-infant death linked files).

*Data for Newfoundland were excluded because data were not available prior to 1991. Data for Ontario were excluded because of data quality concerns.

TABLE E9 **Birth cohort-based causes of infant death among singleton live births ≥ 500 g,**
Canada (excluding Newfoundland and Ontario),* 1985-1988 to 1996-1999

Cause of death (ICD-9 code)	1985-1988		1989-1992		1993-1995		1996-1999	
	Number of infant deaths	Deaths per 1,000 live births	Number of infant deaths	Deaths per 1,000 live births	Number of infant deaths	Deaths per 1,000 live births	Number of infant deaths	Deaths per 1,000 live births
Congenital anomalies (740-759)	2,088	2.31	1,869	1.97	1,157	1.71	1,080	1.32
Short gestation and low birth weight (765)	213	0.24	215	0.23	138	0.20	144	0.18
Sudden infant death syndrome (798.0)	900	0.99	863	0.91	462	0.68	380	0.47
Maternal complications of pregnancy (761)	84	0.09	95	0.10	74	0.11	68	0.08
Respiratory distress syndrome (769)	538	0.59	398	0.42	188	0.28	151	0.19
Complications of placenta/cord/membranes (762)	195	0.22	183	0.19	102	0.15	146	0.18
Infections — perinatal period (771)	82	0.09	106	0.11	56	0.08	59	0.07
Injury and poisoning (E800-E999)	199	0.22	167	0.18	114	0.17	97	0.12
Intrauterine hypoxia and birth asphyxia (768)	164	0.18	147	0.15	132	0.20	139	0.17
Pneumonia (480.0)	25	0.03	18	0.02	13	0.02	11	0.01
Neonatal hemorrhage (772)	44	0.05	32	0.03	30	0.04	30	0.04
Birth trauma (767)	66	0.07	70	0.07	42	0.06	72	0.09
Other	1,487	1.64	1,175	1.24	866	1.28	1,019	1.25
TOTAL	6,085	6.73	5,338	5.62	3,374	4.99	3,396	4.16
Number of live births	904,680		950,072		676,295		815,466	

Source: Statistics Canada, Canadian Vital Statistics System, 1985-1999 (birth-infant death linked files).

*Data for Newfoundland were excluded because data were not available nationally prior to 1991. Data for Ontario were excluded because of data quality concerns.

TABLE E10 **Birth cohort-based causes of infant death among twin live births ≥ 500 g,**
Canada (excluding Newfoundland and Ontario), 1985-1988 to 1996-1999*

Cause of death (ICD-9 code)	1985-1988		1989-1992		1993-1995		1996-1999	
	Number of infant deaths	Deaths per 1,000 live births	Number of infant deaths	Deaths per 1,000 live births	Number of infant deaths	Deaths per 1,000 live births	Number of infant deaths	Deaths per 1,000 live births
Congenital anomalies (740-759)	105	5.92	97	5.04	62	4.30	89	4.54
Short gestation and low birth weight (765)	44	2.48	33	1.72	19	1.32	22	1.12
Sudden infant death syndrome (798.0)	31	1.75	39	2.03	18	1.25	15	0.77
Maternal complications of pregnancy (761)	76	4.28	76	3.95	50	3.47	47	2.40
Respiratory distress syndrome (769)	128	7.21	95	4.94	58	4.02	49	2.50
Complications of placenta/ cord/membranes (762)	23	1.30	18	0.94	28	1.94	25	1.28
Infections — perinatal period (771)	9	0.51	9	0.47	8	0.55	7	0.36
Injury and poisoning (E800-E999)	5	0.28	7	0.36	4	0.28	7	0.36
Intrauterine hypoxia and birth asphyxia (768)	17	0.96	12	0.62	8	0.55	7	0.36
Pneumonia (480.0)	2	0.11	0	0.00	0	0.00	2	0.10
Neonatal hemorrhage (772)	6	0.34	5	0.26	4	0.28	13	0.66
Birth trauma (767)	10	0.56	13	0.68	5	0.35	13	0.66
Other	138	7.78	96	4.99	74	5.13	104	5.31
TOTAL	594	33.47	500	25.99	338	23.44	400	20.42
Number of live births	17,749		19,235		14,421		19,592	

Source: Statistics Canada, Canadian Vital Statistics System, 1985-1999 (birth-infant death linked files).

*Data for Newfoundland were excluded because data were not available nationally prior to 1991. Data for Ontario were excluded because of data quality concerns.

TABLE E11 **Birth cohort-based declines in stillbirth, neonatal mortality and perinatal mortality rates by gestational age among singleton births ≥ 500 g,**
Canada (excluding Newfoundland and Ontario), 1985-1988 vs. 1996-1999*

Death categories by post-conceptual age	1985-1988			1996-1999			Relative risk (95% CI) 1985-1988 vs. 1996-1999
	Number of deaths	Fetuses at risk	Deaths per 1,000 births**	Number of deaths	Fetuses at risk	Deaths per 1,000 births**	
Stillbirths ≥ 22 weeks	4,265	906,286	4.71	3,233	816,584	3.96	0.84 (0.80-0.88)
Stillbirths ≥ 34 weeks	2,366	892,330	2.65	1,679	803,779	2.09	0.79 (0.74-0.83)
Stillbirths ≥ 40 weeks	757	512,507	1.48	435	512,507	1.07	0.73 (0.64-0.81)
Neonatal mortality ≥ 22 weeks	3,485	906,286	3.85	2,032	816,584	2.49	0.65 0.61-0.68)
Neonatal mortality ≥ 34 weeks	1,805	892,330	2.02	1,022	803,779	1.27	0.63 (0.58-0.68)
Neonatal mortality ≥ 40 weeks	710	512,507	1.39	343	512,507	0.85	0.61 (0.54-0.69)
Perinatal mortality ≥ 22 weeks	7,062	906,286	7.79	4,815	816,584	5.90	0.76 (0.73-0.78)
Perinatal mortality ≥ 34 weeks	3,691	892,330	4.14	2,386	803,779	2.97	0.72 (0.68-0.76)
Perinatal mortality ≥ 40 weeks	1,263	512,507	2.46	678	512,507	1.67	0.68 (0.62-0.74)

Source: Statistics Canada, Canadian Vital Statistics System, 1985-1999 (birth-infant death linked files).
*Data for Newfoundland were excluded because data were not available nationally prior to 1991. Data for Ontario were excluded because of data quality concerns.
**Stillbirth and perinatal mortality rates are expressed per 1,000 total births, while neonatal mortality rates are expressed per 1,000 live births. Perinatal mortality includes stillbirth plus early neonatal death.

TABLE E12 **Birth cohort-based declines in stillbirth, neonatal mortality and perinatal mortality rates by gestational age among twin births ≥ 500 g,**
Canada (excluding Newfoundland and Ontario), 1985-1988 vs. 1996-1999*

Death categories by post-conceptual age	1985-1988			1996-1999			Relative risk (95% CI) 1985-1988 vs. 1996-1999
	Number of deaths	Fetuses at risk	Deaths per 1,000 births**	Number of deaths	Fetuses at risk	Deaths per 1,000 births**	
Stillbirths ≥ 22 weeks	294	17,980	16.35	247	19,776	12.49	0.76 (0.65-0.90)
Stillbirths ≥ 32 weeks	165	16,382	10.07	129	17,928	7.20	0.71 (0.57-0.90)
Stillbirths ≥ 36 weeks	105	12,388	8.48	64	12,853	4.98	0.59 (0.43-0.80)
Neonatal mortality ≥ 22 weeks	448	17,980	24.92	315	19,776	15.93	0.64 (0.55-0.74)
Neonatal mortality ≥ 32 weeks	91	16,382	5.55	63	17,928	3.51	0.63 (0.46-0.87)
Neonatal mortality ≥ 36 weeks	50	12,388	4.04	25	12,853	1.95	0.48 (0.30-0.78)
Perinatal mortality ≥ 22 weeks	676	17,980	37.60	507	19,776	25.64	0.68 (0.61-0.76)
Perinatal mortality ≥ 32 weeks	234	16,382	14.28	176	17,928	9.82	0.69 (0.57-0.83)
Perinatal mortality ≥ 36 weeks	142	12,388	11.46	81	12,853	6.30	0.55 (0.42-0.72)

Source: Statistics Canada, Canadian Vital Statistics System, 1985-1999 (birth-infant death linked files).
*Data for Newfoundland were excluded because data were not available nationally prior to 1991. Data for Ontario were excluded because of data quality concerns.
**Stillbirth and perinatal mortality rates are expressed per 1,000 total births, while neonatal mortality rates are expressed per 1,000 live births. Perinatal mortality includes stillbirth plus early neonatal death.

Appendix F

Data Tables for the Figures Presented in the Report

Appendix F

Data Tables

TABLE F1.1 **Rate of maternal smoking, by maternal age,**
Canada (excluding the territories),* 1994-1995, 1996-1997 and 1998-1999

Maternal age (years)	Percentage of children < 2 years of age whose mother reported smoking during pregnancy		
	1994-1995	1996-1997	1998-1999
< 20**	44.1	38.2	53.2
20-24	34.7	32.0	31.7
25-29	22.8	22.7	20.3
30-34	20.3	14.1	14.6
≥ 35	18.3	15.2	11.8
All ages	23.5	19.9	19.4

Source: Statistics Canada. NLSCY, 1994-1995, 1996-1997, 1998-1999 (custom tabulations).
*Data from the territories were not available from the NLSCY.
**This estimate has low precision since it is based on a small number of subjects.

TABLE F1.2 **Rate of maternal smoking, by region/province,**
Canada (excluding the territories),* 1994-1995, 1996-1997 and 1998-1999

Region/province	Percentage of children < 2 years of age whose mother reported smoking during pregnancy		
	1994-1995	1996-1997	1998-1999
Atlantic provinces	26.1	26.9	24.8
Quebec	27.9	23.1	24.2
Ontario	21.3	17.0	15.8
Prairie provinces	23.8	20.7	23.5
British Columbia	19.2	17.9	13.0
All provinces	23.5	19.9	19.4

Source: Statistics Canada. NLSCY, 1994-1995, 1996-1997, 1998-1999 (custom tabulations).
*Data from the territories were not available from the NLSCY.

TABLE F1.3 **Rate of maternal alcohol consumption, by maternal age,**
Canada (excluding the territories), 1994-1995, 1996-1997 and 1998-1999*

Maternal age (years)	Percentage of children < 2 years of age whose mother reported drinking any alcohol during pregnancy		
	1994-1995	1996-1997	1998-1999
< 25**	14.3	10.4	14.1
25-29	14.1	14.2	11.5
30-34	19.0	14.6	13.6
≥ 35	24.7	24.5	21.6
All ages	17.4	15.6	14.6

Source: Statistics Canada. NLSCY, 1994-1995, 1996-1997, 1998-1999 (custom tabulations).
*Data from the territories were not available from the NLSCY.
**Further categorization of age was not possible because of small numbers.

TABLE F1.4 **Rate of maternal alcohol consumption, by region/province,**
Canada (excluding the territories), 1994-1995, 1996-1997 and 1998-1999*

Region/province	Percentage of children < 2 years of age whose mother reported drinking any alcohol during pregnancy		
	1994-1995	1996-1997	1998-1999
Atlantic provinces**	8.2	7.7	7.7
Quebec	26.3	23.7	25.1
Ontario	14.5	12.8	13.6
Prairie provinces	16.9	16.7	10.2
British Columbia**	15.9	12.7	9.2
All provinces	17.4	15.6	14.6

Source: Statistics Canada. NLSCY, 1994-1995, 1996-1997, 1998-1999 (custom tabulations).
*Data from the territories were not available from the NLSCY.
**This estimate has low precision since it is based on a small number of subjects.

TABLE F1.5 **Rate and duration of breastfeeding, by maternal age,**
Canada (excluding the territories), 1994-1995, 1996-1997 and 1998-1999*

Maternal age (years)	Percentage of children < 2 years of age whose mother reported breastfeeding regardless of duration			Percentage of breastfed children < 2 years of age whose mother reported breastfeeding three months or more**		
	1994-1995	1996-1997	1998-1999	1994-1995	1996-1997	1998-1999
< 20	66.3	72.4	73.4	39.6***	46.8***	49.1***
20-24	67.9	74.2	75.3			
25-29	73.4	74.6	81.4	57.7	58.5	59.5
30-34	77.7	81.7	83.5	64.4	69.4	67.1
≥ 35	80.9	82.8	86.5	69.0	71.6	74.9
All ages	75.1	78.5	81.9	58.7	63.0	63.0

Source: Statistics Canada. NLSCY, 1994-1995, 1996-1997, 1998-1999 (custom tabulations).
*Data from the territories were not available from the NLSCY.
**Estimates based on children who were breastfed, but were no longer being breastfed at the time of the survey.
***Further categorization of age was not possible because of small numbers.

TABLE F1.6 **Rate and duration of breastfeeding, by region/province,**
Canada (excluding the territories), 1994-1995, 1996-1997 and 1998-1999*

Region/ province	Percentage of children < 2 years of age whose mother reported breastfeeding regardless of duration			Percentage of breastfed children < 2 years of age whose mother reported breastfeeding three months or more**		
	1994-1995	1996-1997	1998-1999	1994-1995	1996-1997	1998-1999
Atlantic provinces	60.8	68.0	64.5	56.6	56.1	61.2
Quebec	56.7	60.7	71.0	54.4	52.1	53.3
Ontario	80.5	82.3	84.1	58.4	67.2	64.6
Prairie provinces	86.2	88.9	88.2	63.1	64.1	65.9
British Columbia	87.9	89.5	95.2	60.3	65.4	69.2
All provinces	75.1	78.5	81.9	58.7	63.0	63.0

Source: Statistics Canada. NLSCY, 1994-1995, 1996-1997, 1998-1999 (custom tabulations).
*Data from the territories were not available from the NLSCY.
**Estimates based on children who were breastfed, but were no longer being breastfed at the time of the survey.

TABLE F1.7 **Rate of low maternal education and other categories of maternal education,** *Canada (excluding the territories),* 1994-1995, 1996-1997 and 1998-1999*

Highest level of maternal education	Percentage of children < 2 years of age whose mother had a particular educational level		
	1994-1995	1996-1997	1998-1999
Less than high school	17.2	14.9	13.4
High school graduate (no postsecondary education)	16.9	17.2	16.8
Some postsecondary (no college or university degree)	23.0	24.0	23.3
University/college graduate	42.9	43.9	46.5

Source: Statistics Canada. NLSCY, 1994-1995, 1996-1997, 1998-1999 (custom tabulations).
*Data from the territories were not available from the NLSCY.

TABLE F1.8 **Rate of maternal smoking, by maternal education,** *Canada (excluding the territories),* 1994-1995, 1996-1997 and 1998-1999*

Highest level of maternal education	Percentage of children < 2 years of age whose mother reported smoking during pregnancy		
	1994-1995	1996-1997	1998-1999
Less than high school	35.0	31.4	35.9
High school graduate (no postsecondary education)	21.5	19.2	18.1
Some postsecondary (no college or university degree)	21.0	19.1	19.5
University/college graduate	13.6	10.6	9.0

Source: Statistics Canada. NLSCY, 1994-1995, 1996-1997, 1998-1999 (custom tabulations).
*Data from the territories were not available from the NLSCY.

TABLE F1.9 **Rate of maternal alcohol consumption, by maternal education,** *Canada (excluding the territories),* 1994-1995, 1996-1997 and 1998-1999*

Highest level of maternal education	Percentage of children < 2 years of age whose mother reported drinking any alcohol during pregnancy		
	1994-1995	1996-1997	1998-1999
Less than high school**	11.1	11.2	9.9
High school graduate** (no postsecondary education)	12.6	12.9	12.8
Some postsecondary (no college or university degree)	21.0	15.8	11.4
University/college graduate	20.5	17.9	17.7

Source: Statistics Canada. NLSCY, 1994-1995, 1996-1997, 1998-1999 (custom tabulations).
*Data from the territories were not available from the NLSCY.
**These estimates have low precision since they are based on a small number of subjects.

TABLE F1.10 **Rate of breastfeeding, by maternal education,** *Canada (excluding the territories),* 1994-1995, 1996-1997 and 1998-1999*

Highest level of maternal education	Percentage of children < 2 years of age whose mother reported breastfeeding regardless of duration			Percentage of breastfed children < 2 years of age whose mother reported breastfeeding three months or more**		
	1994-1995	1996-1997	1998-1999	1994-1995	1996-1997	1998-1999
Less than high school	63.0	69.8	70.5	56.2	46.9	49.9
High school graduate (no postsecondary education)	71.8	75.4	81.0	57.7	62.5	63.8
Some postsecondary (no college or university degree)	78.6	79.8	82.7	59.2	65.6	60.0
University/college graduate	81.8	85.7	89.0	65.9	70.3	71.1

Source: Statistics Canada. NLSCY, 1994-1995, 1996-1997, 1998-1999 (custom tabulations).
*Data from the territories were not available from the NLSCY.
**Estimates based on children who were breastfed, but were no longer being breastfed at the time of the survey.

TABLE F1.11 **Number of live births by maternal age,** *Canada (excluding Ontario),* 1991-2000*

Year	≤ 14 years	15-17 years	18-19 years	20-24 years	25-29 years	30-34 years	35-39 years	40-44 years	≥ 45 years	Unknown age	Total
1991	222	5,489	11,119	54,353	94,139	64,223	18,968	2,314	75	148	251,050
1992	212	5,574	10,799	52,032	90,527	66,127	20,017	2,571	51	133	248,043
1993	205	5,303	10,480	50,430	84,548	65,743	20,921	2,733	73	106	240,542
1994	197	5,218	10,796	49,347	80,865	66,590	22,017	2,930	66	16	238,042
1995	182	5,124	10,535	48,008	75,803	66,240	22,634	3,088	108	25	231,747
1996	176	4,786	9,844	46,188	73,433	64,339	23,896	3,383	122	21	226,188
1997	170	4,422	9,212	43,762	69,586	60,756	24,047	3,517	114	4	215,590
1998	153	4,343	9,160	42,954	67,078	58,149	24,118	3,609	123	102	209,789
1999	142	4,079	8,890	42,016	65,466	56,630	24,915	3,867	140	12	206,157
2000	111	3,663	8,369	40,621	63,710	54,839	24,855	4,138	129	19	200,454

Source: Statistics Canada. Canadian Vital Statistics System, 1991-2000 (unlinked live birth files).
*Data for Ontario were excluded because of data quality concerns; they are presented in *Appendix G.*

TABLE F1.12 **Number of females, by age,** *Canada (excluding Ontario),* 1991-2000*

Year	14 years	15-17 years	18-19 years	20-24 years	25-29 years	30-34 years	35-39 years	40-44 years	45-49 years
1991	118,869	355,875	237,700	631,046	759,864	805,003	741,016	663,490	523,270
1992	118,495	360,031	235,838	625,540	735,700	807,453	763,175	672,887	558,716
1993	121,465	361,277	239,394	621,533	707,553	811,429	783,218	688,364	589,248
1994	124,859	365,424	243,858	617,256	681,993	809,724	797,454	708,257	618,653
1995	125,959	371,479	246,287	614,983	662,997	801,405	808,900	730,788	646,077
1996	124,778	379,026	248,729	617,708	655,419	781,964	820,079	751,105	668,245
1997	124,473	381,261	251,010	624,198	650,020	758,665	824,275	774,707	677,651
1998	125,026	379,773	255,873	629,287	644,023	728,402	826,343	793,348	691,117
1999	124,264	378,100	258,909	638,399	639,650	701,295	823,187	805,629	709,751
2000	123,627	377,100	258,291	645,264	637,336	681,336	812,630	814,975	730,914

Source: Statistics Canada. Annual Demographics Statistics, 2001. Demography Division, Catalogue No. 91-213-XPB, Annual, Ottawa, 2002.
*Data for Ontario were excluded because of data quality concerns; they are presented in *Appendix G.*

TABLE F1.13 **Proportion (%)* of live births, by maternal age,** *Canada (excluding Ontario),** 1991-2000*

Year	≤ 14 years	15-17 years	18-19 years	20-24 years	25-29 years	30-34 years	35-39 years	40-44 years	≥ 45 years
1991	0.09	2.19	4.43	21.66	37.52	25.60	7.56	0.92	0.03
1992	0.08	2.25	4.36	20.99	36.52	26.67	8.07	1.04	0.02
1993	0.09	2.21	4.36	20.97	35.16	27.34	8.70	1.14	0.03
1994	0.08	2.19	4.54	20.73	33.97	27.98	9.25	1.23	0.03
1995	0.08	2.20	4.55	20.72	32.71	28.59	9.77	1.33	0.05
1996	0.08	2.12	4.35	20.41	32.47	28.45	10.57	1.50	0.05
1997	0.08	2.05	4.27	20.31	32.28	28.18	11.15	1.63	0.05
1998	0.07	2.07	4.37	20.48	32.00	27.73	11.50	1.72	0.06
1999	0.06	1.98	4.31	20.38	31.76	27.47	12.09	1.88	0.07
2000	0.05	1.83	4.18	20.27	31.79	27.36	12.40	2.06	0.06

Source: Statistics Canada. Canadian Vital Statistics System, 1991-2000 (unlinked live birth files).
*Excludes live births with unknown maternal age.
**Data for Ontario were excluded because of data quality concerns; they are presented in *Appendix G.*

TABLE F1.14 **Maternal age-specific live birth rate per 1,000 females,** *Canada (excluding Ontario),* 1991-2000*

Year	≤ 14 years**	15-17 years	18-19 years	20-24 years	25-29 years	30-34 years	35-39 years	40-44 years	≥ 45 years***
1991	1.9	15.4	46.8	86.1	123.9	79.8	25.6	3.5	0.14
1992	1.8	15.5	45.8	83.2	123.0	81.9	26.2	3.8	0.09
1993	1.7	14.7	43.8	81.1	119.5	81.0	26.7	4.0	0.12
1994	1.6	14.3	44.3	79.9	118.6	82.2	27.6	4.1	0.11
1995	1.4	13.8	42.8	78.1	114.3	82.7	28.0	4.2	0.17
1996	1.4	12.6	39.6	74.8	112.0	82.3	29.1	4.5	0.18
1997	1.4	11.6	36.7	70.1	107.1	80.1	29.2	4.5	0.17
1998	1.2	11.4	35.8	68.3	104.2	79.8	29.2	4.5	0.18
1999	1.1	10.8	34.3	65.8	102.3	80.8	30.3	4.8	0.20
2000	0.9	9.7	32.4	63.0	100.0	80.5	30.6	5.1	0.18

Sources: Statistics Canada. Canadian Vital Statistics System, 1991-2000 (unlinked live birth files).
Statistics Canada. Annual Demographics Statistics, 2001. Demography Division, Catalogue No. 91-213-XPB, Annual, Ottawa, 2002.
*Data for Ontario were excluded because of data quality concerns; they are presented in *Appendix G.*
**Rates based on female population aged 14 years.
***Rates based on female population aged 45-49 years.

Appendix F

Number of live births, by maternal age and province/territory,
Canada (excluding Ontario),* 2000

Province/territory	< 18 years**	18-19 years	20-24 years	25-29 years	30-34 years	35-39 years	≥ 40 years***	Unknown age	Total
Newfoundland	125	266	1,084	1,580	1,343	435	36	0	4,869
Prince Edward Island	44	77	335	430	376	152	27	0	1,441
Nova Scotia	196	388	1,893	2,906	2,497	1,061	173	1	9,115
New Brunswick	143	414	1,795	2,496	1,768	660	71	0	7,347
Quebec	779	2,423	14,696	24,230	19,893	8,530	1,452	2	72,005
Manitoba	503	837	3,185	4,369	3,458	1,502	235	1	14,090
Saskatchewan	531	832	3,088	3,878	2,509	1,098	189	14	12,139
Alberta	761	1,696	7,565	11,414	10,124	4,659	786	1	37,006
British Columbia	563	1,287	6,527	11,952	12,514	6,564	1,265	0	40,672
Yukon	11	22	70	92	96	72	7	0	370
Northwest Territories	39	45	160	173	155	85	16	0	673
Nunavut	79	82	223	190	106	37	10	0	727
CANADA	3,774	8,369	40,621	63,710	54,839	24,855	4,267	19	200,454

Source: Statistics Canada. Canadian Vital Statistics System, 2000 (unlinked live birth file).
*Data for Ontario were excluded because of data quality concerns; they are presented in *Appendix G*.
**Age groups ≤ 14 years and 15-17 years have been collapsed because of small numbers.
***Age groups 40-44 years and ≥ 45 years have been collapsed because of small numbers.

Number of females, by age and province/territory,
Canada (excluding Ontario),* 2000

Province/territory	14-17 years	18-19 years	20-24 years	25-29 years	30-34 years	35-39 years	40-49 years
Newfoundland	15,714	8,136	19,070	18,197	20,166	22,846	45,398
Prince Edward Island	4,114	2,010	4,722	4,542	4,559	5,729	10,637
Nova Scotia	24,765	12,588	31,059	32,029	33,818	40,671	75,902
New Brunswick	20,019	9,988	25,165	26,300	26,773	31,805	61,135
Quebec	178,253	97,221	246,897	234,128	255,638	315,148	613,843
Manitoba	32,032	15,545	38,188	38,375	38,490	45,323	85,679
Saskatchewan	31,150	14,885	35,893	32,675	31,912	39,104	73,644
Alberta	87,332	43,206	108,306	109,564	112,890	131,773	239,323
British Columbia	104,194	53,265	132,326	137,570	152,853	175,758	333,461
Yukon	977	396	884	1,090	1,260	1,570	2,796
Northwest Territories	1,125	572	1,567	1,749	1,803	1,970	2,826
Nunavut	1,052	479	1,187	1,117	1,174	933	1,245
CANADA	500,727	258,291	645,264	637,336	681,336	812,630	1,545,889

Source: Statistics Canada. Annual Demographics Statistics, 2001. Demography Division, Catalogue No. 91-213-XPB, Annual, Ottawa, 2002.
*Data for Ontario were excluded because of data quality concerns; they are presented in *Appendix G*.

Appendix F

TABLE F1.17 **Proportion (%)* of live births,** by maternal age and province/territory,**
Canada (excluding Ontario),*** 2000

Province/territory	< 18 years****	18-19 years	20-24 years	25-29 years	30-34 years	35-39 years	≥ 40 years*****
Newfoundland	2.6 (2.1-3.1)	5.5 (4.8-6.1)	22.3 (21.1-23.5)	32.4 (31.1-33.8)	27.6 (26.3-28.9)	8.9 (8.1-9.8)	0.7 (0.5-1.0)
Prince Edward Island	3.1 (2.2-4.1)	5.3 (4.2-6.6)	23.3 (21.1-25.5)	29.8 (27.5-32.3)	26.1 (23.8-28.4)	10.5 (9.0-12.3)	1.9 (1.2-2.7)
Nova Scotia	2.1 (1.9-2.5)	4.3 (3.9-4.7)	20.8 (19.9-21.6)	31.9 (30.9-32.9)	27.4 (26.5-28.3)	11.6 (11.0-12.3)	1.9 (1.6-2.2)
New Brunswick	1.9 (1.6-2.3)	5.6 (5.1-6.2)	24.4 (23.5-25.4)	34.0 (32.9-35.1)	24.1 (23.1-25.1)	9.0 (8.3-9.7)	1.0 (0.8-1.2)
Quebec	1.1 (1.0-1.2)	3.4 (3.2-3.5)	20.4 (20.1-20.7)	33.7 (33.3-34.0)	27.6 (27.3-28.0)	11.8 (11.6-12.1)	2.0 (1.9-2.1)
Manitoba	3.6 (3.3-3.9)	5.9 (5.6-6.3)	22.6 (21.9-23.3)	31.0 (30.2-31.8)	24.5 (23.8-25.3)	10.7 (10.2-11.2)	1.7 (1.5-1.9)
Saskatchewan	4.4 (4.0-4.8)	6.7 (6.4-7.3)	25.5 (24.7-26.3)	32.0 (31.2-32.8)	20.7 (20.0-21.4)	9.1 (8.6-9.6)	1.6 (1.3-1.8)
Alberta	2.1 (1.9-2.2)	4.6 (4.4-4.8)	20.4 (20.0-20.9)	30.8 (30.4-31.3)	27.4 (26.9-27.8)	12.6 (12.3-12.9)	2.1 (2.0-2.3)
British Columbia	1.4 (1.3-1.5)	3.2 (3.0-3.3)	16.0 (15.7-16.4)	29.4 (28.9-29.8)	30.8 (30.3-31.2)	16.1 (15.8-16.5)	3.1 (2.9-3.3)
Yukon	3.0 (1.5-5.3)	5.9 (3.8-8.9)	18.9 (15.1-23.3)	24.9 (20.5-29.6)	25.9 (21.6-30.7)	19.5 (15.5-23.9)	1.9 (0.8-3.9)
Northwest Territories	5.8 (4.2-7.8)	6.7 (4.9-8.8)	23.8 (20.6-27.2)	25.7 (22.4-29.2)	23.0 (19.9-26.4)	12.6 (10.2-15.4)	2.4 (1.4-3.8)
Nunavut	10.8 (8.7-13.4)	11.3 (9.1-13.8)	30.7 (27.3-34.2)	26.1 (23.0-29.5)	14.6 (12.1-17.4)	5.1 (3.6-6.9)	1.4 (0.7-2.5)
CANADA	1.9 (1.8-1.9)	4.2 (4.1-4.3)	20.3 (20.1-20.4)	31.8 (31.6-32.0)	27.3 (27.2-27.6)	12.4 (12.3-12.5)	2.1 (2.1-2.2)

Source: Statistics Canada. Canadian Vital Statistics System, 2000 (unlinked live birth file).
*Excludes live births with unknown maternal age.
**With 95% confidence intervals.
***Data for Ontario were excluded because of data quality concerns; they are presented in *Appendix G*.
****Age groups ≤ 14 years and 15-17 years have been collapsed because of small numbers.
*****Age groups 40-44 years and ≥ 45 years have been collapsed because of small numbers.

TABLE F1.18 **Maternal age-specific live birth rate,* by province/territory,** *Canada* *(excluding Ontario),** 2000*

Province/territory	< 18 years***	18-19 years	20-24 years	25-29 years	30-34 years	35-39 years	≥ 40 years****
Newfoundland	8.0 (6.6-9.5)	32.7 (28.9-36.8)	56.8 (53.6-60.2)	86.8 (82.8-91.0)	66.6 (63.2-70.1)	19.0 (17.3-20.9)	0.8 (0.6-1.1)
Prince Edward Island	10.7 (7.8-14.3)	38.3 (30.3-47.6)	70.9 (63.8-78.6)	94.7 (86.3-103.6)	82.5 (74.6-90.8)	26.5 (22.5-31.0)	2.5 (1.7-3.7)
Nova Scotia	7.9 (6.8-9.1)	30.8 (27.9-34.0)	60.9 (58.3-63.7)	90.7 (87.6-93.9)	73.8 (71.1-76.7)	26.1 (24.6-27.7)	2.3 (2.0-2.6)
New Brunswick	7.1 (6.0-8.4)	41.4 (37.6-45.5)	71.3 (68.2-74.6)	94.9 (91.4-98.5)	66.0 (63.1-69.1)	20.8 (19.2-22.4)	1.2 (0.9-1.5)
Quebec	4.4 (4.1-4.7)	24.9 (24.0-25.9)	59.5 (58.6-60.5)	103.5 (102.3-104.7)	77.8 (76.8-78.9)	27.1 (26.5-27.6)	2.4 (2.2-2.5)
Manitoba	15.7 (14.4-17.1)	53.8 (50.3-57.5)	83.4 (80.6-86.2)	113.9 (110.7-117.1)	89.8 (87.0-92.7)	33.1 (31.5-34.8)	2.7 (2.4-3.1)
Saskatchewan	17.0 (15.6-18.5)	55.9 (52.3-59.7)	86.0 (83.2-89.0)	118.7 (115.2-122.2)	78.6 (75.7-81.6)	28.1 (26.5-29.8)	2.6 (2.2-3.0)
Alberta	8.7 (8.1-9.4)	39.3 (37.4-41.1)	69.8 (68.3-71.4)	104.2 (102.4-106.0)	89.7 (88.0-91.4)	35.4 (34.4-36.4)	3.3 (3.1-3.5)
British Columbia	5.4 (5.0-5.9)	24.2 (22.9-25.5)	49.3 (48.2-50.5)	86.9 (85.4-88.4)	81.9 (80.5-83.3)	37.3 (36.5-38.2)	3.8 (3.6-4.0)
Yukon	11.3 (5.6-20.1)	55.6 (35.1-82.9)	79.2 (62.2-99.0)	84.4 (68.6-102.5)	76.2 (62.1-92.2)	45.9 (36.1-57.4)	2.5 (1.5-5.2)
Northwest Territories	34.7 (24.8-47.1)	78.7 (58.8-103.9)	102.1 (87.6-118.2)	98.9 (85.3-113.9)	86.0 (73.4-99.9)	43.1 (34.6-53.1)	5.7 (3.2-9.2)
Nunavut	75.1 (59.9-92.7)	171.2 (138.5-208.0)	187.9 (166.0-211.3)	170.1 (148.5-193.4)	90.3 (74.5-108.2)	39.7 (28.1-54.2)	8.0 (3.9-14.7)
CANADA	7.5 (7.3-7.8)	32.4 (31.7-33.1)	63.0 (62.4-63.5)	100.0 (99.2-100.7)	80.5 (79.8-81.1)	30.6 (30.2-31.0)	2.8 (2.7-2.8)

Sources: Statistics Canada. Canadian Vital Statistics System, 2000 (unlinked live birth file).
        Statistics Canada. Annual Demographics Statistics, 2001. Demography Division, Catalogue No. 91-213-XPB, Annual, Ottawa, 2002.
*With 95% confidence intervals.
**Data for Ontario were excluded because of data quality concerns; they are presented in *Appendix G.*
***Age groups ≤ 14 years and 15-17 years have been collapsed because of small numbers. Rates based on female population
        14-17 years of age.
****Age groups 40-44 years and ≥ 45 years have been collapsed because of small numbers. Rates based on female population
        40-49 years of age.

Appendix F

TABLE F2.1 **Rate of labour induction,** *Canada, 1991-1992 to 2000-2001*

Fiscal year	Number of medical inductions	Number of hospital deliveries	Medical inductions per 100 hospital deliveries	Number of surgical inductions (AROM)*	Surgical inductions per 100 hospital deliveries
1991-1992	51,312	398,878	12.9	25,271	6.3
1992-1993	51,504	391,015	13.2	25,562	6.5
1993-1994	54,624	383,235	14.3	29,328	7.7
1994-1995	59,662	381,890	15.6	30,620	8.0
1995-1996	63,061	372,580	16.9	29,910	8.0
1996-1997	63,048	358,161	17.6	27,090	7.6
1997-1998	64,473	344,797	18.7	28,076	8.1
1998-1999	63,381	337,261	18.7	25,559	7.6
1999-2000	65,973	334,476	19.7	25,354	7.6
2000-2001	63,622	323,455	19.7	24,772	7.7

Sources: Canadian Institute of Health Information. Discharge Abstract Database (DAD), 1991-1992 to 2000-2001.
    Population Health Research Unit, Dalhousie University, Nova Scotia. ASD, 1991-1992 to 2000-2001.
    Ministère de la Santé et des Services sociaux (Québec). Banque de données sur les hospitalisations du système MED-ÉCHO, 1991-1992
      to 2000-2001.
    Manitoba Health, Health Information Management. Manitoba Hospital Abstract System, 1991-1992 to 2000-2001.
*Artificial rupture of membranes before onset of labour (CCP Code: 85.01).

TABLE F2.2 **Rate of labour induction, by province/territory,** *Canada, 2000-2001*

Province/territory	Number of medical inductions	Number of hospital deliveries	Medical inductions (95% CI) per 100 hospital deliveries		Number of surgical inductions (AROM)*	Surgical inductions (95% CI) per 100 hospital deliveries	
Newfoundland	940	4,751	19.8	(18.7-20.9)	502	10.6	(9.7-11.5)
Prince Edward Island	299	1,365	21.9	(19.7-24.2)	189	13.8	(12.1-15.8)
Nova Scotia	1,702	8,523	20.0	(19.2-20.8)	780	9.2	(8.5-9.8)
New Brunswick	1,208	7,390	16.3	(15.5-17.2)	572	7.7	(7.1-8.4)
Quebec	14,671	69,352	21.2	(20.9-21.5)	6,484	9.3	(9.1-9.6)
Ontario	24,660	128,734	19.2	(18.9-19.4)	12,195	9.5	(9.3-9.6)
Manitoba	2,679	13,813	19.4	(18.7-20.1)	371	2.7	(2.4-3.0)
Saskatchewan	2,305	11,931	19.3	(18.6-20.0)	319	2.7	(2.4-3.0)
Alberta	8,590	36,561	23.5	(23.1-23.9)	2,008	5.5	(5.3-5.7)
British Columbia	6,422	39,597	16.2	(15.9-16.6)	1,345	3.4	(3.2-3.6)
Yukon	37	353	10.5	(7.5-14.2)	0	0.0	(0.0-1.0)
Northwest Territories	99	750	13.2	(10.9-15.8)	7	0.9	(0.4-1.9)
Nunavut	10	335	3.0	(1.4-5.4)	0	0.0	(0.0-1.1)
CANADA	63,622	323,455	19.7	(19.5-19.8)	24,772	7.7	(7.6-7.8)

Sources: Canadian Institute of Health Information. Discharge Abstract Database (DAD), 2000-2001.
    Population Health Research Unit, Dalhousie University, Nova Scotia. ASD, 2000-2001.
    Ministère de la Santé et des Services sociaux (Québec). Banque de données sur les hospitalisations du système MED-ÉCHO, 2000-2001.
    Manitoba Health, Health Information Management. Manitoba Hospital Abstract System, 2000-2001.
*Artificial rupture of membranes before onset of labour (CCP Code: 85.01).
CI — confidence interval.

TABLE F2.3 **Rate of total and primary cesarean delivery (CD),** *Canada, 1991-1992 to 2000-2001*

Fiscal year	Number of CD	Number of hospital deliveries	CD per 100 hospital deliveries	Number of primary CD	Number of deliveries, no previous CD	Primary CD per 100 hospital deliveries
1991-1992	72,466	398,878	18.2	44,783	361,047	12.4
1992-1993	70,043	391,015	17.9	43,588	353,064	12.3
1993-1994	68,238	383,235	17.8	43,081	346,168	12.4
1994-1995	66,974	381,890	17.5	42,664	345,147	12.4
1995-1996	65,755	372,580	17.6	42,408	335,955	12.6
1996-1997	65,131	358,161	18.2	42,218	322,825	13.1
1997-1998	63,812	344,797	18.5	41,713	310,749	13.4
1998-1999	64,026	337,261	19.0	41,884	303,371	13.8
1999-2000	65,871	334,476	19.7	43,548	301,101	14.5
2000-2001	68,455	323,455	21.2	45,353	290,476	15.6

Sources: Canadian Institute of Health Information. Discharge Abstract Database (DAD), 1991-1992 to 2000-2001.
Population Health Research Unit, Dalhousie University, Nova Scotia. ASD, 1991-1992 to 2000-2001.
Ministère de la Santé et des Services sociaux (Québec). Banque de données sur les hospitalisations du système MED-ÉCHO, 1991-1992 to 2000-2001.
Manitoba Health, Health Information Management. Manitoba Hospital Abstract System, 1991-1992 to 2000-2001.

TABLE F2.4 **Rate of repeat cesarean delivery (CD),** *Canada, 1991-1992 to 2000-2001*

Fiscal year	Number of delivering women with previous CD	Number of hospital deliveries	Percentage of delivering women with a previous CD	Number of repeat CD	Repeat CD rate (%)
1991-1992	37,831	398,878	9.5	27,683	73.2
1992-1993	37,951	391,015	9.7	26,455	69.7
1993-1994	37,067	383,235	9.7	25,157	67.9
1994-1995	36,812	381,890	9.6	24,310	66.0
1995-1996	36,071	372,580	9.7	23,347	64.7
1996-1997	35,326	358,161	9.9	22,913	64.9
1997-1998	34,048	344,797	9.9	22,099	64.9
1998-1999	33,890	337,261	10.0	22,142	65.3
1999-2000	33,375	334,476	10.0	22,323	66.9
2000-2001	32,979	323,455	10.2	23,102	70.1

Sources: Canadian Institute of Health Information. Discharge Abstract Database (DAD), 1991-1992 to 2000-2001.
Population Health Research Unit, Dalhousie University, Nova Scotia. ASD, 1991-1992 to 2000-2001.
Ministère de la Santé et des Services sociaux (Québec). Banque de données sur les hospitalisations du système MED-ÉCHO, 1991-1992 to 2000-2001.
Manitoba Health, Health Information Management. Manitoba Hospital Abstract System, 1991-1992 to 2000-2001.

TABLE F2.5 **Rate of primary cesarean delivery (CD), by maternal age,** *Canada, 1991-1992 to 2000-2001*

| Fiscal year | Maternal age (years) | | | | | | | | |
| | < 25 | | | 25-34 | | | ≥ 35 | | |
	Number of primary CD	Number of hospital deliveries, no previous CD	Primary CDs per 100 hospital deliveries*	Number of primary CD	Number of hospital deliveries, no previous CD	Primary CDs per 100 hospital deliveries*	Number of primary CD	Number of hospital deliveries, no previous CD	Primary CDs per 100 hospital deliveries*
1991-1992	12,041	99,545	12.1	27,971	229,821	12.2	4,769	31,671	15.1
1992-1993	11,399	95,957	11.9	27,312	224,019	12.2	4,877	33,088	14.7
1993-1994	10,860	93,335	11.6	26,784	217,891	12.3	5,437	34,939	15.6
1994-1995	10,553	93,378	11.3	26,538	215,012	12.3	5,573	36,757	15.2
1995-1996	10,215	89,614	11.4	26,051	207,611	12.5	6,141	38,725	15.9
1996-1997	9,604	84,220	11.4	26,024	198,374	13.1	6,590	40,236	16.4
1997-1998	9,530	80,408	11.9	25,417	189,532	13.4	6,766	40,807	16.6
1998-1999	9,464	79,634	11.9	25,206	182,182	13.8	7,214	41,551	17.4
1999-2000	9,515	77,263	12.3	26,223	180,626	14.5	7,810	43,211	18.1
2000-2001	9,822	73,431	13.4	27,103	173,651	15.6	8,427	43,389	19.4

Sources: Canadian Institute for Health Information. Discharge Abstract Database (DAD), 1991-1992 to 2000-2001.
    Population Health Research Unit, Dalhousie University, Nova Scotia. ASD, 1991-1992 to 2000-2001.
    Ministère de la Santé et des Services sociaux (Québec). Banque de données sur les hospitalisations du système MED-ÉCHO, 1991-1992
    to 2000-2001.
    Manitoba Health, Health Information Management. Manitoba Hospital Abstract System, 1991-1992 to 2000-2001.
*Excludes hospital deliveries with unknown maternal age.

TABLE F2.6 **Proportion of live births that were first births, by maternal age,*** *Canada (excluding Ontario),** 1991-2000*

| Year | Maternal age (years) | | | | | | | | |
| | < 25 | | | 25-34 | | | ≥ 35 | | |
	Number of live births that were first births***	Number of live births	First births per 100 live births	Number of live births that were first births***	Number of live births	First births per 100 live births	Number of live births that were first births***	Number of live births	First births per 100 live births
1991	44,686	71,183	62.8	57,908	158,362	36.6	4,960	21,357	23.2
1992	42,330	68,617	61.7	57,252	156,654	36.6	5,168	22,639	22.8
1993	40,914	66,418	61.6	55,250	150,291	36.8	5,632	23,727	23.7
1994	40,497	65,558	61.8	54,169	147,455	36.7	6,025	25,013	24.1
1995	39,626	63,849	62.1	52,957	142,043	37.3	6,374	25,830	24.7
1996	37,735	60,994	61.9	51,927	137,772	37.7	6,798	27,401	24.8
1997	35,582	57,566	61.8	49,582	130,342	38.0	7,054	27,678	25.5
1998	33,830	56,610	59.8	46,198	125,227	36.9	6,973	27,849	25.0
1999	32,937	55,127	59.8	45,586	122,096	37.3	7,387	28,922	25.5
2000	31,827	52,764	60.3	45,795	118,549	38.6	7,479	29,122	25.7

Source: Statistics Canada. Canadian Vital Statistics System, 1991-2000 (unlinked live birth files).
*Excludes live births with unknown maternal age.
**Data for Ontario were excluded because of data quality concerns; they are presented in *Appendix G.*
***Live births to women who have not had a previous live birth or stillbirth.

TABLE F2.7 **Rate of cesarean delivery (CD), by province/territory,** *Canada, 2000-2001*

Province/territory	Number of CDs	Number of hospital deliveries	CDs (95% CI) per 100 hospital deliveries	
Newfoundland	1,209	4,751	25.4	(24.2-26.7)
Prince Edward Island	329	1,365	24.1	(21.9-26.5)
Nova Scotia	1,998	8,523	23.4	(22.5-24.4)
New Brunswick	1,907	7,390	25.8	(24.8-26.8)
Quebec	12,864	69,352	18.5	(18.3-18.8)
Ontario	27,995	128,734	21.7	(21.5-22.0)
Manitoba	2,549	13,813	18.5	(17.8-19.1)
Saskatchewan	2,153	11,931	18.0	(17.4-18.7)
Alberta	7,642	36,561	20.9	(20.5-21.3)
British Columbia	9,613	39,597	24.3	(23.9-24.7)
Yukon	66	353	18.7	(14.8-23.2)
Northwest Territories	103	750	13.7	(11.3-16.4)
Nunavut	27	335	8.1	(5.4-11.5)
CANADA	**68,455**	**323,455**	**21.2**	**(21.0-21.3)**

Sources: Canadian Institute of Health Information. Discharge Abstract Database (DAD), 2000-2001.
   Population Health Research Unit, Dalhousie University, Nova Scotia. ASD, 2000-2001.
   Ministère de la Santé et des Services sociaux (Québec). Banque de données sur les hospitalisations du système MED-ÉCHO, 2000-2001.
   Manitoba Health, Health Information Management. Manitoba Hospital Abstract System, 2000-2001.
CI — confidence interval.

TABLE F2.8 **Rate of operative vaginal delivery,** *Canada, 1991-1992 to 2000-2001*

Fiscal year	Number of hospital vaginal deliveries	Number of operative vaginal deliveries	Operative vaginal deliveries per 100 hospital vaginal deliveries	Number of forceps deliveries	Forceps use per 100 hospital vaginal deliveries	Number of vacuum extractions	Vacuum extractions per 100 hospital vaginal deliveries
1991-1992	326,412	56,678	17.4	36,478	11.2	22,223	6.8
1992-1993	320,972	55,665	17.3	33,708	10.5	24,005	7.5
1993-1994	314,997	53,409	16.9	30,723	9.7	25,113	8.0
1994-1995	314,916	53,066	16.8	27,587	8.8	27,393	8.7
1995-1996	306,825	50,770	16.5	23,893	7.8	28,766	9.4
1996-1997	293,030	48,861	16.7	20,911	7.1	29,827	10.2
1997-1998	280,985	47,788	17.0	19,235	6.8	30,381	10.8
1998-1999	273,235	46,365	17.0	17,406	6.4	30,695	11.2
1999-2000	268,605	44,466	16.5	17,226	6.4	28,851	10.7
2000-2001	255,000	41,626	16.3	15,856	6.2	27,138	10.6

Sources: Canadian Institute for Health Information. Discharge Abstract Database (DAD), 1991-1992 to 2000-2001.
   Population Health Research Unit, Dalhousie University, Nova Scotia. ASD, 1991-1992 to 2000-2001.
   Ministère de la Santé et des Services sociaux (Québec). Banque de données sur les hospitalisations du système MED-ÉCHO, 1991-1992
      to 2000-2001.
   Manitoba Health, Health Information Management. Manitoba Hospital Abstract System, 1991-1992 to 2000-2001.

TABLE F2.9 **Rate of operative vaginal delivery, by province/territory,** *Canada, 2000-2001*

Province/territory	Number of operative vaginal deliveries	Number of hospital vaginal deliveries	Operative vaginal deliveries (95% CI) per 100 hospital vaginal deliveries	
Newfoundland	667	3,542	18.8	(17.6-20.2)
Prince Edward Island	103	1,036	9.9	(8.2-11.9)
Nova Scotia	904	6,525	13.9	(13.0-14.7)
New Brunswick	933	5,483	17.0	(16.0-18.0)
Quebec	9,001	56,488	15.9	(15.6-16.2)
Ontario	17,046	100,739	16.9	(16.7-17.2)
Manitoba	1,030	11,264	9.1	(8.6-9.7)
Saskatchewan	1,676	9,778	17.1	(16.4-17.9)
Alberta	5,338	28,919	18.5	(18.0-18.9)
British Columbia	4,835	29,984	16.1	(15.7-16.6)
Yukon	40	287	13.9	(10.2-18.5)
Northwest Territories	48	647	7.4	(5.5-9.7)
Nunavut	5	308	1.6	(0.5-3.8)
CANADA	**41,626**	**255,000**	**16.3**	**(16.2-16.5)**

Sources: Canadian Institute for Health Information. Discharge Abstract Database (DAD), 2000-2001.
   Population Health Research Unit, Dalhousie University, Nova Scotia. ASD, 2000-2001.
   Ministère de la Santé et des Services sociaux (Québec). Banque de données sur les hospitalisations du système MED-ÉCHO, 2000-2001.
   Manitoba Health, Health Information Management. Manitoba Hospital Abstract System, 2000-2001.
CI — confidence interval.

TABLE F2.10 **Rate of vaginal delivery by forceps, by province/territory,** *Canada, 2000-2001*

Province/territory	Number of forceps deliveries	Number of hospital vaginal deliveries	Forceps use (95% CI) per 100 hospital vaginal deliveries	
Newfoundland	315	3,542	8.9	(8.0-9.9)
Prince Edward Island	62	1,036	6.0	(4.6-7.6)
Nova Scotia	514	6,525	7.9	(7.2-8.6)
New Brunswick	414	5,483	7.6	(6.9-8.3)
Quebec	2,840	56,488	5.0	(4.8-5.2)
Ontario	6,921	100,739	6.9	(6.7-7.1)
Manitoba	466	11,264	4.1	(3.8-4.5)
Saskatchewan	419	9,778	4.3	(3.9-4.7)
Alberta	1,890	28,919	6.5	(6.3-6.8)
British Columbia	2,001	29,984	6.7	(6.4-7.0)
Yukon	4	287	1.4	(0.4-3.6)
Northwest Territories	8	647	1.2	(0.5-2.4)
Nunavut	2	308	0.7	(0.1-2.3)
CANADA	**15,856**	**255,000**	**6.2**	**(6.1-6.3)**

Sources: Canadian Institute for Health Information. Discharge Abstract Database (DAD), 2000-2001.
   Population Health Research Unit, Dalhousie University, Nova Scotia. ASD, 2000-2001.
   Ministère de la Santé et des Services sociaux (Québec). Banque de données sur les hospitalisations du système MED-ÉCHO, 2000-2001.
   Manitoba Health, Health Information Management. Manitoba Hospital Abstract System, 2000-2001.
CI — confidence interval.

TABLE F2.11 **Rate of vaginal delivery by vacuum extraction, by province/territory,** *Canada, 2000-2001*

Province/territory	Number of vacuum extractions	Number of hospital vaginal deliveries	Vacuum extractions (95% CI) per 100 hospital vaginal deliveries	
Newfoundland	358	3,542	10.1	(9.1-11.2)
Prince Edward Island	50	1,036	4.8	(3.6-6.3)
Nova Scotia	390	6,525	6.0	(5.4-6.6)
New Brunswick	551	5,483	10.1	(9.3-10.9)
Quebec	6,465	56,488	11.4	(11.2-11.7)
Ontario	10,662	100,739	10.6	(10.4-10.8)
Manitoba	564	11,264	5.0	(4.6-5.4)
Saskatchewan	1,348	9,778	13.8	(13.2-14.5)
Alberta	3,685	28,919	12.7	(12.4-13.1)
British Columbia	2,985	29,984	10.0	(9.7-10.4)
Yukon	36	287	12.5	(9.0-17.1)
Northwest Territories	41	647	6.3	(4.6-8.5)
Nunavut	3	308	1.0	(0.2-2.9)
CANADA	**27,138**	**255,000**	**10.6**	**(10.5-10.8)**

Sources: Canadian Institute for Health Information. Discharge Abstract Database (DAD), 2000-2001.
Population Health Research Unit, Dalhousie University, Nova Scotia. ASD, 2000-2001.
Ministère de la Santé et des Services sociaux (Québec). Banque de données sur les hospitalisations du système MED-ÉCHO, 2000-2001.
Manitoba Health, Health Information Management. Manitoba Hospital Abstract System, 2000-2001.
CI — confidence interval.

TABLE F2.12 **Rate of perineal laceration,** *Canada, 1991-1992 to 2000-2001*

Fiscal year	Number of first- and second-degree lacerations	Number of third-degree lacerations	Number of fourth-degree lacerations	Number of hospital vaginal deliveries	First- and second-degree lacerations per 100 hospital vaginal deliveries	Third-degree lacerations per 100 hospital vaginal deliveries	Fourth-degree lacerations per 100 hospital vaginal deliveries
1991-1992	107,851	12,427	4,623	326,412	33.0	3.8	1.4
1992-1993	118,431	12,088	4,261	320,972	36.9	3.8	1.3
1993-1994	126,785	11,148	3,830	314,997	40.2	3.5	1.2
1994-1995	134,258	11,146	3,506	314,916	42.6	3.5	1.1
1995-1996	137,694	10,420	3,111	306,825	44.9	3.4	1.0
1996-1997	135,326	10,356	2,952	293,030	46.2	3.5	1.0
1997-1998	131,470	9,926	2,772	280,985	46.8	3.5	1.0
1998-1999	128,634	9,753	2,731	273,235	47.1	3.6	1.0
1999-2000	127,776	9,547	2,713	268,605	47.6	3.5	1.0
2000-2001	126,722	9,586	2,509	255,000	49.7	3.7	1.0

Sources: Canadian Institute of Health Information. Discharge Abstract Database (DAD), 1991-1992 to 2000-2001.
Population Health Research Unit, Dalhousie University, Nova Scotia. ASD, 1991-1992 to 2000-2001.
Ministère de la Santé et des Services sociaux (Québec). Banque de données sur les hospitalisations du système MED-ÉCHO, 1991-1992 to 2000-2001.
Manitoba Health, Health Information Management. Manitoba Hospital Abstract System, 1991-1992 to 2000-2001.

Appendix F

Rate of episiotomy, *Canada, 1991-1992 to 2000-2001*

Fiscal year	Number of episiotomies	Number of hospital vaginal deliveries	Episiotomies per 100 hospital vaginal deliveries
1991-1992	160,363	326,412	49.1
1992-1993	142,161	320,972	44.3
1993-1994	123,692	314,997	39.3
1994-1995	108,868	314,916	34.6
1995-1996	94,786	306,825	30.9
1996-1997	84,529	293,030	28.8
1997-1998	76,356	280,985	27.2
1998-1999	71,950	273,235	26.3
1999-2000	67,611	268,605	25.2
2000-2001	60,829	255,000	23.8

Sources: Canadian Institute of Health Information. Discharge Abstract Database (DAD), 1991-1992 to 2000-2001.
　　　　Population Health Research Unit, Dalhousie University, Nova Scotia. ASD, 1991-1992 to 2000-2001.
　　　　Ministère de la Santé et des Services sociaux (Québec). Banque de données sur les hospitalisations du système MED-ÉCHO, 1991-1992
　　　　　to 2000-2001.
　　　　Manitoba Health, Health Information Management. Manitoba Hospital Abstract System, 1991-1992 to 2000-2001.

Rate of episiotomy, by province/territory, *Canada, 2000-2001*

Province/territory	Number of episiotomies	Number of hospital vaginal deliveries	Episiotomies (95% CI) per 100 hospital vaginal deliveries	
Newfoundland	892	3,542	25.2	(23.8-26.7)
Prince Edward Island	257	1,036	24.8	(22.2-27.5)
Nova Scotia	1,451	6,525	22.2	(21.2-23.3)
New Brunswick	1,477	5,483	26.9	(25.8-28.1)
Quebec	17,013	56,488	30.1	(29.7-30.5)
Ontario	24,523	100,739	24.3	(24.1-24.6)
Manitoba	1,629	11,264	14.5	(13.8-15.1)
Saskatchewan	1,913	9,778	19.6	(18.8-20.4)
Alberta	5,911	28,919	20.4	(20.0-20.9)
British Columbia	5,699	29,984	19.0	(18.6-19.5)
Yukon	15	287	5.2	(3.0-8.5)
Northwest Territories	40	647	6.2	(4.5-8.4)
Nunavut	9	308	2.9	(1.4-5.6)
CANADA	60,829	255,000	23.8	(23.7-24.0)

Sources: Canadian Institute for Health Information. Discharge Abstract Database (DAD), 2000-2001.
　　　　Population Health Research Unit, Dalhousie University, Nova Scotia. ASD, 2000-2001.
　　　　Ministère de la Santé et des Services sociaux (Québec). Banque de données sur les hospitalisations du système MED-ÉCHO, 2000-2001.
　　　　Manitoba Health, Health Information Management. Manitoba Hospital Abstract System, 2000-2001.
CI — confidence interval.

Appendix F

TABLE F2.15 **Rate of short maternal length of stay (LOS) in hospital for childbirth,** *Canada, 1991-1992 to 2000-2001*

Fiscal year	Vaginal delivery			Cesarean delivery		
	Number of women with LOS < 2 days	Number of hospital deliveries	Women with LOS < 2 days per 100 hospital vaginal deliveries	Number of women with LOS < 4 days	Number of hospital deliveries	Women with LOS < 4 days per 100 hospital cesarean deliveries
1991-1992	12,159	326,412	3.7	1,970	72,466	2.7
1992-1993	15,501	320,972	4.8	3,041	70,043	4.3
1993-1994	22,159	314,997	7.0	5,181	68,238	7.6
1994-1995	39,953	314,916	12.7	9,178	66,974	13.7
1995-1996	51,340	306,825	16.7	12,301	65,755	18.7
1996-1997	52,286	293,030	17.8	14,156	65,131	21.7
1997-1998	55,777	280,985	19.9	16,899	63,812	26.5
1998-1999	58,796	273,235	21.5	19,377	64,026	30.3
1999-2000	55,027	268,605	20.5	21,494	65,871	32.6
2000-2001	50,454	255,000	19.8	24,410	68,455	35.7

Sources: Canadian Institute for Health Information. Discharge Abstract Database, (DAD) 1991-1992 to 2000-2001.
Population Health Research Unit, Dalhousie University, Nova Scotia. ASD, 1991-1992 to 2000-2001.
Ministère de la Santé et des Services sociaux (Québec). Banque de données sur les hospitalisations du système MED-ÉCHO, 1991-1992 to 2000-2001.
Manitoba Health, Health Information Management. Manitoba Hospital Abstract System, 1991-1992 to 2000-2001.

TABLE F2.16 **Rate of short maternal length of stay (LOS) in hospital for childbirth (vaginal delivery), by province/territory,** *Canada, 2000-2001*

Province/territory	Number of women with LOS < 2 days	Number of hospital vaginal deliveries	Women with LOS < 2 days (95% CI) per 100 hospital vaginal deliveries	
Newfoundland	226	3,542	6.4	(5.6-7.2)
Prince Edward Island	23	1,036	2.2	(1.4-3.3)
Nova Scotia	815	6,525	12.5	(11.7-13.3)
New Brunswick	303	5,483	5.5	(4.9-6.2)
Quebec	2,490	56,488	4.4	(4.2-4.6)
Ontario	25,263	100,739	25.1	(24.8-25.3)
Manitoba	1,468	11,264	13.0	(12.4-13.7)
Saskatchewan	1,109	9,778	11.3	(10.7-12.0)
Alberta	10,536	28,919	36.4	(35.9-37.0)
British Columbia	7,927	29,984	26.4	(25.9-26.9)
Yukon	32	287	11.1	(7.8-15.4)
Northwest Territories	84	647	13.0	(10.5-15.8)
Nunavut	178	308	57.8	(52.1-63.4)
CANADA	50,454	255,000	19.8	(19.6-19.9)

Sources: Canadian Institute of Health Information. Discharge Abstract Database (DAD), 2000-2001.
Population Health Research Unit, Dalhousie University, Nova Scotia. ASD, 2000-2001.
Ministère de la Santé et des Services sociaux (Québec). Banque de données sur les hospitalisations du système MED-ÉCHO, 2000-2001.
Manitoba Health, Health Information Management. Manitoba Hospital Abstract System, 2000-2001.
CI — confidence interval.

TABLE F2.17 **Rate of short maternal length of stay (LOS) in hospital for childbirth (cesarean delivery), by province/territory,** *Canada, 2000-2001*

Province/territory	Number of women with LOS < 4 days	Number of hospital cesarean deliveries	Women with LOS < 4 days (95% CI) per 100 hospital cesarean deliveries	
Newfoundland	305	1,209	25.2	(22.8-27.8)
Prince Edward Island	7	329	2.1	(0.9-4.3)
Nova Scotia	663	1,998	33.2	(31.1-35.3)
New Brunswick	633	1,907	33.2	(31.1-35.4)
Quebec	1,982	12,864	15.4	(14.8-16.0)
Ontario	11,344	27,995	40.5	(40.0-41.1)
Manitoba	846	2,549	33.2	(31.4-35.1)
Saskatchewan	618	2,153	28.7	(26.8-30.7)
Alberta	3,924	7,642	51.4	(50.2-52.5)
British Columbia	4,040	9,613	42.0	(41.0-43.0)
Yukon	12	66	18.2	(9.8-29.6)
Northwest Territories	21	103	20.4	(13.1-29.5)
Nunavut	15	27	55.6	(35.3-74.5)
CANADA	**24,410**	**68,455**	**35.7**	**(35.3-36.0)**

Sources: Canadian Institute of Health Information. Discharge Abstract Database (DAD), 2000-2001.
Population Health Research Unit, Dalhousie University, Nova Scotia. ASD, 2000-2001.
Ministère de la Santé et des Services sociaux (Québec). Banque de données sur les hospitalisations du système MED-ÉCHO, 2000-2001.
Manitoba Health, Health Information Management. Manitoba Hospital Abstract System, 2000-2001.
CI — confidence interval.

TABLE F2.18 **Average maternal length of stay (LOS) in hospital for childbirth,** *Canada, 1991-1992 to 2000-2001*

Year	Vaginal delivery		Cesarean delivery	
	Number of hospital deliveries	Mean LOS in days (SD)	Number of hospital deliveries	Mean LOS in days (SD)
1991-1992	326,412	3.6 (1.8)	72,466	6.3 (2.7)
1992-1993	320,972	3.3 (1.7)	70,043	6.0 (2.7)
1993-1994	314,997	3.1 (1.7)	68,238	5.6 (2.6)
1994-1995	314,916	2.8 (1.6)	66,974	5.3 (2.6)
1995-1996	306,825	2.6 (1.6)	65,755	5.0 (2.5)
1996-1997	293,030	2.5 (1.5)	65,131	4.8 (2.5)
1997-1998	280,985	2.4 (1.5)	63,812	4.6 (2.5)
1998-1999	273,235	2.4 (1.5)	64,026	4.5 (2.5)
1999-2000	268,605	2.4 (1.5)	65,871	4.5 (2.4)
2000-2001	255,000	2.4 (1.5)	68,455	4.4 (2.4)

Sources: Canadian Institute of Health Information. Discharge Abstract Database (DAD), 1991-1992 to 2000- 2001.
Population Health Research Unit, Dalhousie University, Nova Scotia. ASD, 1991-1992 to 2000-2001.
Ministère de la Santé et des Services sociaux (Québec). Banque de données sur les hospitalisations du système MED-ÉCHO, 1991-1992 to 2000-2001.
Manitoba Health, Health Information Management, Manitoba Hospital Abstract System, 1991-1992 to 2000-2001.
SD — standard deviation.

TABLE F2.19 **Average maternal length of stay (LOS) in hospital for childbirth, by province/territory,** *Canada, 2000-2001*

Province/territory	Number of vaginal deliveries	Mean LOS in days (SD) vaginal deliveries	Number of hospital cesarean deliveries	Mean LOS in days (SD) cesarean deliveries
Newfoundland	3,542	3.4 (2.3)	1,209	5.5 (3.6)
Prince Edward Island	1,036	3.1 (1.6)	329	5.5 (2.3)
Nova Scotia	6,525	2.9 (2.0)	1,998	4.7 (2.9)
New Brunswick	5,483	2.8 (1.6)	1,907	4.6 (2.5)
Quebec	56,488	2.7 (1.4)	12,864	4.8 (2.3)
Ontario	100,739	2.2 (1.4)	27,995	4.2 (2.3)
Manitoba	11,264	2.6 (1.4)	2,549	4.6 (2.7)
Saskatchewan	9,778	2.8 (1.6)	2,153	4.6 (2.4)
Alberta	28,919	2.0 (1.4)	7,642	4.0 (2.5)
British Columbia	29,984	2.3 (1.6)	9,613	4.2 (2.4)
Yukon	287	3.1 (1.4)	66	4.7 (1.6)
Northwest Territories	647	2.7 (1.4)	103	4.9 (2.0)
Nunavut	308	1.6 (0.9)	27	3.9 (2.9)
CANADA	**255,000**	**2.4 (1.5)**	**68,455**	**4.4 (2.4)**

Sources: Canadian Institute of Health Information. Discharge Abstract Database (DAD), 2000-2001.
Population Health Research Unit, Dalhousie University, Nova Scotia. ASD, 2000-2001.
Ministère de la Santé et des Services sociaux (Québec). Banque de données sur les hospitalisations du système MED-ÉCHO, 2000-2001.
Manitoba Health, Health Information Management. Manitoba Hospital Abstract System, 2000-2001.
SD — standard deviation.

TABLE F2.20 **Rate of early neonatal discharge from hospital after birth,** *Canada, 1991-1992 to 2000-2001*

Fiscal year	Birth weight 1,000-2,499 g			Birth weight ≥ 2,500 g		
	Number of newborns with LOS < 2 days	Number of hospital live births	Newborns with LOS < 2 days per 100 hospital live births	Number of newborns with LOS < 2 days	Number of hospital live births	Newborns with LOS < 2 days per 100 hospital live births
1991-1992*	1,874	20,101	9.3	15,633	367,385	4.3
1992-1993	1,942	20,257	9.6	21,731	372,764	5.8
1993-1994	2,006	20,131	10.0	31,348	365,004	8.6
1994-1995	2,400	20,700	11.6	54,762	362,772	15.1
1995-1996	2,500	20,083	12.4	70,886	354,003	20.0
1996-1997	2,279	19,217	11.9	70,143	341,042	20.6
1997-1998	2,124	18,707	11.4	75,056	327,900	22.9
1998-1999	2,118	18,116	11.7	78,802	321,080	24.5
1999-2000	2,069	17,762	11.6	74,649	318,682	23.4
2000-2001	1,526	16,912	9.0	68,872	308,236	22.3

Sources: Canadian Institute of Health Information. Discharge Abstract Database (DAD), 1991-1992 to 2000-2001.
Population Health Research Unit, Dalhousie University, Nova Scotia. ASD, 1992-1993 to 2000-2001.
Ministère de la Santé et des Services sociaux (Québec). Banque de données sur les hospitalisations du système MED-ÉCHO, 1991-1992 to 2000-2001.
Manitoba Health, Health Information Management. Manitoba Hospital Abstract System, 1991-1992 to 2000-2001.
*Complete data for Nova Scotia were not available for 1991-1992 and were not included in the estimates for that year.
LOS — length of stay.

Canadian Perinatal Health Report, 2003 **177**

TABLE F2.21 **Rate of early neonatal discharge from hospital after birth, by province/territory,** *Canada, 2000-2001*

Province/territory	Birth weight 1,000-2,499 g			Birth weight ≥ 2,500 g		
	Number of newborns with LOS < 2 days	Number of hospital live births	Newborns with LOS < 2 days (95% CI) per 100 hospital live births	Number of newborns with LOS < 2 days	Number of hospital live births	Newborns with LOS < 2 days (95% CI) per 100 hospital live births
Newfoundland	15	233	6.4 (3.7-10.4)	401	4,521	8.9 (8.1-9.7)
Prince Edward Island	1	51	2.0 (0.1-10.5)	26	1,320	2.0 (1.3-2.9)
Nova Scotia	28	448	6.3 (4.2-8.9)	1,264	8,233	15.4 (14.6-16.1)
New Brunswick	17	356	4.8 (2.8-7.5)	438	7,074	6.2 (5.6-6.8)
Quebec	229	3,706	6.2 (5.4-7.0)	3,966	66,378	6.0 (5.8-6.2)
Ontario	677	6,805	9.9 (9.3-10.7)	33,167	122,568	27.1 (26.8-27.3)
Manitoba	50	650	7.7 (5.8-10.0)	2,117	13,034	16.2 (15.6-16.9)
Saskatchewan	37	565	6.5 (4.7-8.9)	1,658	11,382	14.6 (13.9-15.2)
Alberta	290	2,115	13.7 (12.3-15.3)	14,596	34,579	42.2 (41.7-42.7)
British Columbia	168	1,930	8.7 (7.5-10.1)	10,825	37,769	28.7 (28.2-29.2)
Yukon	1	13	7.7 (0.2-36.0)	49	338	14.5 (10.9-18.7)
Northwest Territories	3	24	12.5 (2.7-32.4)	120	719	16.7 (14.0-19.6)
Nunavut	10	16	62.5 (35.4-84.8)	245	321	76.3 (71.3-80.9)
CANADA	1,526	16,912	9.0 (8.6-9.5)	68,872	308,236	22.3 (22.2-22.5)

Sources: Canadian Institute of Health Information. Discharge Abstract Database (DAD), 2000-2001.
Population Health Research Unit, Dalhousie University, Nova Scotia. ASD, 2000-2001.
Ministère de la Santé et des Services sociaux (Québec). Banque de données sur les hospitalisations du système MED-ÉCHO, 2000-2001.
Manitoba Health, Health Information Management, Manitoba Hospital Abstract System, 2000-2001.
CI — confidence interval.
LOS — length of stay.

TABLE F2.22 **Average neonatal length of stay (LOS) in hospital after birth,** *Canada, 1991-1992 to 2000-2001*

Fiscal year	Birth weight 1,000-2,499 g		Birth weight ≥ 2,500 g	
	Number of hospital live births	Mean LOS in days (SD)	Number of hospital live births	Mean LOS in days (SD)
1991-1992*	20,101	8.5 (6.6)	367,385	3.5 (1.8)
1992-1993	20,257	8.2 (6.7)	372,764	3.2 (1.7)
1993-1994	20,131	8.1 (6.8)	365,004	2.9 (1.7)
1994-1995	20,700	7.8 (6.8)	362,772	2.6 (1.6)
1995-1996	20,083	7.7 (6.8)	354,003	2.5 (1.6)
1996-1997	19,217	7.8 (6.8)	341,042	2.4 (1.6)
1997-1998	18,707	7.9 (6.8)	327,900	2.3 (1.6)
1998-1999	18,116	7.9 (6.8)	321,080	2.3 (1.6)
1999-2000	17,762	8.0 (6.8)	318,682	2.3 (1.6)
2000-2001	16,912	8.5 (6.8)	308,236	2.4 (1.7)

Sources: Canadian Institute for Health Information. Discharge Abstract Database (DAD), 1991-1992 to 2000-2001.
Population Health Research Unit, Dalhousie University, Nova Scotia. ASD, 1992-1993 to 2000-2001.
Ministère de la Santé et des Services sociaux (Québec). Banque de données sur les hospitalisations du système MED-ÉCHO, 1991-1992 to 2000-2001.
Manitoba Health, Health Information Management. Manitoba Hospital Abstract System, 1991-1992 to 2000-2001.
*Complete data for Nova Scotia were not available for 1991-1992 and were not included in the estimates for that year.
SD — standard deviation.

TABLE F2.23 **Average neonatal length of stay (LOS) in hospital after birth, by province/ territory,** *Canada, 2000-2001*

Province/territory	Birth weight 1,000-2,499 g		Birth weight ≥ 2,500 g	
	Number of hospital live births	**Mean LOS in days (SD)**	**Number of hospital live births**	**Mean LOS in days (SD)**
Newfoundland	233	9.7 (6.8)	4,521	3.0 (1.7)
Prince Edward Island	51	11.5 (7.2)	1,320	3.4 (2.0)
Nova Scotia	448	10.5 (7.2)	8,233	2.9 (1.9)
New Brunswick	356	12.2 (7.3)	7,074	3.0 (2.1)
Quebec	3,706	9.3 (7.0)	66,378	2.8 (1.6)
Ontario	6,805	8.1 (6.7)	122,568	2.3 (1.6)
Manitoba	650	9.6 (7.0)	13,034	2.6 (1.9)
Saskatchewan	565	9.5 (7.2)	11,382	2.7 (1.8)
Alberta	2,115	7.6 (6.5)	34,579	2.1 (1.6)
British Columbia	1,930	9.0 (6.7)	37,769	2.4 (1.7)
Yukon	13	4.6 (3.3)	338	3.0 (1.8)
Northwest Territories	24	5.8 (5.9)	719	1.4 (1.2)
Nunavut	16	5.5 (8.3)	321	2.6 (1.7)
CANADA	**16,912**	**8.5 (6.8)**	**308,236**	**2.4 (1.7)**

Sources: Canadian Institute of Health Information. Discharge Abstract Database (DAD), 2000-2001.
Population Health Research Unit, Dalhousie University, Nova Scotia. ASD, 2000-2001.
Ministère de la Santé et des Services sociaux (Québec). Banque de données sur les hospitalisations du système MED-ÉCHO, 2000-2001.
Manitoba Health, Health Information Management. Manitoba Hospital Abstract System, 2000-2001.
SD — standard deviation.

TABLE F3.1 **Number of maternal deaths and maternal mortality ratios (MMR), by direct and indirect causes,** *Canada (excluding Ontario),* 1979-1981 to 1997-1999*

Period	Number of maternal deaths				Maternal deaths (95% CI) per 100,000 live births			
	Due to direct causes	**Due to indirect causes**	**Total**	**Number of live births**	**Due to direct causes only**		**Due to direct and indirect causes**	
1979-1981	43	2	45	740,965	5.8	(4.2-7.9)	6.1	(4.4-8.1)
1982-1984	23	0	23	740,824	3.1	(2.0-4.7)	3.1	(2.0-4.7)
1985-1987	25	1	26	717,675	3.5	(2.3-5.2)	3.6	(2.4-5.3)
1988-1990	29	2	31	740,615	3.9	(2.6-5.6)	4.2	(2.8-6.0)
1991-1993	27	2	29	739,635	3.7	(2.4-5.3)	3.9	(2.6-5.6)
1994-1996	19	1	20	695,977	2.7	(1.7-4.3)	2.9	(1.8-4.4)
1997-1999	14	2	16	631,536	2.2	(1.2-3.7)	2.5	(1.5-4.1)

Sources: For years 1979-1990: see references 3-11 in the *Maternal Mortality* section.
For years 1991-1999: Statistics Canada. Canadian Vital Statistics System, 1991-1999 (unlinked live birth and death files).
*Data for Ontario were excluded because of data quality concerns; they are presented in *Appendix G*.
CI — confidence interval.

TABLE F3.2 **Incidence and case fatality rate of amniotic fluid embolism,** *Canada, 1991-1992 to 2000-2001*

Fiscal year	Number of cases	Number of hospital deliveries	Incidence per 100,000 deliveries	Number of deaths	Case fatality rate* per 100 cases
1991-1992	13	398,878	3.3	1	7.7
1992-1993	30	391,015	7.7	7	23.3
1993-1994	16	383,235	4.2	2	12.5
1994-1995	18	381,890	4.7	2	11.1
1995-1996	25	372,580	6.7	4	16.0
1996-1997	23	358,161	6.4	5	21.7
1997-1998	26	344,797	7.5	2	7.7
1998-1999	19	337,261	5.6	0	0.0
1999-2000	11	334,476	3.3	0	0.0
2000-2001	16	323,455	4.9	1	6.3
TOTAL	197	3,625,748	5.4	24	12.2

Sources: Canadian Institute for Health Information. Discharge Abstract Database (DAD), 1991-1992 to 2000-2001.
Population Health Research Unit, Dalhousie University, Nova Scotia. ASD, 1991-1992 to 2000-2001.
Ministère de la Santé et des Services sociaux (Québec). Banque de données sur les hospitalisations du système MED-ÉCHO, 1991-1992 to 2000-2001.
Manitoba Health, Health Information Management. Manitoba Hospital Abstract System, 1991-1992 to 2000-2001.

*The overall case fatality rate of 12.2% and the case fatality rates for each year are low in comparison with case fatality rates of approximately 80% reported in hospital-based studies. This suggests that amniotic fluid embolism may be over-reported in hospitalization data, perhaps because of a tendency to diagnose less serious events as amniotic fluid embolisms (see reference 5 in *Severe Maternal Morbidity* section).

TABLE F3.3 **Incidence and case fatality rate of postpartum hemorrhage requiring hysterectomy,** *Canada, 1991-1992 to 2000-2001*

Fiscal year	Number of cases	Number of hospital deliveries	Incidence per 100,000 deliveries	Number of deaths	Case fatality rate per 100 cases
1991-1992	93	398,878	23.3	1	1.1
1992-1993	105	391,015	26.9	3	2.9
1993-1994	109	383,235	28.4	2	1.8
1994-1995	112	381,890	29.3	3	2.7
1995-1996	130	372,580	34.9	2	1.5
1996-1997	125	358,161	34.9	2	1.6
1997-1998	128	344,797	37.1	1	0.8
1998-1999	133	337,261	39.4	3	2.3
1999-2000	157	334,476	46.9	0	0.0
2000-2001	143	323,455	44.2	1	0.7
TOTAL	1,235	3,625,748	34.1	18	1.5

Sources: Canadian Institute for Health Information. Discharge Abstract Database (DAD), 1991-1992 to 2000-2001.
Population Health Research Unit, Dalhousie University, Nova Scotia. ASD, 1991-1992 to 2000-2001.
Ministère de la Santé et des Services sociaux (Québec). Banque de données sur les hospitalisations du système MED-ÉCHO, 1991-1992 to 2000-2001.
Manitoba Health, Health Information Management. Manitoba Hospital Abstract System, 1991-1992 to 2000-2001.

TABLE F3.4 **Ratio and rate* of induced abortion,** *Canada (excluding Ontario),** 1992-2000*

Year***	Number of induced abortions	Number of live births	Number of females 15-44 years	Induced abortions per 100 live births	Induced abortions per 1,000 females 15-44 years
1992	59,102	248,043	4,200,624	23.8	14.1
1993	59,512	240,542	4,212,768	24.7	14.1
1994	61,149	238,042	4,223,966	25.7	14.5
1995	62,153	231,747	4,236,839	26.8	14.7
1996	64,741	226,188	4,254,030	28.6	15.2
1997	67,663	215,590	4,264,136	31.4	15.9
1998	67,879	209,789	4,255,457	32.4	16.0
1999	65,627	206,157	4,245,169	31.8	15.5
2000	65,883	200,454	4,227,539	32.9	15.6

Sources: Canadian Institute for Health Information and Statistics Canada. Therapeutic Abortion Survey. (Custom tabulation, Health Statistics Division, Statistics Canada, 2003).
  Statistics Canada. CANSIM II, table 051-0001 — Canadian population estimates, 1992-2000.
  Statistics Canada. Canadian Vital Statistics System, 1992-2000 (unlinked live birth files).
*Includes cases of unknown area of residence and abortions performed on Canadian residents in selected U.S. states. Includes cases with age not specified as well as abortions to females ≤ 14 years of age and ≥ 45 years of age. Rate based on female population 15-44 years of age. Excludes abortions performed in Canada on non-Canadian residents.
**Data for Ontario residents were excluded because of data quality concerns; they are presented in *Appendix G*.
***1991 data were not presented because data on province of residence for clinic abortions were not available before 1992.

TABLE F3.5 **Ratio and rate* of induced abortion, by province/territory,** *Canada (excluding Ontario),** 2000*

Province/territory	Number of induced abortions	Number of live births	Number of females 15-44 years	Induced abortions (95% CI) per 100 live births		Induced abortions (95% CI) per 1,000 live females 15-44 years	
Newfoundland	898	4,869	123,269	18.4	(17.4-19.6)	7.3	(6.8-7.8)
Prince Edward Island	158	1,441	30,134	11.0	(9.4-12.7)	5.2	(4.5-6.1)
Nova Scotia	1,989	9,115	208,612	21.8	(21.0-22.7)	9.5	(9.1-10.0)
New Brunswick	1,098	7,347	166,572	14.9	(14.1-15.8)	6.6	(6.2-7.0)
Quebec	31,125	72,005	1,606,900	43.2	(42.9-43.6)	19.4	(19.2-19.6)
Manitoba	3,366	14,090	244,586	23.9	(23.2-24.6)	13.8	(13.3-14.2)
Saskatchewan	1,956	12,139	216,931	16.1	(15.5-16.8)	9.0	(8.6-9.4)
Alberta	10,432	37,006	701,795	28.2	(27.7-28.7)	14.9	(14.6-15.2)
British Columbia	14,009	40,672	904,913	34.4	(34.0-34.9)	15.5	(15.2-15.7)
Yukon	135	370	7,405	36.5	(31.6-41.6)	18.2	(15.3-21.5)
Northwest Territories	281	673	10,105	41.8	(38.0-45.6)	27.8	(24.7-31.2)
Nunavut	178	727	6,317	24.5	(21.4-27.8)	28.2	(25.6-34.1)
CANADA***	65,883	200,454	4,227,539	32.9	(32.7-33.1)	15.6	(15.5-15.7)

Sources: Canadian Institute for Health Information and Statistics Canada. Therapeutic Abortion Survey. (Custom tabulation, Health Statistics Division, Statistics Canada, 2003).
  Statistics Canada. CANSIM II, table 051-0001 — Canadian population estimates, 2000.
  Statistics Canada. Canadian Vital Statistics System, 2000 (unlinked live birth file).
*Includes cases with age not specified as well as abortions to females ≤ 14 years of age and ≥ 45 years of age. Rate based on female population 15-44 years of age. Excludes abortions performed in Canada on non-Canadian residents.
**Data for Ontario residents were excluded because of data quality concerns; they are presented in *Appendix G*.
***Includes cases of unknown area of residence and abortions performed on Canadian residents in selected U.S. states.
CI — confidence interval.

Appendix F

TABLE F3.6 **Age-specific induced abortion rate,** *Canada (excluding Ontario),** 2000*

Age (years)	Number of induced abortions	Number of females	Induced abortions (95% CI) per 1,000 females	
< 15***	282	123,624	2.3	(2.0-2.6)
15-19	13,149	635,540	20.7	(20.3-21.0)
20-24	20,938	645,696	32.4	(32.0-32.9)
25-29	13,436	636,921	21.1	(20.7-21.5)
30-34	9,488	682,115	13.9	(13.6-14.2)
35-39	6,198	812,780	7.6	(7.4-7.8)
40-44****	2,173	814,487	2.7	(2.6-2.8)

Sources: Canadian Institute for Health Information and Statistics Canada. Therapeutic Abortion Survey. (Custom tabulation, Health Statistics Division, Statistics Canada, 2003).
Statistics Canada. CANSIM II, table 051-0001 — Canadian population estimates, 2000.
*Includes cases of unknown area of residence. Excludes abortions performed in Canada on non-Canadian residents and abortions performed on Canadian residents in the United States.
**Data for Ontario were excluded because of data quality concerns.
***Rate based on female population aged 14 years.
****Includes induced abortions to women ≥ 45 years of age. Rate based on female population aged 40-44 years.
CI — confidence interval.

TABLE F3.7 **Rate of ectopic pregnancy,** *Canada, 1991-1992 to 2000-2001*

Fiscal year	Number of reported pregnancies*	Number of ectopic pregnancies	Ectopic pregnancies per 1,000 reported pregnancies
1991-1992	498,467	8,191	16.4
1992-1993	488,075	8,151	16.7
1993-1994	482,468	7,838	16.2
1994-1995	477,691	7,720	16.2
1995-1996	466,041	7,364	15.8
1996-1997	444,385	6,911	15.6
1997-1998	424,102	6,436	15.2
1998-1999	409,268	6,199	15.1
1999-2000	401,766	5,665	14.1
2000-2001	387,978	5,364	13.8

Sources: Canadian Institute of Health Information. Discharge Abstract Database (DAD), 1991-1992 to 2000-2001.
Population Health Research Unit, Dalhousie University, Nova Scotia. ASD, 1991-1992 to 2000-2001.
Ministère de la Santé et des Services sociaux (Québec). Banque de données sur les hospitalisations du système MED-ÉCHO, 1991-1992 to 2000-2001.
Manitoba Health, Health Information Management. Manitoba Hospital Abstract System, 1991-1992 to 2000-2001.
*Reported pregnancies include all hospital deliveries, hospital-based induced abortions and ectopic pregnancies, but not spontaneous abortions and clinic-based induced abortions.

TABLE F3.8 **Rate of ectopic pregnancy, by province/territory,** *Canada, 2000-2001*

Province/territory	Number of reported pregnancies*	Number of ectopic pregnancies	Ectopic pregnancies (95% CI) per 1,000 reported pregnancies	
Newfoundland	5,322	71	13.3	(10.4-16.8)
Prince Edward Island	1,451	13	9.0	(4.8-15.3)
Nova Scotia	10,792	139	12.9	(10.8-15.2)
New Brunswick	8,374	106	12.7	(10.4-15.3)
Quebec	79,793	1,102	13.8	(13.0-14.6)
Ontario	157,940	1,985	12.6	(12.0-13.1)
Manitoba	17,061	259	15.2	(13.4-17.1)
Saskatchewan	14,715	205	13.9	(12.1-16.0)
Alberta	38,990	685	17.6	(16.3-18.9)
British Columbia	51,442	762	14.8	(13.8-15.9)
Yukon	537	5	9.3	(3.0-21.6)
Northwest Territories	1,094	20	18.3	(11.2-28.1)
Nunavut	467	12	25.7	(13.4-44.5)
CANADA	**387,978**	**5,364**	**13.8**	**(13.5-14.2)**

Sources: Canadian Institute of Health Information. Discharge Abstract Database (DAD), 2000-2001.
Population Health Research Unit, Dalhousie University, Nova Scotia. ASD, 2000-2001.
Ministère de la Santé et des Services sociaux (Québec). Banque de données sur les hospitalisations du système MED-ÉCHO, 2000-2001.
Manitoba Health, Health Information Management. Manitoba Hospital Abstract System, 2000-2001.

*Reported pregnancies include all hospital deliveries, hospital-based induced abortions and ectopic pregnancies, but not spontaneous abortions and clinic-based induced abortions.

CI — confidence interval.

TABLE F3.9 **Rate of ectopic pregnancy, by maternal age,** *Canada, 2000-2001*

Age (years)	Number of reported pregnancies*	Number of ectopic pregnancies	Ectopic pregnancies (95% CI) per 1,000 reported pregnancies	
15-19	27,475	259	9.4	(8.3-10.6)
20-24	75,807	877	11.6	(10.8-12.4)
25-29	113,266	1,307	11.5	(10.9-12.2)
30-34	106,759	1,533	14.4	(13.7-15.1)
35-39	53,237	1,104	20.7	(19.5-22.0)
40-44	10,558	270	25.6	(22.6-28.8)
45-49	445	10	22.5	(10.8-40.9)

Sources: Canadian Institute of Health Information. Discharge Abstract Database (DAD), 2000-2001.
Population Health Research Unit, Dalhousie University, Nova Scotia. ASD, 2000-2001.
Ministère de la Santé et des Services sociaux (Québec). Banque de données sur les hospitalisations du système MED-ÉCHO, 2000-2001.
Manitoba Health, Health Information Management. Manitoba Hospital Abstract System, 2000-2001.

*Excludes reported pregnancies with unknown maternal age. Reported pregnancies include all hospital deliveries, hospital-based induced abortions and ectopic pregnancies, but not spontaneous abortions and clinic-based induced abortions.

CI — confidence interval.

TABLE F3.10 **Rate of maternal readmission within three months of discharge from hospital following childbirth,** *Canada (excluding Manitoba),* 1991-1992 to 2000-2001*

Fiscal year	Vaginal deliveries			Cesarean deliveries		
	Number of readmissions	Number of hospital deliveries	Readmissions per 100 hospital deliveries	Number of readmissions	Number of hospital deliveries	Readmissions per 100 hospital deliveries
1991-1992	6,315	310,014	2.0	1,772	68,516	2.6
1992-1993	7,033	307,530	2.3	1,931	67,102	2.9
1993-1994	6,885	300,380	2.3	1,968	65,150	3.0
1994-1995	6,584	300,574	2.2	1,958	63,958	3.1
1995-1996	6,500	294,290	2.1	2,100	62,601	3.4
1996-1997	5,946	282,560	2.1	1,986	62,420	3.2
1997-1998	5,769	269,564	2.1	1,969	60,363	3.3
1998-1999	5,524	262,234	2.1	2,018	60,793	3.3
1999-2000	5,288	256,633	2.1	2,078	62,172	3.3
2000-2001	5,012	245,512	2.0	2,088	64,056	3.3

Sources: Canadian Institute of Health Information. Discharge Abstract Database (DAD), 1991-1992 to 2000-2001.
Population Health Research Unit, Dalhousie University, Nova Scotia. ASD, 1991-1992 to 2000-2001.
Ministère de la Santé et des Services sociaux (Québec). Banque de données sur les hospitalisations du système MED-ÉCHO, 1991-1992 to 2000-2001.

*Data for Manitoba were not included because the Manitoba Hospital Abstract System does not distinguish readmitted patients from those transferred from one facility to another.

Note: 1. The number of deliveries was based on calendar year. The number of readmissions was calculated for three months after discharge from hospital.

2. Women who were directly transferred to another hospital after childbirth and women with initial length of hospital stay > 20 days were excluded.

3. Hospital discharge records with day surgery were not counted as readmission in the analysis.

TABLE F3.11 **Rate of maternal readmission within three months of discharge from hospital following childbirth (vaginal deliveries), by province/territory,** *Canada (excluding Manitoba),* 1998-1999 to 2000-2001 combined*

Province/territory	Number of readmissions	Number of hospital vaginal deliveries	Readmissions (95% CI) per 100 hospital deliveries	
Newfoundland	284	11,162	2.5	(2.3-2.9)
Prince Edward Island	90	3,389	2.7	(2.1-3.3)
Nova Scotia	504	21,166	2.4	(2.2-2.6)
New Brunswick	480	17,521	2.7	(2.5-3.0)
Quebec	3,359	175,304	1.9	(1.9-2.0)
Ontario	5,282	315,960	1.7	(1.6-1.7)
Saskatchewan	862	30,804	2.8	(2.6-3.0)
Alberta	2,806	90,192	3.1	(3.0-3.2)
British Columbia	2,075	95,143	2.2	(2.1-2.3)
Yukon	24	900	2.7	(1.7-4.0)
Northwest Territories	41	2,293	1.8	(1.3-2.4)
Nunavut	17	545	3.1	(1.8-5.0)
CANADA	15,824	764,379	2.1	(2.0-2.1)

Sources: Canadian Institute of Health Information. Discharge Abstract Database (DAD), 1998-1999 to 2000-2001.
      Population Health Research Unit, Dalhousie University, Nova Scotia. ASD, 1998-1999 to 2000-2001.
      Ministère de la Santé et des Services sociaux (Québec). Banque de données sur les hospitalisations du système MED-ÉCHO, 1998-1999 to 2000-2001.

*Data for Manitoba were not included because the Manitoba Hospital Abstract System does not distinguish readmitted patients from those transferred from one facility to another.

Note: 1. The number of deliveries was based on calendar year. The number of readmissions was calculated for three months after discharge from hospital.
    2. Women who were directly transferred to another hospital after childbirth and women with initial length of hospital stay > 20 days were excluded.
    3. Hospital discharge records with day surgery were not counted as readmission in the analysis.

CI — confidence interval.

TABLE F3.12 **Rate of maternal readmission within three months of discharge from hospital following childbirth (cesarean deliveries), by province/territory,**
Canada (excluding Manitoba),* 1998-1999 to 2000-2001combined

Province/territory	Number of readmissions	Number of hospital cesarean deliveries	Readmissions (95% CI) per 100 hospital deliveries	
Newfoundland	152	3,557	4.3	(3.6-5.0)
Prince Edward Island	42	965	4.4	(3.2-5.8)
Nova Scotia	226	5,497	4.1	(3.6-4.7)
New Brunswick	241	5,522	4.4	(3.8-4.9)
Quebec	1,268	37,434	3.4	(3.2-3.6)
Ontario	2,123	78,710	2.7	(2.6-2.8)
Saskatchewan	240	6,173	3.9	(3.4-4.4)
Alberta	944	20,769	4.5	(4.3-4.8)
British Columbia	931	27,799	3.3	(3.1-3.6)
Yukon	3	206	1.5	(0.3-4.2)
Northwest Territories	12	343	3.5	(1.9-6.0)
Nunavut	2	46	4.3	(0.5-14.8)
CANADA	**6,184**	**187,021**	**3.3**	**(3.2-3.4)**

Sources: Canadian Institute for Health Information. Discharge Abstract Database (DAD), 2000-2001.
Population Health Research Unit, Dalhousie University, Nova Scotia. ASD, 2000-2001.
Ministère de la Santé et des Services sociaux (Québec). Banque de données sur les hospitalisations du système MED-ÉCHO, 2000-2001.

*Data for Manitoba were not included because the Manitoba Hospital Abstract System does not distinguish readmitted patients from those transferred from one facility to another.

Note: 1. The number of deliveries was based on calendar year. The number of readmissions was calculated for three months after discharge from hospital.
2. Women who were directly transferred to another hospital after childbirth and women with initial length of hospital stay > 20 days were excluded.
3. Hospital discharge records with day surgery were not counted as readmissions in the analysis.

CI — confidence interval.

TABLE F3.13 **Rate of maternal readmission within three months of discharge from hospital following childbirth, by primary diagnosis,** *Canada (excluding Manitoba),* 1998-1999 to 2000-2001 combined*

Primary diagnosis at readmission (ICD-9 code)	All		Cesarean		Vaginal	
	Number of read-missions	Percentage of maternal read-mission	Number of read-missions	Percentage of maternal read-mission	Number of read-missions	Percentage of maternal read-mission
1. Postpartum hemorrhage (666)	3,174	14.4	379	6.1	2,795	17.7
2. Cholelithiasis (574)	2,890	13.1	740	12.0	2,150	13.6
3. Major puerperal infection (670)	2,668	12.8	786	12.7	1,882	11.9
4. Other and unspecified complications of the puerperium, not elsewhere classified (674)	1,807	8.2	1,355	21.9	452	2.9
5. Infections of the breast and nipple associated with childbirth (675)	646	2.9	123	2.0	523	3.3
6. Persons seeking consultation without complaint of sickness (V65)	546	2.5	81	1.3	465	2.9
7. Other current conditions in the mother classifiable elsewhere, but complicating pregnancy, childbirth or the puerperium (648)	533	2.4	160	2.6	373	2.4
8. Complications of pregnancy, not elsewhere classified (646)	514	2.3	140	2.3	374	2.4
9. Symptoms involving abdomen and pelvis (789)	376	1.7	120	1.9	256	1.6
10. Complications of procedures, not elsewhere classified (998)	328	1.5	202	3.3	126	0.8
11. Postpartum care and examination (V24)	184	0.9	45	0.7	139	0.9
12. Venous complications in pregnancy and the puerperium (671)	183	0.9	68	1.1	115	0.7
13. Encounter for contraceptive management (V25)	137	0.6	14	0.2	123	0.8
14. Other diagnoses	8,022	36.5	1,971	31.9	6,051	38.2
TOTAL	22,008	100.0	6,184	100.0	15,824	100.0

Sources: Canadian Institute for Health Information. Discharge Abstract Database (DAD), 2000-2001.
Population Health Research Unit, Dalhousie University, Nova Scotia. ASD, 2000-2001.
Ministère de la Santé et des Services sociaux (Québec). Banque de données sur les hospitalisations du système MED-ÉCHO, 2000-2001.

*Data for Manitoba were not included because the Manitoba Hospital Abstract System does not distinguish readmitted patients from those transferred from one facility to another.

Note: 1. The number of deliveries was based on calendar year. The number of readmissions was calculated for three months after discharge from hospital.
2. Women who were directly transferred to another hospital after childbirth and women with initial length of hospital stay > 20 days were excluded.
3. Hospital discharge records with day surgery were not counted as readmissions in the analysis.

TABLE F4.1 **Rate of preterm birth,** *Canada (excluding Ontario),* 1991-2000*

Year	Number of preterm births	Number of live births**	Preterm births per 100 live births
1991	16,405	247,584	6.6
1992	16,361	244,989	6.7
1993	15,862	238,409	6.6
1994	16,100	237,633	6.8
1995	16,125	231,436	7.0
1996	15,892	224,520	7.1
1997	15,174	214,414	7.1
1998	15,009	209,629	7.2
1999	15,213	206,004	7.4
2000	15,289	200,355	7.6

Source: Statistics Canada, Canadian Vital Statistics System, 1991-2000 (unlinked live birth files).
*Data for Ontario were excluded because of data quality concerns; they are presented in *Appendix G.*
**Excludes live births with unknown gestational age.

TABLE F4.2 **Rate of preterm birth (singleton and multiple births),** *Canada (excluding Ontario),* 2000*

Plurality	Number of preterm births	Number of live births**	Preterm births per 100 live births
Singletons	12,420	195,076	6.4
Twins	2,710	5,115	53.0
Triplet or higher	159	164	97.0
All live births	15,289	200,355	7.6

Source: Statistics Canada, Canadian Vital Statistics System, 2000 (unlinked live birth file).
*Data for Ontario were excluded because of data quality concerns; they are presented in *Appendix G.*
**Excludes live births with unknown gestational age.

TABLE F4.3 **Rate of preterm birth, by province/territory,** *Canada (excluding Ontario),* 2000*

Province/territory	Number of preterm births	Number of live births**	Preterm births (95% CI) per 100 live births	
Newfoundland	387	4,864	8.0	(7.2-8.8)
Prince Edward Island	83	1,438	5.8	(4.6-7.1)
Nova Scotia	614	9,109	6.7	(6.2-7.3)
New Brunswick	495	7,347	6.7	(6.2-7.3)
Quebec	5,604	72,003	7.8	(7.6-8.0)
Manitoba	1,121	14,048	8.0	(7.5-8.4)
Saskatchewan	824	12,139	6.8	(6.3-7.3)
Alberta	3,120	37,004	8.4	(8.2-8.7)
British Columbia	2,892	40,651	7.1	(6.9-7.4)
Yukon	27	370	7.3	(4.9-10.4)
Northwest Territories	48	669	7.2	(5.3-9.4)
Nunavut	74	713	10.4	(8.2-12.9)
CANADA	**15,289**	**200,355**	**7.6**	**(7.5-7.7)**

Source: Statistics Canada, Canadian Vital Statistics System, 2000 (unlinked live birth file).
*Data for Ontario were excluded because of data quality concerns; they are presented in *Appendix G.*
**Excludes live births with unknown gestational age.
CI — confidence interval.

TABLE F4.4 **Rate of postterm birth,** *Canada (excluding Ontario),* 1991-2000*

Year	Number of postterm births	Number of live births**	Postterm births per 100 live births
1991	10,788	247,584	4.4
1992	9,149	244,989	3.7
1993	9,132	238,409	3.8
1994	7,388	237,633	3.1
1995	5,751	231,436	2.5
1996	4,353	224,520	1.9
1997	3,928	214,414	1.8
1998	3,439	209,629	1.6
1999	2,999	206,004	1.5
2000	2,397	200,355	1.2

Source: Statistics Canada, Canadian Vital Statistics System, 1991- 2000 (unlinked live birth files).
*Data for Ontario were excluded because of data quality concerns; they are presented in *Appendix G.*
**Excludes live births with unknown gestational age.

TABLE F4.5 **Rate of postterm birth, by province/territory,** *Canada (excluding Ontario),* 2000*

Province/territory	Number of postterm births	Number of live births**	Postterm births (95% CI) per 100 live births	
Newfoundland	31	4,864	0.6	(0.4-0.9)
Prince Edward Island	29	1,438	2.0	(1.4-2.9)
Nova Scotia	263	9,109	2.9	(2.6-3.3)
New Brunswick	93	7,347	1.3	(1.0-1.6)
Quebec	352	72,003	0.5	(0.4-0.5)
Manitoba	317	14,048	2.3	(2.0-2.5)
Saskatchewan	223	12,139	1.8	(1.6-2.1)
Alberta	565	37,004	1.5	(1.4-1.7)
British Columbia	494	40,651	1.2	(1.1-1.3)
Yukon	16	370	4.3	(2.5-6.9)
Northwest Territories	9	669	1.3	(0.6-2.5)
Nunavut	5	713	0.7	(0.2-1.6)
CANADA	2,397	200,355	1.2	(1.2-1.2)

Source: Statistics Canada, Canadian Vital Statistics System, 2000 (unlinked live birth file).
*Data for Ontario were excluded because of data quality concerns; they are presented in *Appendix G.*
**Excludes live births with unknown gestational age.
CI — confidence interval.

TABLE F4.6 **Rates of small for gestational age (SGA) and large for gestational age (LGA),** *Canada (excluding Ontario),* 1991-2000*

Year	Number of SGA singleton live births	Number of LGA singleton live births	Number of singleton live births**	SGA singleton live births per 100 singleton live births**	LGA singleton live births per 100 singleton live births**
1991	25,798	22,830	241,378	10.7	9.5
1992	23,808	24,228	238,946	10.0	10.1
1993	23,979	22,729	232,460	10.3	9.8
1994	23,657	22,876	232,200	10.2	9.9
1995	22,704	22,137	224,864	10.1	9.8
1996	20,726	22,966	218,246	9.5	10.5
1997	19,783	21,111	207,926	9.5	10.2
1998	18,639	22,012	204,004	9.1	10.8
1999	16,904	22,310	200,486	8.4	11.1
2000	15,354	23,351	194,917	7.9	12.0

Source: Statistics Canada. Canadian Vital Statistics System, 1991-2000 (unlinked live birth files).
*Data for Ontario were excluded because of data quality concerns; they are presented in *Appendix G.*
**Excludes live births with unknown gestational age or birth weight, or gestational age < 22 weeks or > 43 weeks.

Appendix F

TABLE F4.7 **Rates of small for gestational age (SGA) and large for gestational age (LGA), by province/territory,** *Canada (excluding Ontario),* 2000*

Province/ territory	Number of SGA singleton live births	Number of LGA singleton live births	Number of singleton live births**	SGA singleton live births (95% CI) per 100 singleton live births**		LGA singleton live births (95% CI) per 100 singleton live births**	
Newfoundland	335	727	4,735	7.1	(6.4-7.8)	15.4	(14.3-16.4)
Prince Edward Island	89	230	1,413	6.3	(5.1-7.7)	16.3	(14.4-18.3)
Nova Scotia	735	1,193	8,848	8.3	(7.7-8.9)	13.5	(12.8-14.2)
New Brunswick	533	1,017	7,157	7.4	(6.8-8.1)	14.2	(13.4-15.0)
Quebec	5,677	7,322	70,119	8.1	(7.9-8.3)	10.4	(10.2-10.7)
Manitoba	998	2,021	13,678	7.3	(6.9-7.7)	14.8	(14.2-15.4)
Saskatchewan	872	1,622	11,819	7.4	(6.9-7.9)	13.7	(13.1-14.4)
Alberta	3,090	4,027	35,852	8.6	(8.3-8.9)	11.2	(10.9-11.6)
British Columbia	2,917	4,937	39,590	7.4	(7.1-7.6)	12.5	(12.1-12.8)
Yukon	29	49	357	8.1	(5.5-11.5)	13.7	(10.3-17.7)
Northwest Territories	33	119	656	5.0	(3.5-7.0)	18.1	(15.3-21.3)
Nunavut	46	87	693	6.6	(4.9-8.8)	12.6	(10.2-15.3)
CANADA	15,354	23,351	194,917	7.9	(7.8-8.0)	12.0	(11.8-12.1)

Source: Statistics Canada. Canadian Vital Statistics System, 2000 (unlinked live birth file).
*Data for Ontario were excluded because of data quality concerns; they are presented in *Appendix G.*
**Excludes live births with unknown gestational age or birth weight, or gestational age < 22 weeks or > 43 weeks.
CI — confidence interval.

TABLE F4.8 **Rate of fetal death,** *Canada (excluding Ontario),* 1991-2000*

Year	All fetal deaths			Fetal deaths ≥ 500 g**		
	Number of fetal deaths	Total births	Deaths per 1,000 total births	Number of fetal deaths	Total births	Deaths per 1,000 total births
1991	1,492	252,542	5.9	1,226	252,121	4.9
1992	1,450	249,493	5.8	1,175	249,082	4.7
1993	1,363	241,905	5.6	1,135	241,518	4.7
1994	1,355	239,397	5.7	1,135	239,025	4.7
1995	1,380	233,127	5.9	1,082	232,636	4.7
1996	1,220	227,408	5.4	972	226,967	4.3
1997	1,263	216,853	5.8	983	216,373	4.5
1998	1,146	210,935	5.4	866	210,493	4.1
1999	1,230	207,387	5.9	933	206,903	4.5
2000	1,175	201,629	5.8	903	201,180	4.5

Source: Statistics Canada. Canadian Vital Statistics System, 1991-2000 (unlinked live birth and stillbirth files).
*Data for Ontario were excluded because of data quality concerns; they are presented in *Appendix G.*
**Fetal death rates ≥ 500 g exclude stillbirths and live births with a birth weight < 500 g or, if birth weight was unknown, those with a gestational age of < 22 weeks.

TABLE F4.9 | **Rate of fetal death, by province/territory,** *Canada (excluding Ontario),* 2000*

Province/territory	All fetal deaths			Fetal deaths ≥ 500 g**		
	Number of fetal deaths	Total births	Deaths (95% CI) per 1,000 total births	Number of fetal deaths	Total births	Deaths (95% CI) per 1,000 total births
Newfoundland	23	4,892	4.7 (3.0-7.0)	19	4,886	3.9 (2.3-6.1)
Prince Edward Island	6	1,447	4.1 (1.5-9.0)	5	1,445	3.5 (1.1-8.1)
Nova Scotia	52	9,167	5.7 (4.2-7.4)	32	9,132	3.5 (2.4-4.9)
New Brunswick	37	7,384	5.0 (3.5-6.9)	27	7,371	3.7 (2.4-5.3)
Quebec	311	72,316	4.3 (3.8-4.8)	308	72,250	4.3 (3.8-4.8)
Manitoba	134	14,224	9.4 (7.9-11.1)	93	14,171	6.6 (5.3-8.0)
Saskatchewan	73	12,212	6.0 (4.7-7.5)	71	12,206	5.8 (4.5-7.3)
Alberta	244	37,250	6.6 (5.8-7.4)	167	37,125	4.5 (3.8-5.2)
British Columbia	281	40,953	6.9 (6.1-7.7)	169	40,815	4.1 (3.5-4.8)
Yukon	3	373	8.0 (1.7-23.3)	3	372	8.1 (1.7-23.4)
Northwest Territories	8	681	11.7 (5.1-23.0)	6	678	8.8 (3.3-19.2)
Nunavut	3	730	4.1 (0.8-12.0)	3	729	4.1 (0.8-12.0)
CANADA	1,175	201,629	5.8 (5.5-6.2)	903	201,180	4.5 (4.2-4.8)

Source: Statistics Canada. Canadian Vital Statistics System, 1991-2000 (unlinked live birth and stillbirth files).
*Data for Ontario were excluded because of data quality concerns; they are presented in *Appendix G*.
**Fetal death rates ≥ 500 g exclude stillbirths and live births with a birth weight < 500 g or, if birth weight was unknown, those with a gestational age of < 22 weeks.
CI — confidence interval.

TABLE F4.10 | **Rate of neonatal (0-27 days) death,** *Canada (excluding Ontario),* 1991-2000*

Year	Number of neonatal deaths	Number of live births	Neonatal deaths per 1,000 live births
1991	987	251,050	3.9
1992	983	248,043	4.0
1993	964	240,542	4.0
1994	1,016	238,042	4.3
1995	976	231,747	4.2
1996	857	226,188	3.8
1997	840	215,590	3.9
1998	762	209,789	3.6
1999	712	206,157	3.5
2000	687	200,454	3.4

Source: Statistics Canada. Canadian Vital Statistics System, 1991-2000 (period calculation using unlinked live birth and death files).
*Data for Ontario were excluded because of data quality concerns; they are presented in *Appendix G*.

TABLE F4.11 **Rate of neonatal (0-27 days) death, by province/territory,** *Canada (excluding Ontario),* 2000*

Province/territory	Number of neonatal deaths	Number of live births	Neonatal deaths (95% CI) per 1,000 live births	
Newfoundland	17	4,869	3.5	(2.0-5.6)
Prince Edward Island	4	1,441	2.8	(0.8-7.1)
Nova Scotia	31	9,115	3.4	(2.3-4.8)
New Brunswick	22	7,347	3.0	(1.9-4.6)
Quebec	248	72,005	3.4	(3.0-3.9)
Manitoba	54	14,090	3.8	(2.9-5.0)
Saskatchewan	41	12,139	3.4	(2.4-4.6)
Alberta	154	37,006	4.2	(3.5-4.9)
British Columbia	106	40,672	2.6	(2.1-3.2)
Yukon	0	370	0.0	(0.0-9.9)
Northwest Territories	5	673	7.4	(2.4-17.3)
Nunavut	5	727	6.9	(2.2-16.0)
CANADA	687	200,454	3.4	(3.2-3.7)

Source: Statistics Canada. Canadian Vital Statistics System, 2000 (period calculation using unlinked live birth and death files).
*Data for Ontario were excluded because of data quality concerns; they are presented in *Appendix G.*
CI — confidence interval.

TABLE F4.12 **Rate of postneonatal (28-364 days) death,** *Canada (excluding Ontario),* 1991-2000*

Year	Number of postneonatal deaths	Number of neonatal survivors	Postneonatal deaths per 1,000 neonatal survivors
1991	633	250,063	2.5
1992	562	247,060	2.3
1993	560	239,578	2.3
1994	523	237,026	2.2
1995	475	230,771	2.1
1996	392	225,331	1.7
1997	359	214,750	1.7
1998	382	209,027	1.8
1999	359	205,445	1.7
2000	336	199,767	1.7

Source: Statistics Canada. Canadian Vital Statistics System, 1991-2000 (period calculation using unlinked live birth and death files).
*Data for Ontario were excluded because of data quality concerns; they are presented in *Appendix G.*

TABLE F4.13 **Rate of postneonatal (28-364) death, by province/territory,** *Canada (excluding Ontario),* * 2000*

Province/territory	Number of postneonatal deaths	Number of neonatal survivors	Postneonatal deaths per 1,000 neonatal survivors	
Newfoundland	7	4,852	1.4	(0.6-3.0)
Prince Edward Island	1	1,437	0.7	(0.0-3.9)
Nova Scotia	14	9,084	1.5	(0.8-2.6)
New Brunswick	4	7,325	0.6	(0.2-1.4)
Quebec	91	71,757	1.3	(1.0-1.6)
Manitoba	38	14,036	2.7	(1.9-3.7)
Saskatchewan	41	12,098	3.4	(2.4-4.6)
Alberta	90	36,852	2.4	(2.0-3.0)
British Columbia	44	40,566	1.1	(0.8-1.5)
Yukon	1	370	2.7	(0.1-15.0)
Northwest Territories	1	668	1.5	(0.0-8.3)
Nunavut	4	722	5.5	(1.5-14.1)
CANADA	336	199,767	1.7	(1.5-1.9)

Source: Statistics Canada. Canadian Vital Statistics System, 2000 (period calculation using unlinked live birth and death files).
*Data for Ontario were excluded because of data quality concerns; they are presented in *Appendix G*.
CI — confidence interval.

TABLE F4.14 **Rate of infant (0-364 days) death,** *Canada (excluding Ontario),* * 1991-2000*

Year	Number of infant deaths	Number of live births	Infant deaths per 1,000 live births
1991	1,620	251,050	6.5
1992	1,545	248,043	6.2
1993	1,524	240,542	6.3
1994	1,539	238,042	6.5
1995	1,451	231,747	6.3
1996	1,249	226,188	5.5
1997	1,199	215,590	5.6
1998	1,144	209,789	5.5
1999	1,071	206,157	5.2
2000	1,023	200,454	5.1

Source: Statistics Canada. Canadian Vital Statistics System, 1991-2000 (period calculation using unlinked live birth and death files).
*Data for Ontario were excluded because of data quality concerns; they are presented in *Appendix G*.

TABLE F4.15 **Rate of infant (0-364 days) death, by province/territory,** *Canada (excluding Ontario),* 2000*

Province/territory	Number of infant deaths	Number of live births	Deaths (95% CI) per 1,000 live births	
Newfoundland	24	4,869	4.9	(3.2-7.3)
Prince Edward Island	5	1,441	3.5	(1.1-8.1)
Nova Scotia	45	9,115	4.9	(3.6-6.6)
New Brunswick	26	7,347	3.5	(2.3-5.2)
Quebec	339	72,005	4.7	(4.2-5.2)
Manitoba	92	14,090	6.5	(5.3-8.0)
Saskatchewan	82	12,139	6.8	(5.4-8.4)
Alberta	244	37,006	6.6	(5.8-7.5)
British Columbia	150	40,672	3.7	(3.1-4.3)
Yukon	1	370	2.7	(0.1-15.0)
Northwest Territories	6	673	8.9	(3.3-19.3)
Nunavut	9	727	12.4	(5.7-23.4)
CANADA	1,023	200,454	5.1	(4.8-5.4)

Source: Statistics Canada. Canadian Vital Statistics System, 2000 (period calculation using unlinked live birth and death files).
*Data for Ontario were excluded because of data quality concerns; they are presented in *Appendix G.*
CI — confidence interval.

TABLE F4.16 **Causes of infant death,** *Canada (excluding Ontario),* 1999***

Cause according to modified ICE classification***	Number of infant deaths	Percentage of infant deaths	Number of neonatal deaths	Percentage of neonatal deaths	Number of post-neonatal deaths	Percentage of post-neonatal deaths
Congenital anomalies	284	26.5	203	28.5	81	22.6
Asphyxia	108	10.1	105	14.7	3	0.8
Immaturity	251	23.4	232	32.6	19	5.3
Infection	72	6.7	27	3.8	45	12.5
Sudden infant death syndrome (SIDS)	120	11.2	15	2.1	105	29.2
Other sudden unexplained infant death	28	2.6	8	1.1	20	5.6
External causes	30	2.8	5	0.7	25	7.0
Other	178	16.6	117	16.4	61	17.0
TOTAL	1,071	100.0	712	100.0	359	100.0

Source: Statistics Canada. Canadian Vital Statistics System, 1999 (period calculation using unlinked death files).
*Data for Ontario were excluded because of data quality concerns; they are presented in *Appendix G.*
**Causes of infant death are presented for 1999 because the ICE classification is based on ICD-9. In 2000, causes of death in the Statistics Canada death file were coded using ICD-10.
***See reference 4 in the *Infant Mortality Rate and Causes of Death* section.

TABLE F4.17 **Birth cohort-based infant death rate,* by gestational age,** *Canada (excluding Ontario),** 1997-1999 combined*

Gestational age (weeks)	Number of infant deaths	Number of live births	Deaths (95% CI) per 1,000 live births	
< 22	342	345	991.3	(974.8-998.2)
22-23	432	472	915.3	(886.4-938.8)
24-25	364	791	460.2	(425.0-495.6)
26-27	199	1,108	179.6	(157.4-203.5)
28-31	238	3,959	60.1	(52.9-68.00)
32-33	141	5,445	25.9	(21.84-30.5)
34-36	327	33,350	9.8	(8.8-10.9)
37-41	1,315	575,228	2.3	(2.2-2.4)
≥ 42	30	10,379	2.9	(2.0-4.1)
Unknown gestational age	13	475	27.4	(14.7-46.3)
Unlinked	41	—	—	
All gestational ages	3,442	631,552	5.4	(5.3-5.6)

Source: Statistics Canada. Canadian Vital Statistics System, 1997-1999 (birth-infant death linked files).

*In the birth-infant death linked files, all live births at < 22 weeks and < 500 g were assumed to have died on the first day of life and were classified as such.

**Data for Ontario were excluded because of data quality concerns; they are presented in *Appendix G*.

CI — confidence interval.

TABLE F4.18 **Birth cohort-based infant death rate,* by birth weight,** *Canada (excluding Ontario),** 1997-1999 combined*

Birth weight (grams)	Number of infant deaths	Number of live births	Deaths (95% CI) per 1,000 live births	
< 500	513	544	943.0	(920.1-961.0)
500-749	575	1,041	552.4	(521.6-582.9)
750-999	254	1,206	210.6	(187.9-234.7)
1,000-1,249	135	1,387	97.3	(82.2-114.2)
1,250-1,499	70	1,720	40.7	(31.9-51.1)
1,500-1,999	203	6,965	29.1	(25.3-33.4)
2,000-2,499	284	22,821	12.4	(11.1-14.0)
2,500-3,999	1,191	515,148	2.3	(2.2-2.5)
≥ 4,000	149	80,100	1.9	(1.6-2.2)
Unknown birth weight	27	620	43.5	(28.9-62.7)
Unlinked	41	—	—	
All births weights	3,442	631,552	5.4	(5.3-5.6)

Source: Statistics Canada. Canadian Vital Statistics System, 1997-1999 (birth-infant death linked files).

*In the birth-infant death linked files, all live births at < 22 weeks and < 500 g were assumed to have died on the first day of life and were classified as such.

**Data for Ontario were excluded because of data quality concerns; they are presented in *Appendix G*.

CI — confidence interval.

TABLE F4.19

Birth cohort-based number of infant deaths,* by gestational age and province/territory, *Canada (excluding Ontario),** 1995-1999 combined*

Gestational age (weeks)	NF	PE	NS	NB	QC	MB	SK	AB	BC	YT	NT
< 22	8	6	19	16	213	58	23	111	96	2	7
22-23	15	8	30	20	263	69	50	150	129	0	5
24-25	28	3	14	24	218	51	58	108	115	0	2
26-27	11	4	15	9	123	34	36	61	54	0	7
28-31	16	8	19	16	151	30	40	77	76	1	10
32-33	7	2	11	10	75	13	32	43	41	2	7
34-36	23	3	32	24	214	69	41	110	100	2	8
37-41	48	12	93	85	772	205	211	440	419	9	48
≥ 42	4	1	4	3	12	10	6	12	8	0	0
Unknown gestational age	0	0	0	0	9	3	0	1	12	0	0
Unlinked	11	0	0	1	18	0	16	3	14	0	5
All gestational ages	171	47	237	208	2,068	542	513	1,116	1,064	16	99

Source: Statistics Canada. Canadian Vital Statistics System, 1995-1999 (birth-infant death linked files).

*In the birth-infant death linked files, all live births at < 22 weeks and < 500 g were assumed to have died on the first day of life and were classified as such.

**Data for Ontario were excluded because of data quality concerns; they are presented in *Appendix G*.

TABLE F4.20

Birth cohort-based number of live births,* by gestational age and province/territory, *Canada (excluding Ontario),** 1995-1999 combined*

Gestational age (weeks)	NF	PE	NS	NB	QC	MB	SK	AB	BC	YT	NT
< 22	9	6	19	16	214	59	24	111	99	2	8
22-23	18	9	32	22	291	73	52	164	143	0	5
24-25	47	10	41	41	466	108	91	260	262	1	7
26-27	60	14	77	58	622	152	141	336	362	3	19
28-31	213	57	328	248	2,381	442	389	1,299	1,348	15	81
32-33	276	65	418	299	3,265	647	523	1,750	1,770	8	76
34-36	1,356	334	2,748	1,885	22,233	4,116	3,243	10,054	10,503	87	477
37-41	24,800	7,341	44,246	36,462	366,855	66,851	58,924	172,093	203,018	1,939	6,575
≥ 42	289	219	2,501	1,129	3,778	2,506	1,651	3,669	4,539	111	91
Unknown gestational age	7	6	23	2	1,771	85	2	12	495	1	48
All gestational ages	27,075	8,061	50,433	40,162	401,876	75,039	65,040	189,748	222,537	2,167	7,386

Source: Statistics Canada. Canadian Vital Statistics System, 1995-1999 (birth-infant death linked files).

*In the birth-infant death linked files, all live births at < 22 weeks and < 500 g were assumed to have died on the first day of life and were classified as such.

**Data for Ontario were excluded because of data quality concerns; they are presented in *Appendix G*.

Appendix F

TABLE F4.21 **Birth cohort-based infant death rate,* by gestational age and province/territory,**
*Canada (excluding Ontario),** 1995-1999 combined*

Gestational age (weeks)	NF	PE	NS	NB	QC
< 22	888.9 (517.5-997.2)	1,000.0 (540.7-1,000.0)	1,000.0 (823.5-1,000.0)	1,000.0 (794.1-1,000.0)	995.3 (974.2-999.9)
22-23	833.3 (585.8-964.2)	888.9 (517.5-997.2)	937.5 (791.9-992.3)	909.1 (708.4-988.8)	903.8 (863.9-935.1)
24-25	595.7 (442.7-736.3)	300.0 (66.7-652.5)	341.5 (200.8-506.0)	585.4 (421.1-736.8)	467.8 (421.8-514.3)
26-27	183.3 (95.2-304.4)	285.7 (83.9-581.0)	194.8 (113.3-300.9)	155.2 (73.5-274.2)	197.7 (167.1-231.3)
28-31	75.1 (43.5-119.1)	140.4 (62.6-258.0)	57.9 (35.2-89.0)	64.5 (37.3-102.7)	63.4 (54.0-74.0)
32-33	25.4 (10.3-51.6)	30.8 (3.8-106.8)	26.3 (13.2-46.6)	33.4 (16.2-60.6)	23.0 (18.1-28.7)
34-36	17.0 (10.8-25.3)	9.0 (1.9-26.0)	11.6 (8.0-16.4)	12.7 (8.2-18.9)	9.6 (8.4-11.0)
37-41	1.9 (2.6-1.9)	1.6 (0.8-2.9)	2.1 (1.7-2.6)	2.3 (1.9-2.9)	2.1 (2.0-2.3)
≥ 42	13.8 (3.8-35.1)	4.6 (0.1-25.2)	1.6 (0.4-4.1)	2.7 (0.6-7.8)	3.2 (1.6-5.5)
Unknown gestational age	0.0 (0.0-409.6)	0.0 (0.0-459.3)	0.0 (0.0-148.2)	0.0 (0.0-841.9)	5.1 (2.3-9.6)
All gestational ages	6.3 (5.4-7.3)	5.8 (4.3-7.8)	4.7 (4.1-5.3)	5.2 (4.5-5.9)	5.1 (4.9-5.4)

Gestational age (weeks)	MB	SK	AB	BC	YT	NT
< 22	983.1 (909.1-999.6)	958.3 (788.8-999.0)	1,000.0 (967.3-1,000.0)	969.7 (914.0-993.7)	1,000.0 (158.1-1,000.0)	875.0 (473.5-996.8)
22-23	945.2 (865.6-984.9)	961.5 (867.9-995.3)	914.6 (860.9-952.5)	902.1 (841.2-945.4)	0.0 (0.0-975.0)	1000.0 (478.2-1000.0)
24-25	472.2 (375.4-570.6)	637.4 (529.9-735.6)	415.4 (354.8-477.9)	438.9 (377.9-501.3)	0.0 (0.0-975.0)	285.7 (36.7-709.6)
26-27	223.7 (160.2-298.3)	255.3 (185.7-335.5)	181.5 (141.8-227.0)	149.2 (114.1-190.1)	0.0 (0.0-707.6)	368.4 (162.9-616.4)
28-31	67.9 (46.3-95.5)	102.8 (74.8-137.4)	59.3 (47.1-73.53)	56.4 (44.7-70.1)	66.7 (1.7-319.5)	123.5 (60.8-215.4)
32-33	20.1 (10.7-34.1)	61.2 (42.2-85.3)	24.6 (17.8-33.0)	23.2 (16.7-31.3)	250.0 (31.9-650.9)	92.1 (37.8-180.6)
34-36	16.8 (13.1-21.2)	12.6 (9.1-17.1)	10.9 (9.00-13.2)	9.5 (7.8-11.6)	23.0 (2.8-80.6)	16.8 (7.3-32.8)
37-41	3.1 (2.7-3.5)	3.6 (3.1-4.1)	2.6 (2.3-2.8)	2.1 (1.9-2.3)	4.6 (2.1-8.8)	7.3 (5.4-9.7)
≥ 42	4.0 (1.9-7.3)	3.6 (1.3-7.9)	3.3 (1.7-5.7)	1.8 (0.8-3.5)	0.0 (0.0-32.7)	0.0 (0.0-39.7)
Unknown gestational age	35.3 (7.3-99.7)	0.0 (0.0-841.9)	83.3 (2.1-384.8)	24.2 (12.6-42.0)	0.0 (0.0-975.0)	0.0 (0.0-74.0)
All gestational ages	7.2 (6.6-7.9)	7.9 (7.2-8.6)	5.9 (5.5-6.2)	4.8 (4.5-5.1)	7.4 (4.2-12.0)	13.4 (10.9-16.3)

Source: Statistics Canada. Canadian Vital Statistics System, 1995-1999 (birth-infant death linked files).

*Deaths (95% confidence interval) per 1,000 live births. In the birth-infant death linked files, all live births at < 22 weeks and < 500 g were assumed to have died on the first day of life and were classified as such.

**Data for Ontario were excluded because of data quality concerns; they are presented in *Appendix G.*

TABLE F4.22 **Birth cohort-based number of infant deaths,* by birth weight and province/territory,** *Canada (excluding Ontario),** 1995-1999 combined*

Birth weight (grams)	NF	PE	NS	NB	QC	MB	SK	AB	BC	YT	NT
< 500	12	6	36	29	320	100	42	166	144	1	7
500-749	35	12	29	24	354	78	76	190	174	0	6
750-999	15	3	19	19	146	37	44	68	63	1	3
1,000-1,249	7	2	10	12	75	19	23	51	43	0	7
1,250-1,499	7	3	7	4	59	12	15	27	23	0	3
1,500-1,999	9	4	18	13	135	28	30	72	77	1	10
2,000-2,499	15	2	18	26	162	40	44	96	87	3	10
2,500-3,999	47	12	85	73	698	200	192	402	369	9	43
≥ 4,000	7	2	13	7	72	26	29	39	50	1	5
Unknown birth weight	6	1	2	0	29	2	2	2	20	0	0
Unlinked	11	0	0	1	18	0	16	3	14	0	5
All birth weights	171	47	237	208	2,068	542	513	1,116	1,064	16	99

Source: Statistics Canada. Canadian Vital Statistics System, 1995-1999 (birth-infant death linked files).

*In the birth-infant death linked files, all live births at < 22 weeks and < 500 g were assumed to have died on the first day of life and were classified as such.

**Data for Ontario were excluded because of data quality concerns; they are presented in *Appendix G.*

TABLE F4.23 **Birth cohort-based number of live births,* by birth weight and province/territory,** *Canada (excluding Ontario),** 1995-1999 combined*

Birth weight (grams)	NF	PE	NS	NB	QC	MB	SK	AB	BC	YT	NT
< 500	18	6	37	30	335	107	43	175	163	1	7
500-749	54	18	56	43	619	157	127	335	319	1	10
750-999	53	18	108	78	713	162	128	379	354	4	8
1,000-1,249	75	22	114	93	836	171	169	457	448	3	25
1,250-1,499	94	18	135	120	1,130	206	166	541	576	3	24
1,500-1,999	305	83	556	406	4,473	790	641	2,199	2,224	15	109
2,000-2,499	919	242	1817	1,325	15,618	2,513	2,144	7,417	7,352	69	268
2,500-3,999	21,286	6,273	39,882	31,927	335,092	59,596	52,280	155,643	180,403	1,732	5,758
≥ 4,000	4,242	1,357	7,689	6,134	41,556	11,320	9,333	22,594	30,195	338	1,038
Unknown birth weight	29	24	39	6	1,504	17	9	8	505	1	140
All birth weights	27,075	8,061	50,433	40,162	401,876	75,039	65,040	189,748	222,537	2,167	7,386

Source: Statistics Canada. Canadian Vital Statistics System, 1995-1999 (birth-infant death linked files).

*In the birth-infant death linked files, all live births at < 22 weeks and < 500 g were assumed to have died on the first day of life and were classified as such.

**Data for Ontario were excluded because of data quality concerns; they are presented in *Appendix G.*

Appendix F

Birth cohort-based infant death rate,* by birth weight and province/territory,
Canada (excluding Ontario),** 1995-1999 combined

Birth weight (grams)	NF	PE	NS	NB	QC
< 500	666.7 (409.9-866.6)	1,000.0 (540.7-1,000.0)	973.0 (858.4-999.3)	966.7 (827.8-999.2)	955.2 (927.2-974.7)
500-749	648.1 (506.2-773.2)	666.7 (409.9-866.6)	517.9 (380.3-653.5)	558.1 (398.8-709.2)	571.9 (531.8-611.3)
750-999	283.0 (167.9-423.5)	166.7 (35.8-414.2)	175.9 (109.4-261.0)	243.6 (153.5-354.0)	204.8 (175.7-236.3)
1,000-1,249	93.3 (38.4-182.9)	90.9 (11.2-291.6)	87.7 (42.9-155.4)	129.0 (68.5-214.6)	89.7 71.2-111.2)
1,250-1,499	74.5 (30.5-147.4)	166.7 (35.8-414.2)	51.9 (21.1-103.9)	33.3 (9.2-83.2)	52.2 (40.0-66.8)
1,500-1,999	29.5 (13.6-55.3)	48.2 (13.3-118.8)	32.4 (19.3-50.7)	32.0 (17.2-54.1)	30.2 (25.4-35.6)
2,000-2,499	16.3 (9.2-26.8)	8.3 (1.0-29.5)	9.9 (5.9-15.6)	19.6 (12.9-28.6)	10.4 (8.8-12.1)
2,500-3,999	2.2 (1.6-2.9)	1.9 (1.0-3.3)	2.1 (1.7-2.6)	2.3 (1.8-2.9)	2.1 (1.9-2.2)
≥ 4,000	1.7 (0.7-3.4)	1.5 (0.2-5.3)	1.7 (0.9-2.9)	1.1 (0.5-2.4)	1.7 (1.4-2.2)
Unknown birth weight	206.9 (79.9-397.3)	41.7 (1.1-211.2)	51.3 (6.3-173.3)	0.0 (0.0-459.3)	19.3 (13.0-27.6)
All birth weights	6.3 (5.4-7.3)	5.8 (4.3-7.8)	4.7 (4.1-5.3)	5.2 (4.5-5.9)	5.1 (4.9-5.4)

Birth weight (grams)	MB	SK	AB	BC	YT	NT
< 500	934.6 (869.9-973.3)	976.7 (877.1-999.4)	948.6 (904.6-976.2)	883.4 (824.0-928.3)	1,000.0 (25.0-1,000.0)	1,000.0 (590.4-1,000.0)
500-749	496.8 (416.1-577.6)	598.4 (507.8-684.4)	567.2 (512.2-620.9)	545.5 (489.0-601.0)	0.0 (0.0-975.0)	600.0 (262.4-878.5)
750-999	228.4 (166.2-300.8)	343.8 (262.1-432.8)	179.4 (142.1-221.8)	178.0 (139.6-221.9)	250.0 (6.3-805.9)	375.0 (85.2-755.1)
1,000-1,249	111.1 (68.2-168.1)	136.1 (88.3-197.2)	111.6 (84.2-144.1)	96.0 (70.3-127.1)	0.0 (0.0-707.6)	280.0 (120.7-493.9)
1,250-1,499	58.3 (30.5-99.54)	90.4 (51.5-144.66)	49.9 (33.1-71.8)	39.9 (25.5-59.3)	0.0 (0.0-707.6)	125.0 (26.6-323.6)
1,500-1,999	35.4 (23.7-50.8)	46.8 (31.8-66.1)	32.7 (25.7-41.1)	34.6 (27.4-43.1)	66.7 (1.7-319.5)	91.7 (44.9-162.3)
2,000-2,499	15.9 (11.4-21.6)	20.5 (15.0-27.5)	12.9 (10.5-15.8)	11.8 (9.5-14.6)	43.5 (9.1-121.9)	37.3 (18.0-67.6)
2,500-3,999	3.4 (2.9-3.9)	3.7 (3.2-4.2)	2.6 (2.3-2.9)	2.0 (1.8-2.3)	5.2 (2.4-9.8)	7.5 (5.4-10.1)
≥ 4,000	2.3 (1.5-3.4)	3.1 (2.1-4.5)	1.7 (1.2-2.4)	1.7 (1.2-2.2)	3.0 (0.1-16.4)	4.8 (1.6-11.2)
Unknown birth weight	117.6 (14.6-364.4)	222.2 (28.2-600.1)	250.0 (31.9-650.9)	39.6 (24.4-60.5)	0.0 (0.0-975.0)	0.0 (0.0-26.0)
All birth weights	7.2 (6.6-7.9)	7.9 (7.2-8.6)	5.9 (5.5-6.2)	4.8 (4.5-5.1)	7.4 (4.2-12.0)	13.4 (10.9-16.3)

Source: Statistics Canada. Canadian Vital Statistics System, 1995-1999 (birth-infant death linked files).

*Deaths (95% confidence interval) per 1,000 live births. In the birth-infant death linked files, all live births < 22 weeks and < 500 g were assumed to have died on the first day of life and were classified as such.

**Data for Ontario were excluded because of data quality concerns; they are presented in *Appendix G*.

TABLE F4.25 **Rates of respiratory distress syndrome (RDS) and neonatal sepsis,** *Canada, 1991-1992 to 2000-2001*

Fiscal year	Number of RDS cases	Number of hospital live births	RDS cases per 1,000 hospital live births	Number of sepsis cases	Sepsis cases per 1,000 hospital live births
1991-1992*	5,268	389,776	13.5	6,568	16.9
1992-1993	5,215	394,290	13.2	7,346	18.6
1993-1994	4,553	386,519	11.8	7,186	18.6
1994-1995	4,520	384,583	11.8	7,485	19.5
1995-1996	4,286	375,463	11.4	7,687	20.5
1996-1997	4,064	361,582	11.2	8,126	22.5
1997-1998	3,918	347,948	11.3	8,022	23.1
1998-1999	3,854	340,464	11.3	7,869	23.1
1999-2000	3,813	337,723	11.3	7,692	22.8
2000-2001	3,797	326,410	11.6	8,104	24.8

Sources: Canadian Institute for Health Information. Discharge Abstract Database (DAD), 1991-1992 to 2000-2001.
    Population Health Research Unit, Dalhousie University, Nova Scotia. ASD, 1992-1993 to 2000-2001.
    Ministère de la Santé et des Services sociaux (Québec). Banque de données sur les hospitalisations du système MED-ÉCHO,
        1991-1992 to 2000-2001.
    Manitoba Health, Health Information Management. Manitoba Hospital Abstract System, 1991-1992 to 2000-2001.
Note: 1. Live births with birth weight < 500 g were excluded.
    2. RDS and neonatal sepsis cases include infants whose condition was diagnosed during the birth admission only.
*Complete data for Nova Scotia were not available for 1991-1992 and were not included in the estimates for that year.

TABLE F4.26 **Rates of respiratory distress syndrome (RDS) and neonatal sepsis, by province/territory,** *Canada, 2000-2001*

Province/ territory	Number of hospital live births	Number of RDS cases	RDS cases (95% CI) per 1,000 hospital live births		Number of sepsis cases	Sepsis cases (95% CI) per 1,000 hospital live births	
Newfoundland	4,769	64	13.4	(10.4-17.1)	33	6.9	(4.8-9.7)
Prince Edward Island	1,372	12	8.7	(4.5-15.2)	7	5.1	(2.1-10.5)
Nova Scotia	8,714	102	11.7	(9.6-14.2)	71	8.1	(6.4-10.3)
New Brunswick	7,451	82	11.0	(8.8-13.6)	142	19.1	(16.1-22.4)
Quebec	70,346	786	11.2	(10.4-12.0)	936	13.3	(12.5-14.2)
Ontario	129,914	1,508	11.6	(11.0-12.2)	5,632	43.4	(42.3-44.5)
Manitoba	13,749	153	11.1	(9.4-13.0)	96	7.0	(5.7-8.5)
Saskatchewan	11,988	120	10.0	(8.3-12.0)	120	10.0	(8.3-12.0)
Alberta	36,858	482	13.1	(11.9-14.3)	308	8.4	(7.5-9.3)
British Columbia	39,817	478	12.0	(11.0-13.1)	756	19.0	(17.7-20.4)
Yukon	351	3	8.5	(1.8-24.8)	0	0.0	(0.0-10.5)
Northwest Territories	338	1	3.0	(0.1-16.4)	0	0.0	(0.0-10.9)
Nunavut	743	6	8.1	(3.0-17.5)	3	4.0	(0.8-11.8)
CANADA	326,410	3,797	11.6	(11.3-12.0)	8,104	24.8	(24.3-25.4)

Sources: Canadian Institute for Health Information. Discharge Abstract Database (DAD), 2000-2001.
    Population Health Research Unit, Dalhousie University, Nova Scotia. ASD, 2000-2001.
    Ministère de la Santé et des Services sociaux (Québec). Banque de données sur les hospitalisations du système MED-ÉCHO,
        2000-2001.
    Manitoba Health, Health Information Management. Manitoba Hospital Abstract System, 2000-2001.
Note: 1. Live births with birth weight < 500 g were excluded.
    2. RDS and neonatal sepsis cases include infants whose condition was diagnosed during the birth admission only.
CI — confidence interval.

Appendix F

TABLE F4.27 **Rate of multiple birth,** *Canada (excluding Ontario), * 1991-2000*

Year	Number of multiple births	Total births	Multiple births per 100 total births
1991	5,271	252,542	2.1
1992	5,286	249,493	2.1
1993	5,231	241,905	2.2
1994	5,278	239,397	2.2
1995	5,230	233,127	2.2
1996	5,235	227,408	2.3
1997	5,304	216,853	2.4
1998	5,423	210,935	2.6
1999	5,448	207,387	2.6
2000	5,384	201,629	2.7

Source: Statistics Canada. Canadian Vital Statistics System, 1991-2000 (unlinked live birth and stillbirth files).
*Data for Ontario were excluded because of data quality concerns; they are presented in *Appendix G*.

TABLE F4.28 **Rate of multiple birth, by province/territory,** *Canada (excluding Ontario),* 2000*

Province/territory	Number of multiple births	Total births	Multiple births (95% CI) per 100 total births	
Newfoundland	124	4,892	2.5	(2.1-3.0)
Prince Edward Island	24	1,447	1.7	(1.1-2.5)
Nova Scotia	253	9,167	2.8	(2.4-3.1)
New Brunswick	195	7,384	2.6	(2.3-3.0)
Quebec	1,853	72,316	2.6	(2.4-2.7)
Manitoba	372	14,224	2.6	(2.4-2.9)
Saskatchewan	320	12,212	2.6	(2.3-2.9)
Alberta	1,136	37,250	3.0	(2.9-3.2)
British Columbia	1,069	40,953	2.6	(2.5-2.8)
Yukon	13	373	3.5	(1.9-5.9)
Northwest Territories	12	681	1.8	(0.9-3.1)
Nunavut	13	730	1.8	(1.0-3.0)
CANADA	5,384	201,629	2.7	(2.6-2.7)

Source: Statistics Canada. Canadian Vital Statistics System, 2000 (unlinked live birth and stillbirth files).
*Data for Ontario were excluded because of data quality concerns; they are presented in *Appendix G*.
CI — confidence interval.

TABLE F4.29 **Rate of Down syndrome (DS),** *Canada,* 1991-1999*

Year	Number of DS cases (excluding NS)	Total births (excluding NS)	DS cases per 10,000 total births (excluding NS)	Number of DS cases (including NS)	Total births (including NS)	DS cases per 10,000 total births (including NS)
1991	556	389,926	14.3	—	—	—
1992	460	384,740	12.0	—	—	—
1993	490	377,167	13.0	—	—	—
1994	461	375,451	12.3	—	—	—
1995	493	368,100	13.4	—	—	—
1996	430	356,188	12.1	450	366,811	12.3
1997	468	341,122	13.7	478	351,139	13.6
1998	458	334,133	13.7	486	343,822	14.1
1999	466	328,493	14.2	487	338,133	14.4

Source: Health Canada. Canadian Congenital Anomalies Surveillance System, 1991-1999.
*Nova Scotia data were not available to CCASS before 1996.

TABLE F4.30 **Rate of Down syndrome (DS), by province/territory,** *Canada, 1997-1999 combined*

Province/territory	Number of DS cases	Total births	DS cases (95% CI) per 10,000 total births	
Newfoundland	20	15,538	12.9	(7.8-19.9)
Prince Edward Island	8	4,550	17.6	(7.6-34.6)
Nova Scotia	59	29,346	20.1	(15.3-25.9)
New Brunswick	43	24,017	17.9	(12.9-24.1)
Quebec	298	225,053	13.2	(11.8-14.8)
Ontario	553	406,064	13.6	(12.5-14.8)
Manitoba	59	43,232	13.6	(10.4-17.6)
Saskatchewan	61	37,957	16.1	(12.3-20.6)
Alberta	124	113,844	10.9	(9.0-13.0)
British Columbia	218	129,230	16.9	(14.7-19.3)
Yukon	3	1,213	24.7	(5.0-72.3)
Northwest Territories*	5	3,050	16.4	(5.3-38.2)
CANADA	1,451	1,033,094	14.0	(13.3-14.8)

Source: Health Canada. Canadian Congenital Anomalies Surveillance System, 1997-1999.
*Nunavut is included in the Northwest Territories in the data for 1999.
CI — confidence interval.

TABLE F4.31 **Rate of neural tube defects (NTDs),** *Canada,* 1991-1999*

Year	Number of NTD cases (excluding NS)	Total births (excluding NS)	NTD cases per 10,000 total births (excluding NS)	Number of NTD cases (including NS)	Total births (including NS)	NTD cases per 10,000 total births (including NS)
1991	389	389,926	10.0	—	—	—
1992	370	384,740	9.6	—	—	—
1993	345	377,167	9.1	—	—	—
1994	349	375,451	9.3	—	—	—
1995	340	368,100	9.2	—	—	—
1996	257	356,188	7.2	278	366,811	7.6
1997	257	341,122	7.5	267	351,139	7.6
1998	188	334,133	5.6	196	343,822	5.7
1999	185	328,493	5.6	195	338,133	5.8

Source: Health Canada. Canadian Congenital Anomalies Surveillance System, 1991-1999.
*Nova Scotia data were not available to CCASS before 1996.

TABLE F4.32 **Rate of neural tube defects (NTDs), by province/territory,** *Canada, 1997-1999 combined*

Province/territory	Number of NTD cases	Total births	NTD cases (95% CI) per 10,000 total births	
Newfoundland	15	15,538	9.7	(5.4-15.9)
Prince Edward Island	0	4,550	0.0	(0.0-8.1)
Nova Scotia	28	29,346	9.5	(6.3-13.8)
New Brunswick	19	24,017	7.9	(4.8-12.3)
Quebec	121	225,053	5.4	(4.5-6.4)
Ontario	265	406,064	6.5	(5.8-7.4)
Manitoba	36	43,232	8.3	(5.8-11.5)
Saskatchewan	22	37,957	5.8	(3.6-8.8)
Alberta	52	113,844	4.6	(3.4-6.0)
British Columbia	100	129,230	7.7	(6.3-9.4)
Yukon	0	1,213	0.0	(0.0 -30.2)
Northwest Territories*	0	3,050	0.0	(0.0-12.0)
CANADA	658	1,033,094	6.4	(5.9-6.9)

Source: Health Canada. Canadian Congenital Anomalies Surveillance System, 1997-1999.
*Nunavut is included in the Northwest Territories in the data for 1999.
CI — confidence interval.

TABLE F4.33 **Rate of anencephaly,*** *Canada,*** 1991-1999*

Year	Number of cases (excluding NS)	Total births (excluding NS)	Prevalence rate per 10,000 total births (excluding NS)	Number of cases (including NS)	Total births (including NS)	Prevalence rate per 10,000 total births (including NS)
1991	75	389,926	1.9	—	—	—
1992	63	384,740	1.6	—	—	—
1993	72	377,167	1.9	—	—	—
1994	68	375,451	1.8	—	—	—
1995	65	368,100	1.8	—	—	—
1996	40	356,188	1.1	42	366,811	1.1
1997	51	341,122	1.5	54	351,139	1.5
1998	30	334,133	0.9	31	343,822	0.9
1999	31	328,493	0.9	31	338,133	0.9

Source: Health Canada. Canadian Congenital Anomalies Surveillance System, 1991-1999.
*Includes similar cranial neural tube defects such as cranioraschisis and inencephaly.
**Nova Scotia data were not available to CCASS before 1996.

TABLE F4.34 **Rate of anencephaly,* by province/territory,** *Canada, 1997-1999 combined*

Province/territory	Number of cases	Total births	Cases (95% CI) per 10,000 total births	
Newfoundland	3	15,538	1.9	(0.4-5.6)
Prince Edward Island	0	4,550	0.0	(0.0-8.1)
Nova Scotia	4	29,346	1.4	(0.4-3.5)
New Brunswick	2	24,017	0.8	(0.1-3.0)
Quebec	14	225,053	0.6	(0.3-1.0)
Ontario	52	406,064	1.3	(0.9-1.7)
Manitoba	7	43,232	1.6	(0.6-3.3)
Saskatchewan	3	37,957	0.8	(0.1-2.3)
Alberta	13	113,844	1.1	(0.6-1.9)
British Columbia	18	129,230	1.4	(0.8-2.2)
Yukon	0	1,213	0.0	(0.0-30.2)
Northwest Territories**	0	3,050	0.0	(0.0-12.0)
CANADA	116	1,033,094	1.1	(0.9-1.3)

Source: Health Canada. Canadian Congenital Anomalies Surveillance System, 1997-1999.
*Includes similar cranial neural tube defects such as cranioraschisis and inencephaly.
**Nunavut is included in the Northwest Territories in the data for 1999.
CI — confidence interval.

TABLE F4.35 **Rate of spina bifida,** *Canada,* 1991-1999*

Year	Number of cases (excluding NS)	Total births (excluding NS)	Cases per 10,000 total births (excluding NS)	Number of cases (including NS)	Total births (including NS)	Cases per 10,000 total births (including NS)
1991	268	389,926	6.9	—	—	—
1992	265	384,740	6.9	—	—	—
1993	239	377,167	6.3	—	—	—
1994	237	375,451	6.3	—	—	—
1995	238	368,100	6.5	—	—	—
1996	184	356,188	5.2	200	366,811	5.4
1997	182	341,122	5.3	188	351,139	5.3
1998	138	334,133	4.1	144	343,822	4.2
1999	130	328,493	4.0	136	338,133	4.0

Source: Health Canada. Canadian Congenital Anomalies Surveillance System, 1991-1999.
*Nova Scotia data were not available to CCASS before 1996.

TABLE F4.36 **Rate of spina bifida, by province/territory,** *Canada, 1997-1999 combined*

Province/territory	Number of cases	Total births	Cases (95% CI) per 10,000 total births	
Newfoundland	9	15,538	5.8	(2.6-11.0)
Prince Edward Island	0	4,550	0.0	(0.0-8.1)
Nova Scotia	18	29,346	6.1	(3.6-9.7)
New Brunswick	14	24,017	5.8	(3.2-9.8)
Quebec	86	225,053	3.8	(3.0-4.7)
Ontario	190	406,064	4.7	(4.0-5.4)
Manitoba	24	43,232	5.6	(3.5-8.3)
Saskatchewan	17	37,957	4.5	(2.6-7.2)
Alberta	34	113,844	3.0	(2.1-4.2)
British Columbia	76	129,230	5.9	(4.6-7.4)
Yukon	0	1,213	0.0	(0.0-30.2)
Northwest Territories*	0	3,050	0.0	(0.0-12.0)
CANADA	468	1,033,094	4.5	(4.1-4.9)

Source: Health Canada. Canadian Congenital Anomalies Surveillance System. 1997-1999.
*Nunavut is included in the Northwest Territories in the data for 1999.
CI — confidence interval.

TABLE F4.37 **Rate of neonatal hospital readmission after discharge at birth,**
Canada (excluding Manitoba),* 1991-1992 to 2000-2001

Fiscal year	Number of readmitted newborns (excluding NS)**	Number of hospital live births*** (excluding NS)**	Readmitted newborns per 100 hospital live births*** (excluding NS)**	Number of readmitted newborns (including NS)	Number of hospital live births*** (including NS)	Readmitted newborns per 100 hospital live births*** (including NS)
1991-1992	7,039	369,093	1.9	—	—	—
1992-1993	7,293	363,159	2.0	—	—	—
1993-1994	7,980	355,142	2.2	—	—	—
1994-1995	8,881	353,993	2.5	—	—	—
1995-1996	9,656	345,951	2.8	10,107	356,998	2.8
1996-1997	9,971	333,013	3.0	10,466	343,729	3.0
1997-1998	10,046	320,563	3.1	10,457	330,589	3.2
1998-1999	10,548	314,024	3.4	10,969	323,688	3.4
1999-2000	9,933	310,889	3.2	10,369	320,441	3.2
2000-2001	9,609	300,772	3.2	9,927	309,453	3.2

Sources: Canadian Institute for Health Information, Discharge Abstract Database (DAD), 1991-1992 to 2000-2001.
      Population Health Research Unit, Dalhousie University, Nova Scotia. ASD, 1995-1996 to 2000-2001.
      Ministère de la Santé et des Services sociaux (Québec). Banque de données sur les hospitalisations du système MED-ÉCHO, 1991-1992 to 2000-2001

*Data for Manitoba were not included because the Manitoba Hospital Abstract System does not distinguish readmitted patients from those transferred from one facility to another.

**Complete data for Nova Scotia were not available for 1991-1992 to 1994-1995.

***Live birth with birth weight < 1,000 g were excluded. The number of neonatal readmissions was calculated for 28 days after discharge from hospital. Newborns who were directly transferred to another hospital after birth or newborns with initial length of hospital stay > 20 days were excluded. Hospital discharges following day surgery were not counted as readmissions in the analysis.

TABLE F4.38 **Rate of neonatal hospital readmissions after discharge at birth, by province/territory,** *Canada (excluding Manitoba),* 2000-2001*

Province/territory	Number of readmitted newborns**	Number of hospital live births**	Readmitted newborns (95% CI) per 100 live hospital births**	
Newfoundland	101	4,699	2.1	(1.8-2.6)
Prince Edward Island	20	1,367	1.5	(0.9-2.3)
Nova Scotia	318	8,681	3.7	(3.3-4.1)
New Brunswick	245	7,318	3.3	(3.0-3.8)
Quebec	2,185	70,084	3.1	(3.0-3.3)
Ontario	3,674	128,229	2.9	(2.8-3.0)
Saskatchewan	486	11,839	4.1	(3.8-4.5)
Alberta	1,544	36,299	4.3	(4.0-4.5)
British Columbia	1,288	39,501	3.3	(3.1-3.4)
Yukon	13	353	3.7	(2.0-6.2)
Northwest Territories	22	748	2.9	(1.8-4.4)
Nunavut	31	335	9.3	(6.4-12.9)
CANADA	**9,927**	**309,453**	**3.2**	**(3.1-3.3)**

Sources: Canadian Institute for Health Information, Discharge Abstract Database (DAD), 2000-2001.
　　　Population Health Research Unit, Dalhousie University, Nova Scotia. ASD, 2000-2001.
　　　Ministère de la Santé et des Services sociaux (Québec). Banque de données sur les hospitalisations du
　　　　système MED-ÉCHO, 2000-2001.

*Data for Manitoba were not included because the Manitoba Hospital Abstract System does not distinguish readmitted patients from those transferred from one facility to another.

**Live births with birth weight < 1,000 g were excluded. The number of neonatal readmissions was calculated for 28 days after discharge from hospital. Newborns who were directly transferred to another hospital after birth or newborns with initial length of hospital stay > 20 days were excluded. Hospital discharges following day surgery were not counted as readmissions in the analysis.

CI — confidence interval.

TABLE F4.39 **Principal diagnosis for readmitted newborns,** *Canada (excluding Manitoba),* 1991-1992 and 2000-2001*

Principal diagnosis	1991-1992**		2000-2001	
	Number of readmitted newborns***	Percent of readmitted newborns by principal diagnosis***	Number of readmitted newborns***	Percent of readmitted newborns by principal diagnosis***
Jaundice	1,965	27.9	3,855	38.8
Feeding problems	436	6.2	692	7.0
Sepsis	199	2.8	379	3.8
Dehydration	46	0.7	218	2.2
Inadequate weight gain	109	1.6	162	1.6
Others	4,284	60.9	4,621	46.6
TOTAL	7,039	100.0	9,927	100.0

Sources: Canadian Institute for Health Information, Discharge Abstract Database (DAD), 1991-1992 and 2000-2001.
   Population Health Research Unit, Dalhousie University, Nova Scotia. ASD, 2000-2001.
   Ministère de la Santé et des Services sociaux (Québec). Banque de données sur les hospitalisations du système MED-ÉCHO, 1991-1992 and 2000-2001.

*Data for Manitoba were not included because the Manitoba Hospital Abstract System does not distinguish readmitted patients from those transferred from one facility to another.

**Complete data for Nova Scotia were not available for 1991-1992 and were not included in the estimates for that year.

***Live births with birth weight < 1,000 g were excluded. The number of neonatal readmissions was calculated for 28 days after discharge from hospital. Newborns who were directly transferred to another hospital after birth or newborns with initial length of hospital stay > 20 days were excluded. Hospital discharges following day surgery were not counted as readmissions in the analysis.

Appendix G

Ontario Vital Statistics Data

Previous studies have identified problems with the quality of vital statistics data from the province of Ontario.[1-3] Errors in birth weight and gestational age led to large artifactual increases in rates of low birth weight and preterm birth in Ontario during the early and mid-1990s. The problems that led to these data artifacts have been corrected, and recent data on birth weight and gestational age appear to be free from the previously identified concerns. Other concerns persist, including those related to increases in the under-registration of live births and the under-registration of live births among vulnerable populations, such as teenage mothers.[3] In particular, the Canadian Perinatal Surveillance System's project, which links information from live birth registrations with information from infant death registrations, has been successful in all provinces and territories except Ontario, where it has consistently resulted in a substantial rate of infant deaths, i.e., infant deaths for which a birth registration could not be located. Approximately 25% of infant deaths in Ontario result in such non-links (see Tables G18 and G19) as compared with 1% to 2% of unlinked infant deaths in other provinces and territories.

The above-mentioned errors in birth weight and gestational age in Ontario were responsible for the higher than expected values of indicators such as preterm birth (page 217), small for gestational age (page 219), etc., for the years 1993 and 1994. The infant mortality rate in Ontario increased from 5.0 per 1,000 live births in 1998 to 5.4 per 1,000 live births in 1999 and to 5.6 per 1,000 live births in 2000 (page 221). Neonatal and postneonatal death rates (page 220 and 221) also increased during the same period. Detailed analyses show that this increase was not due to an increase in birth registration of live births < 500 g. Infant death due to congenital anomalies, sudden infant death syndrome and respiratory distress syndrome decreased in Ontario between 1998 and 2000. However, infant deaths due to disorders relating to short gestation and unspecified low birth weight increased. Obstetricians and neonatalogists on the CPSS Steering Committee recommend examining gestational age-specific mortality infant rates especially among mild-moderately preterm infants (e.g., 32-33 weeks). Such analyses require a linked live birth-infant death file, however. At present, it is unclear whether this recent increase in infant mortality in Ontario is a true increase or an artifact. Statistics Canada recently reported that the infant mortality rate in Ontario in 2001 was 5.4 per 1,000 live births.

Because of concerns about the quality of gestational age and birth weight data in Ontario, Ontario data were excluded from the indicators in the *Canadian Perinatal Health Report, 2000*, which use these variables. Ontario data are included in this Appendix, along with this cautionary note, as some of the information may be useful in specific contexts.

References

1. Joseph KS, Kramer MS. Recent trends in infant mortality rates and proportions of low-birth-weight live births in Canada. *Can Med Assoc J* 1997;157:535-41.

2. Joseph KS. *Preterm Birth in Canada*. Background papers — Preterm Birth Prevention Consensus Conference. Ottawa, Ontario, 1998.

3. Bienefeld M, Woodward GL, Ardal S. *Under-reporting of Live Births in Ontario: 1991-1997*. Newmarket, Ontario: Central East Health Information Partnership. February 2001. URL: <http://www.cehip.org/Library/missing%20births%20final.PDF>.

List of Data Tables

Appendix G

Data Tables for Ontario Vital Statistics

TABLE G1 **Number of live births, by maternal age,** *Ontario, 1991-2000*

Year	≤ 14 years	15-17 years	18-19 years	20-24 years	25-29 years	30-34 years	35-39 years	≥ 40 years*	Unknown age	Total
1991	43	2,575	4,997	26,370	55,885	43,337	14,139	1,873	2,259	151,478
1992	51	2,627	4,983	25,658	54,951	45,162	14,935	2,025	201	150,593
1993	51	2,672	4,982	24,697	50,949	46,337	15,795	2,193	168	147,844
1994	55	2,686	5,028	23,953	48,848	47,099	16,461	2,418	518	147,066
1995	59	2,722	5,035	23,134	46,172	48,272	17,784	2,626	457	146,261
1996	51	2,383	4,584	21,327	43,290	46,683	18,745	2,762	185	140,010
1997	48	2,005	4,061	19,760	40,623	44,370	19,040	2,967	123	132,997
1998	39	2,110	4,108	20,083	39,814	43,265	19,679	3,112	396	132,606
1999	35	1,907	3,928	19,462	39,202	42,815	20,241	3,366	105	131,061
2000	42	1,708	3,608	18,895	37,355	41,506	20,535	3,654	90	127,393

Source: Statistics Canada. Canadian Vital Statistics System, 1991-2000 (unlinked live birth files).
*Age groups 40-44 years and ≥ 45 years have been collapsed because of small numbers.

TABLE G2 **Number of females, by age,** *Ontario, 1991-2000*

Year	14 years	15-17 years	18-19 years	20-24 years	25-29 years	30-34 years	35-39 years	40-49 years
1991	64,584	201,418	141,783	394,757	477,307	478,625	432,159	703,703
1992	64,880	201,651	139,703	391,590	465,736	485,811	443,582	729,017
1993	66,129	200,461	139,383	384,311	448,146	492,476	454,476	754,025
1994	68,275	201,660	140,650	379,524	432,975	498,688	464,676	781,835
1995	70,021	205,500	140,131	375,031	421,250	500,616	475,627	811,849
1996	70,213	210,808	139,432	368,944	414,384	494,189	488,432	838,268
1997	72,057	214,296	140,516	368,082	411,241	484,761	499,397	854,825
1998	73,302	217,245	143,555	367,688	408,760	470,675	510,347	874,033
1999	74,977	219,909	147,074	370,464	406,687	457,650	519,198	895,786
2000	75,810	224,607	148,977	374,840	407,294	450,701	524,431	920,963

Source: Statistics Canada. Annual Demographics Statistics, 2001. Demography Division, Catalogue No. 91-213-XPB, Annual, Ottawa, 2002.

TABLE G3 ## Proportion (%)* of live births, by maternal age, *Ontario, 1991-2000*

Year	≤ 14 years	15-17 years	18-19 years	20-24 years	25-29 years	30-34 years	35-39 years	≥ 40 years**
1991	0.03	1.73	3.35	17.67	37.45	29.04	9.48	1.25
1992	0.03	1.75	3.31	17.06	36.54	30.03	9.93	1.35
1993	0.03	1.81	3.37	16.72	34.50	31.38	10.70	1.49
1994	0.04	1.83	3.43	16.34	33.33	32.14	11.23	1.66
1995	0.04	1.87	3.45	15.86	31.67	33.11	12.20	1.80
1996	0.04	1.70	3.28	15.25	30.96	33.39	13.41	1.97
1997	0.04	1.51	3.06	14.87	30.57	33.39	14.33	2.23
1998	0.03	1.60	3.11	15.19	30.11	32.72	14.88	2.36
1999	0.03	1.46	3.00	14.86	29.93	32.69	15.46	2.57
2000	0.03	1.34	2.85	14.84	29.34	32.60	16.13	2.87

Sources: Statistics Canada. Canadian Vital Statistics System, 1991-2000 (unlinked live birth files).
Statistics Canada. Annual Demographics Statistics, 2001. Demography Division, Catalogue No. 91-213-XPB, Annual, Ottawa, 2002.
*Excludes live births with unknown maternal age.
**Age groups 40-44 years and ≥ 45 years have been collapsed because of small numbers.

TABLE G4 ## Maternal age-specific live birth rate per 1,000 females, *Ontario, 1991-2000*

Year	≤ 14 years*	15-17 years	18-19 years	20-24 years	25-29 years	30-34 years	35-39 years	≥ 40 years**
1991	0.7	12.8	35.2	66.8	117.1	90.5	32.7	2.7
1992	0.8	13.0	35.7	65.5	118.0	93.0	33.7	2.8
1993	0.8	13.3	35.7	64.3	113.7	94.1	34.8	2.9
1994	0.8	13.3	35.8	63.1	112.8	94.5	35.4	3.1
1995	0.8	13.3	35.9	61.7	109.6	96.4	37.4	3.2
1996	0.7	11.3	32.9	57.8	104.5	94.5	38.4	3.3
1997	0.7	9.4	28.9	53.7	98.8	91.5	38.1	3.5
1998	0.5	9.7	28.6	54.6	97.4	91.9	38.6	3.6
1999	0.5	8.7	26.7	52.5	96.4	93.6	39.0	3.8
2000	0.6	7.6	24.2	50.4	91.7	92.1	39.2	4.0

Sources: Statistics Canada. Canadian Vital Statistics System, 1991-2000 (unlinked live birth files).
Statistics Canada. Annual Demographics Statistics, 2001. Demography Division, Catalogue No. 91-213-XPB, Annual, Ottawa, 2002.
*Rates based on female population aged 14 years.
**Rates based on female population aged 40-49 years. Age groups 40-44 years and ≥ 45 years have been collapsed because of small numbers.

Appendix G

TABLE G5 **Proportion* of live births that were first births, by maternal age,** *Ontario, 1991-2000*

Year	Mothers aged < 25 years			Mothers aged 25-34 years			Mothers aged ≥ 35 years		
	Number of live births that were first births**	Number of live births	First births per 100 live births	Number of live births that were first births**	Number of live births	First births per 100 live births	Number of live births that were first births**	Number of live births	First births per 100 live births
1991	22,499	33,985	66.2	38,933	99,222	39.2	3,749	16,012	23.4
1992	21,664	33,319	65.0	39,060	100,113	39.0	4,033	16,960	23.8
1993	21,138	32,402	65.2	38,212	97,286	39.3	4,396	17,988	24.4
1994	20,482	31,722	64.6	37,641	95,947	39.2	4,585	18,879	24.3
1995	20,013	30,950	64.7	36,911	94,444	39.1	4,925	20,409	24.1
1996	18,369	28,345	64.8	35,560	89,973	39.5	5,391	21,506	25.1
1997	16,537	25,874	63.9	34,064	84,993	40.1	5,411	22,007	24.6
1998	16,975	26,340	64.5	33,156	83,079	39.9	5,707	22,790	25.0
1999	16,457	25,332	65.0	33,816	82,017	41.2	6,030	23,605	25.6
2000	15,920	24,253	65.6	33,310	78,861	42.2	6,241	24,189	25.8

Source: Statistics Canada. Canadian Vital Statistics System, 1991-2000 (unlinked live birth files).
*Excludes live births with unknown maternal age.
**Live births to women who have not had a previous live birth or stillbirth.

TABLE G6 **Number of maternal deaths and maternal mortality ratios (MMR), by direct and indirect causes,** *Ontario, 1979-1981 to 1997-1999*

Period	Number of maternal deaths			Number of live births	Maternal deaths (95% CI) per 100,000 live births			
	Due to direct causes	Due to indirect causes	Total		Due to direct causes only		Due to direct and indirect causes	
1979-1981	26	7	33	367,154	7.1	(4.6-10.4)	9.0	(6.2-12.7)
1982-1984	15	1	16	382,978	3.9	(2.2-6.4)	4.2	(2.4-6.8)
1985-1987	12	3	15	400,707	3.0	(1.5-5.2)	3.7	(2.1-6.2)
1988-1990	13	0	13	434,327	3.0	(1.6-5.1)	3.0	(1.6-5.1)
1991-1993	14	3	17	449,915	3.1	(1.7-5.3)	3.8	(2.2-6.0)
1994-1996	26	3	29	433,337	6.0	(3.9-8.8)	6.7	(4.5-9.6)
1997-1999	22	2	24	396,664	5.5	(3.5-8.4)	6.1	(3.9-9.0)

Sources: For years 1979-1990: see references 3-11 in the *Maternal Mortality* section.
       For years 1991-1999: Statistics Canada. Canadian Vital Statistics System, 1991-1999 (unlinked live birth and death files).
CI — confidence interval.

TABLE G7 **Direct maternal deaths by cause,** *Ontario, 1979-1999**

Cause	1979-1984		1985-1990		1991-1996		1997-1999	
	No. of deaths	Ratio (95% CI) per 1,000,000 live births	No. of deaths	Ratio (95% CI) per 1,000,000 live births	No. of deaths	Ratio (95% CI) per 1,000,000 live births	No. of deaths	Ratio (95% CI) per 1,000,000 live births
Ectopic and molar pregnancy (630-633)	4	5.3 (1.7-13.4)	0	0.0 (0.0-4.3)	2	2.3 (0.3-8.5)	2	5.0 (0.3-17.9)
Other pregnancy with abortive outcome (634-639)	2	2.7 (0.3-9.8)	2	2.4 (0.3-8.6)	1	1.1 (0.3-6.4)	1	2.5 (0.3-14.4)
Antepartum hemorrhage, abruptio placentae and placenta previa (641)	1	1.3 (0.3-7.5)	1	1.2 (0.3-6.4)	3	3.4 (0.4-9.6)	3	7.6 (1.4-22.3)
Hypertension complicating pregnancy, childbirth and the puerperium (642)	6	8.0 (2.5-17.1)	3	3.6 (0.5-10.8)	12	13.6 (7.2-23.6)	5	12.6 (4.3-29.3)
Other complications of pregnancy, NEC (640,643,644,645,646)	1	1.3 (0.3-7.5)	0	0.0 (0.0-4.3)	0	0.0 (0.0-4.3)	0	0.0 (0.0-9.1)
Normal delivery, and other indications for care in pregnancy, labour and delivery (650-659)	3	4.0 (0.5-12.1)	0	0.0 (0.0-4.3)	0	0.0 (0.0-4.3)	1	2.5 (0.3-14.4)
Postpartum hemorrhage (666)	6	8.0 (2.5-17.1)	6	7.2 (2.3-15.3)	1	1.1 (0.3-6.4)	0	0.0 (0.0-9.1)
Complications occurring mainly in the course of labour and delivery, NEC (660-665,667-669)	2	2.7 (0.3-9.8)	3	3.6 (0.5-10.8)	5	5.7 (1.8-12.8)	2	5.0 (0.3-17.9)
Major puerperal infection (670)	0	0.0 (0.0-5.3)	0	0.0 (0.0-4.3)	1	1.1 (0.3-6.4)	1	2.5 (0.3-14.4)
Venous complications in pregnancy and the puerperium (671)	2	2.7 (0.3-9.8)	3	3.6 (0.5-10.8)	4	4.5 (1.4-11.7)	1	2.5 (0.3-14.4)
Obstetrical pulmonary embolism (673)	7	9.3 (3.8-19.4)	6	7.2 (2.3-15.3)	7	7.9 (3.5-16.0)	3	7.6 (1.4-22.3)
Cerebrovascular disorders in the puerperium (674.0)	7	9.3 (3.8-19.4)	1	1.2 (0.3-6.4)	4	4.5 (1.4-11.7)	2	5.0 (0.3-17.9)
Other and unspecified complications of the puerperium, NEC (674.1-674.9)	0	0.0 (0.0-5.3)	0	0.0 (0.0-4.3)	0	0.0 (0.0-4.3)	1	2.5 (0.3-14.4)

Sources: For years 1979-1990: see references 3-11 in the *Maternal Mortality* section.
For years 1991-1999: Statistics Canada. Canadian Vital Statistics System, 1991-1999 (unlinked live birth and death files).
*Maternal deaths are coded using ICD-10 from 2000 onwards, and will be presented in subsequent reports.
CI — confidence interval.

TABLE G8 | **Ratio and rate* of induced abortion,** *Ontario, 1992-2000*

Year**	Number of induced abortions	Number of live births	Number of females 15-44 years	Induced abortions per 100 live births	Induced abortions per 1,000 females 15-44 years
1992	42,983	150,593	2,526,647	28.5	17.0
1993	44,891	147,844	2,523,588	30.4	17.8
1994	45,106	147,066	2,532,706	30.7	17.8
1995	46,095	146,261	2,545,354	31.5	18.1
1996	46,918	140,010	2,555,857	33.5	18.4
1997	44,046	132,997	2,572,297	33.1	17.1
1998	42,452	132,606	2,584,909	32.0	16.4
1999	39,981	131,061	2,599,826	30.5	15.4
2000	39,544	127,393	2,622,915	31.0	15.1

Sources: Canadian Institute for Health Information and Statistics Canada. Therapeutic Abortion Survey. (Custom tabulation, Health Statistics Division, Statistics Canada, 2003).

Statistics Canada. CANSIM II, table 051-0001 — Canadian population estimates, 1992-2000.

Statistics Canada. Canadian Vital Statistics System, 1992-2000 (unlinked live birth files).

*Includes cases with age not specified and abortions to women $\leq$ 14 years of age and $\geq$ 45 years of age. Rates based on women aged 15-44 years. Excludes abortions performed in Ontario on non-residents of Ontario. Caution is required when comparing data for 1999 and later years with data for 1998 and earlier. As of 1999, the Ontario Ministry of Health and Long-term Care no longer maintains a system for the collection of detailed information on abortions performed in clinics in Ontario. Ontario now uses the billing system of the Ontario Health Insurance Plan (OHIP) to provide counts of clinic abortions to the Therapeutic Abortion Survey. As a result, information is no longer available for clinic abortions performed on non-residents of Ontario or on Ontario residents who do not submit a claim to OHIP. A comparison of the data collected using both sources for the years 1995 to 1998 shows that the new data source underestimated the clinic abortions performed on Ontario residents by an average of 5.4% (950 cases) per year, or approximately 1% of all abortions performed in Canada. The new source does not include non-resident cases, which averaged 70 cases per year or 0.4% of total clinic abortions performed in Ontario.

**1991 data are not presented, because data on province of residence for clinic abortions were not available before 1992.

TABLE G9 | **Rate of preterm birth,** *Ontario, 1991-2000*

Year	Number of preterm births	Number of live births*	Preterm births per 100 live births
1991	9,931	149,075	6.7
1992	10,354	150,345	6.9
1993	11,956	147,638	8.1
1994	12,200	146,738	8.3
1995	13,454	145,474	9.2
1996	13,370	139,492	9.6
1997	10,684	132,848	8.0
1998	9,509	132,380	7.2
1999	9,359	130,961	7.1
2000	9,323	127,318	7.3

Source: Statistics Canada. Canadian Vital Statistics System, 1991-2000 (unlinked live birth files).

*Excludes live births with unknown gestational age.

TABLE G10 **Rate of preterm birth (singleton and multiple births),** *Ontario, 2000*

Plurality	Number of preterm births	Number of live births*	Preterm births per 100 live births
Singleton births	7,409	123,639	6.0
Twin births	1,716	3,478	49.3
Triplet or higher-order births	198	201	98.5
All live births	9,323	127,318	7.3

Source: Statistics Canada, Canadian Vital Statistics System, 2000 (unlinked live birth file).
*Excludes live births with unknown gestational age.

TABLE G11 **Rate of postterm birth,** *Ontario, 1991-2000*

Year	Number of postterm births	Number of live births*	Postterm births per 100 live births
1991	7,482	149,075	5.0
1992	6,605	150,345	4.4
1993	8,123	147,638	5.5
1994	6,671	146,738	4.5
1995	5,251	145,474	3.6
1996	3,816	139,492	2.7
1997	3,717	132,848	2.8
1998	2,445	132,380	1.8
1999	1,602	130,961	1.2
2000	1,211	127,318	1.0

Source: Statistics Canada. Canadian Vital Statistics System, 1991-2000 (unlinked live birth files).
*Excludes live births with unknown gestational age.

TABLE G12 **Rates of small for gestational age (SGA) and large for gestational age (LGA),** *Ontario, 1991-2000*

Year	Number of SGA singleton live births	Number of LGA singleton live births	Number of singleton live births*	SGA singleton live births per 100 singleton live births*	LGA singleton live births per 100 singleton live births*
1991	16,263	14,695	145,928	11.1	10.1
1992	15,435	15,945	146,956	10.5	10.9
1993	16,453	15,413	144,385	11.4	10.7
1994	17,609	14,921	142,853	12.3	10.4
1995	NA	NA	NA	NA	NA
1996	13,872	16,303	135,747	10.2	12.0
1997	13,423	14,351	129,261	10.4	11.1
1998	12,315	14,550	128,648	9.6	11.3
1999	11,359	15,083	127,170	8.9	11.9
2000	10,477	15,751	123,594	8.5	12.7

Source: Statistics Canada. Canadian Vital Statistics System, 1991-2000 (unlinked live birth files).
*Excludes live births with unknown gestational age or birth weight, or gestational age < 22 weeks or > 43 weeks.
NA — not available.

TABLE G13 **Rate of fetal death,** *Ontario, 1991-2000*

Year	All fetal deaths			Fetal deaths ≥ 500 g*		
	Number of fetal deaths	Total births	Deaths per 1,000 total births*	Number of fetal deaths	Total births	Deaths per 1,000 total births
1991	802	152,280	5.3	623	151,926	4.1
1992	1,070	151,663	7.1	837	151,359	5.5
1993	972	148,816	6.5	746	148,419	5.0
1994	945	148,011	6.4	708	147,698	4.8
1995	978	147,239	6.6	738	146,947	5.0
1996	905	140,915	6.4	678	140,585	4.8
1997	881	133,878	6.6	651	133,577	4.9
1998	850	133,456	6.4	611	133,115	4.6
1999	837	131,898	6.3	599	131,559	4.6
2000	815	128,208	6.4	564	127,874	4.4

Source: Statistics Canada. Canadian Vital Statistics System, 1991-2000 (unlinked live birth and stillbirth files).
**Fetal death rates ≥ 500 g exclude stillbirths and live births with a birth weight < 500 g or, if birth weight was unknown, those with a gestational age of < 22 weeks.

TABLE G14 **Rate of neonatal (0-27 days) death,** *Ontario, 1991-2000*

Year	Number of neonatal deaths	Number of live births	Neonatal deaths per 1,000 live births
1991	651	151,478	4.3
1992	596	150,593	4.0
1993	647	147,844	4.4
1994	618	147,066	4.2
1995	608	146,261	4.2
1996	584	140,010	4.2
1997	518	132,997	3.9
1998	501	132,606	3.8
1999	510	131,061	3.9
2000	505	127,393	4.0

Source: Statistics Canada. Canadian Vital Statistics System, 1991-2000 (period calculation using unlinked live birth and death files).

TABLE G15 **Rate of postneonatal (28-364 days) death,** *Ontario, 1991-2000*

Year	Number of postneonatal deaths	Number of neonatal survivors	Postneonatal deaths per 1,000 neonatal survivors
1991	302	150,827	2.0
1992	289	149,997	1.9
1993	275	147,197	1.9
1994	261	146,448	1.8
1995	262	145,653	1.8
1996	218	139,426	1.6
1997	210	132,479	1.6
1998	165	132,105	1.2
1999	195	130,551	1.5
2000	208	126,888	1.6

Source: Statistics Canada. Canadian Vital Statistics System, 1991-2000 (period calculation using unlinked live birth and death files).

TABLE G16 **Rate of infant (0-364 days) death,** *Ontario, 1991-2000*

Year	Number of infant deaths	Number of live births	Infant deaths per 1,000 live births
1991	953	151,478	6.3
1992	885	150,593	5.9
1993	922	147,844	6.2
1994	879	147,066	6.0
1995	870	146,261	5.9
1996	802	140,010	5.7
1997	728	132,997	5.5
1998	666	132,606	5.0
1999	705	131,061	5.4
2000	713	127,393	5.6

Source: Statistics Canada. Canadian Vital Statistics System, 1991-2000 (period calculation using unlinked live birth and death files).

TABLE G17 **Causes of infant death,** *Ontario, 1999**

Cause according to modified ICE classification**	Number of infant deaths	Percentage of infant deaths	Number of neonatal deaths	Percentage of neonatal deaths	Number of post-neonatal deaths	Percentage of neonatal deaths
Congenital anomalies	206	29.2	149	29.2	57	29.2
Asphyxia	59	8.4	57	11.2	2	1.0
Immaturity	209	29.6	194	38.0	15	7.7
Infection	60	8.5	33	6.5	27	13.8
Sudden infant death syndrome (SIDS)	46	6.5	7	1.4	39	20.0
Other sudden unexplained infant death	19	2.7	9	1.8	10	5.1
External causes	10	1.4	1	0.2	9	4.6
Other	96	13.6	60	11.8	36	18.5
TOTAL	705	100.0	510	100.0	195	100.0

Source: Statistics Canada. Canadian Vital Statistics System, 1999 (period calculation using unlinked death file).

*Causes of infant death are presented for 1999 because the ICE classification is based on ICD-9. In 2000, causes of death in the Statistics Canada death file were coded using ICD-10.

**See reference 4 in the *Infant Mortality Rate and Causes of Death* section.

Appendix G

TABLE G18 **Birth cohort-based infant death rate,* by gestational age,**
Ontario, 1995-1999 combined

Gestational age (weeks)	Number of infant deaths	Number of live births	Infant deaths (95% CI) per 1,000 live births	
< 22	167	182	917.6	(867.7-953.1)
22-23	367	413	888.6	(854.2-917.3)
24-25	313	866	361.4	(329.4-394.4)
26-27	179	1,302	137.5	(119.2-157.4)
28-31	220	4,723	46.6	(40.8-53.0)
32-33	109	6,249	17.4	(14.3-21.0)
34-36	298	42,612	7.0	(6.2-7.8)
37-41	1,067	608,372	1.8	(1.7-1.9)
≥ 42	35	16,852	2.1	(1.5-2.9)
Unknown gestational age	8	1,784	4.5	(2.0-8.8)
Unlinked	1,014	—	—	—
All gestational ages	3,777	683,355	5.5	(5.4-5.7)

Source: Statistics Canada. Canadian Vital Statistics System, 1995-1999 (birth-infant death linked files).
*In the birth-infant death linked files, all live births at < 22 weeks and < 500 g were assumed to have died on the first day of life and were classified as such.
CI — confidence interval.

TABLE G19 **Birth cohort-based infant death rate,* by birth weight,**
Ontario, 1995-1999 combined

Birth weight (grams)	Number of infant deaths	Number of live births	Infant deaths (95% CI) per 1,000 live births	
< 500	351	520	675.0	(632.9-715.1)
500-749	446	1,088	409.9	(380.5-439.8)
750-999	208	1,356	153.4	(134.6-173.7)
1,000-1,249	112	1,659	67.5	(55.9-80.7)
1,250-1,499	87	2,069	42.0	(33.8-51.6)
1,500-1,999	191	7,959	24.0	(20.8-27.6)
2,000-2,499	232	25,740	9.0	(7.9-10.2)
2,500-3,999	960	554,189	1.7	(1.6-1.9)
≥ 4,000	127	87,841	1.4	(1.2-1.7)
Unknown birth weight	49	934	52.5	(39.1-68.8)
Unlinked	1,014	—	—	—
All birth weights	3,777	683,355	5.5	(5.4-5.7)

Source: Statistics Canada. Canadian Vital Statistics System, 1995-1999 (birth-infant death linked files).
*In the birth-infant death linked files, all live births at < 22 weeks and < 500 g were assumed to have died on the first day of life and were classified as such.
CI — confidence interval.

TABLE G20 **Rate of multiple birth,** *Ontario, 1991-2000*

Year	Number of multiple births	Number of total births	Multiple births per 100 total births
1991	3,039	152,280	2.0
1992	3,198	151,663	2.1
1993	3,069	148,816	2.1
1994	3,610	148,011	2.4
1995	3,592	147,239	2.4
1996	3,711	140,915	2.6
1997	3,583	133,878	2.7
1998	3,764	133,456	2.8
1999	3,829	131,898	2.9
2000	3,734	128,208	2.9

Source: Statistics Canada Vital Statistics System, 1991-2000 (unlinked live birth and stillbirth files).

Appendix H

Canadian Perinatal Surveillance System Publications (as of October 2003)

Papers Published or in Press in Peer-Reviewed Journals

Wen SW, Kramer MS, Platt R, Demissie K, Joseph KS, Liu S, et al. for the Fetal and Infant Health Study Group of the Canadian Perinatal Surveillance System. Secular trends of fetal growth in Canada, 1981 to 1997. *Paediatr Perinat Epidemiol* 2003;17:347-54.

Joseph KS, Liu S, Demissie K, Wen SW, Platt RW, Ananth CV et al. for the Fetal and Infant Health Study Group of the Canadian Perinatal Surveillance System. A parsimonious explanation for intersecting perinatal mortality curves: understanding the effects of plurality and of parity. *BMC Pregnancy and Childbirth* 2003;3:3.

Wen SW, Chen LM, Li CY, Kramer MS, Allen AC, for the Fetal and Infant Health Study Group of the Canadian Perinatal Surveillance System. The impact of missing birth weight in deceased versus surviving fetuses and infants in the comparison of birth weight-specific feto-infant mortality. *Chron Dis Can* 2002;23:146-51.

Kramer MS, Liu S, Luo Z, Yuan H, Platt RW, Joseph KS. Analysis of perinatal mortality and its components: time for a change? *Am J Epidemiol* 2002;156:493-7.

Liu S, Heaman M, Kramer MS, Demissie K, Wen SW, Marcoux S. Length of hospital stay, obstetric conditions at childbirth, and maternal readmission: a population-based cohort study. *Am J Obstet Gynecol* 2002;187:681-7.

Joseph KS, Marcoux S, Ohlsson A, Kramer MS, Allen AC, Liu S, et al. for the Fetal and Infant Health Study Group of the Canadian Perinatal Surveillance System. Preterm birth, stillbirth and infant mortality among triplet births in Canada, 1985-96. *Paediatr Perinat Epidemiol* 2002;16:141-8.

Liu S, Joseph KS, Kramer MS, Allen AC, Sauve R, Rusen ID, et al. for the Fetal and Infant Health Study Group of the Canadian Perinatal Surveillance System. Relationship of prenatal diagnosis and pregnancy termination to overall infant mortality in Canada. *JAMA* 2002;287:1561-7.

Turner LA, Kramer MS, Liu S, for the Maternal Mortality and Morbidity Study Group of the Canadian Perinatal Surveillance System. Cause-specific mortality during and after pregnancy and the definition of maternal death. *Chron Dis Can* 2002;23:31-6.

Turner LA, Cyr M, Kinch RA, Liston R, Kramer MS, Fair M, et al. for the Maternal Mortality and Morbidity Study Group of the Canadian Perinatal Surveillance System. Under-reporting of maternal mortality in Canada: a question of definition. *Chron Dis Can* 2002;23:22-30.

Joseph KS, Marcoux S, Ohlsson A, Liu S, Allen A, Kramer MS, et al. for the Fetal and Infant Health Study Group of the Canadian Perinatal Surveillance System. Changes in stillbirth and infant mortality associated with increases in preterm birth among twins. *Pediatrics* 2001;108:1055-61.

Liu S, Joseph KS, Wen SW, Kramer MS, Marcoux S, Ohlsson A, et al. for the Fetal and Infant Health Study Group. Secular trends in congenital anomaly-related fetal and infant mortality in Canada, 1985-1996. *Am J Med Genet* 2001;104:7-13.

Kramer MS, Platt R, Wen SW, Joseph KS, Allen A, Abrahamowicz M, et al. A new and improved population-based Canadian reference for birth weight for gestational age. *Pediatrics* 2001;108(2):E35.

Wen SW, Joseph KS, Kramer MS, Demissie K, Oppenheimer L, Liston R, et al. for the Fetal and Infant Mortality Study Group, Canadian Perinatal Surveillance System. Recent trends in fetal and infant outcomes following post-term pregnancies. *Chron Dis Can* 2001;22:1-5.

Joseph KS, Kramer MS, Allen AC, Mery LS, Platt RW, Wen SW. Implausible birth weight for gestational age. *Am J Epidemiol* 2001;153:110-3.

Wen SW, Liu S, Kramer MS, Marcoux S, Ohlsson A, Sauve R, et al. Comparison of maternal and infant outcomes between vacuum extraction and forceps deliveries. *Am J Epidemiol* 2001;153:103-7.

Joseph KS, Kramer MS, Allen AC, Cyr M, Fair M, Ohlsson A, et al. for the Fetal and Infant Health Study Group of the Canadian Perinatal Surveillance System. Gestational age- and birth weight-specific declines in infant mortality in Canada, 1985-94. *Pediatr Perinat Epidemiol* 2000;14:332-9.

Wen SW, Liu S, Kramer MS, Joseph KS, Marcoux S, Levitt C, et al. Impact of prenatal glucose screening on the diagnosis of gestational diabetes and on pregnancy outcomes. *Am J Epidemiol* 2000;152:1009-14.

Kramer MS, Marcoux S, Joseph KS, Ohlsson A, McCarthy B. The contribution of mild and moderate preterm birth to infant mortality. *JAMA* 2000;284:843-9.

Dzakpasu S, Joseph KS, Kramer MS, Allen AC. The Matthew effect: infant mortality in Canada and internationally. *Pediatrics* 2000;106:e5.

Wen SW, Rouleau J, Lowry RB, Kinakin B, Anderson-Redick S, Sibbald B, et al. Congenital anomalies ascertained by two record systems run in parallel in the Canadian province of Alberta. *Can J Public Health* 2000;91:193-6.

Liu S, Wen SW, McMillan D, Trouton K, Fowler D, McCourt C. Increased neonatal readmission rate associated with decreased length of hospital stay at birth in Canada. *Can J Public Health* 2000;91:46-50.

Wen SW, Liu S, Joseph KS, Rouleau J, Allen A. Patterns of infant mortality caused by congenital anomalies. *Teratology* 2000;61:342-6.

Wen SW, Kramer MS, Liu S, Dzakpasu S, Sauve R, for the Fetal and Infant Health Study Group. Infant mortality by gestational age and birth weight in Canadian provinces and territories, 1990-1994 births. *Chron Dis Can* 2000; 21:14-22.

Fair M, Cyr M, Allen AC, Wen SW, Guyon G, MacDonald RC, for the Fetal-Infant Mortality Study Group. An assessment of the validity of a computer system for probabilistic record linkage of birth and infant death records in Canada. *Chron Dis Can* 2000;21:8-13.

Wen SW, Liu S, Joseph KS, Trouton K, Allen A. Regional patterns of infant mortality caused by lethal congenital anomalies. *Can J Public Health* 1999;90:316-19.

Wen SW, Mery L, Kramer MS, Jimenez V, Trouton K, Herbert P, et al. Attitudes of Canadian women towards birthing centre and nurse/midwife care for childbirth. *Can Med Assoc J* 1999;161:708-9.

Joseph KS, Allen A, Kramer MS, Cyr M, Fair M. Changes in the registration of stillbirths less than 500 g in Canada, 1985-95. *Paediatr Perinat Epidemiol* 1999;13:278-87.

Liu S, Wen SW. Development of record linkage of hospital discharge data from the study of neonatal readmission. *Chronic Dis Can* 1999;20:77-81.

Joseph KS, Kramer MS, Marcoux S, Ohlsson A, Wen SW, Allen A, et al. Determinants of preterm birth rates in Canada from 1981 through 1983 and from 1992 through 1994. *N Engl J Med* 1998;339:1434-9.

Fair M, Wilkins R, Cyr M, Chen J, and the Fetal-Infant Mortality Study Group of the Canadian Perinatal Surveillance System. Maternal education and fetal and infant mortality in Quebec. *Health Rep* 1998;10:53-64.

Wen SW, Liu S, Marcoux S, Fowler D. Trends and variations in length of hospital stay for childbirth in Canada. *Can Med Assoc J* 1998;158:875-9.

Wen SW, Liu S, Fowler D. Trends and variations in neonatal length of in-hospital stay in Canada. *Can J Public Health* 1998;115-9.

Wen SW, Liu S, Marcoux S, Fowler D. Uses and limitations of routine hospital admission/separation records for perinatal surveillance. *Chronic Dis Can* 1997;18:113-9.

Joseph KS, Kramer MS. Recent trends in infant mortality rates and proportions of low-birth-weight live births in Canada. *Can Med Assoc J* 1997;157:535-41.

Joseph KS, Kramer MS. Canadian infant mortality: 1994 update. *Can Med Assoc J* 1997;156:161-3.

Joseph KS, Kramer MS. Recent trends in Canadian infant mortality rates: effect of changes in registration of live newborns weighing less than 500 g. *Can Med Assoc J* 1996;155:1047-52.

Reports

Health Canada. *Congenital Anomalies in Canada — A Perinatal Health Report, 2002*. Ottawa: Minister of Public Works and Government Services Canada, 2002 (Catalogue No. H39-641/2002E). URL: <http://www.hc-sc.gc.ca/pphb-dgspsp/rhs-ssg/index.html>.

Health Canada. *Canadian Perinatal Health Report, 2000*. Ottawa: Minister of Public Works and Government Services Canada, 2000 (Catalogue No. H49-142/2000E). URL: <http://www.hc-sc.gc.ca/pphb-dgspsp/rhs-ssg/index.html>.

Health Canada. *Perinatal Health Indicators for Canada: A Resource Manual*. Ottawa: Minister of Public Works and Government Services Canada, 2000 (Catalogue No. H49-135/2000E). URL: <http://www.hc-sc.gc.ca/pphb-dgspsp/rhs-ssg/index.html>.

Fair M, Cyr M, Allen AC, Wen SW, Guyon G, MacDonald RC, and the Fetal and Infant Mortality Study Group of the Canadian Perinatal Surveillance System. *Validation Study for a Record Linkage of Births and Infant Deaths in Canada*. Statistics Canada.

Health Canada. *Canadian Perinatal Surveillance System. Progress Report 1997-1998*. Ottawa: Minister of Public Works and Government Services Canada, 1998 (Catalogue No. H21-131/1998E).

Health Canada. Progress Report. *Canadian Perinatal Surveillance System*. Ottawa: Minister of Supply and Services Canada, 1995 (Catalogue No. H21-131/1996E).

Fact Sheets

Physical Abuse during Pregnancy	December 2003
Preterm Birth	October 1999
Sudden Infant Death Syndrome	September 1999
Alcohol and Pregnancy	November 1998
Breastfeeding	November 1998
Induced Abortion	April 1998
Report on Maternal Mortality in Canada	April 1998
Infant Mortality	March 1998